Asian Cooking

Asian Cooking

CUISINES OF THE ORIENT

Edited by
LYDIA DARBYSHIRE

Colour
Library
Direct

A QUINTET BOOK

CLD 21338

This edition published in 1999 for
Colour Library Direct,
Godalming Business Centre,
Woolsack Way, Godalming,
Surrey GU7 1XW

Reprinted 1999

ISBN 1-84100-120-1

This book was designed and produced by
Quintet Publishing Limited
6 Blundell Street
London N7 9BH

Creative Director: Richard Dewing
Designer: Ian Hunt
Art Director: Clare Reynolds
Senior Editor: Anna Briffa
Editor: Lydia Darbyshire

Typeset in Great Britain by
Central Southern Typesetters, Eastbourne
Manufactured in China by
Regent Publishing Services Ltd
Printed in China by
Leefung-Asco Printers Ltd

The material in this publication previously
appeared in: *Korean Cooking; Stir Fry Cooking;
The Soy Sauce Cookbook; Vietnamese Cooking;
Japanese Cooking for Two; The Noodle Cookbook;
Chinese Vegetarian Cooking;* and *Thai Cooking.*

Contents

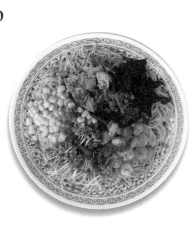

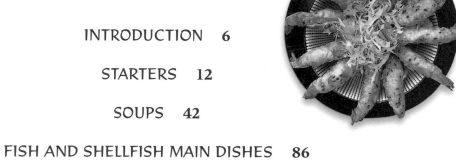

Introduction

The cuisine of southeast Asia has enjoyed a boom in popularity over the past few years, and the sheer diversity of the cooking styles from this enormous geographical area has meant that it is now common to find books on Thai and Indonesian cooking on the shelves in every bookshop along with titles on regional Chinese food as well as books on Korean and Vietnamese cooking.

Japanese cooking has, perhaps, been less well served, and apart from the famous dishes, like tempura and sushi, there are few well-known foods. People invariably think that Japanese cookery and its preparation is an esoteric art, requiring years of training and experience to master. This misunderstanding is a great pity, because Japanese cookery not only encompasses as great a range of flavours and textures as any other country in Asia, but also, for the most part, is easily and quickly prepared.

Thai food has become one of the most popular exotic cuisine in the world. The distinctive flavours, with hints of fresh herbs, coconut, nuoc mam fish sauce and lemon grass, are the result of a special national talent for blending a great variety of herbs and spices. While remaining identifiably Thai, the cuisine is a synthesis of many Asian influences, incorporating as it does dishes and ideas from India, China, Burma and the southern countries of Malaysia and Indonesia.

Laos, Cambodia and Thailand have influenced Vietnamese cuisine, especially in the use of herbs. No Vietnamese meal is complete without there being at least two or three fresh herbs present, either as a garnish or in their own right as part of the meal. The Vietnamese love to wrap up their food in fresh lettuce leaves, and to include one or two herbs in the parcels, especially coriander, mint, basil, dill and fennel. Indian and Portuguese travellers brought spices, which developed the combinations that came to be known as curries. The French, who colonized Vietnam, forced the Vietnamese to be inventive, and it is ironic that dishes, such as steamed or stewed chicken feet, which the peasants were forced to devise from leftovers, are now so highly regarded.

The recipes in this book illustrate this diversity of cooking styles. At the same time, they show how the same basic ingredients can be used in subtly different ways to reflect a particular national preference. Many of the recipes, for example, include noodles in one form or another. Noodles are served all over southeastern Asia: you will find them served from stalls by the roadside in the wastes of northern China, in crowded ramen shops in the heart of Tokyo, on the beach in the sandy resorts of Thailand and in villages on the sub-tropical islands of Indonesia. In south and east Asia the noodle is ubiquitous, challenging rice in many areas as the main staple. Prepared in as little as five minutes, the noodle could even stake a claim to the title of the world's first and fastest fast food, although real noodle dishes bear no resemblance to the bland, anaemic-looking strands lurking in pot noodle tubs on supermarket shelves.

The recipes that follow take advantage of the enormous variety of ingredients available from all over the world—exotic fruits and vegetables, fragrant spices, herbs and preserves; contrasting grains and cereals; and quick-to-cook seafood, meat and poultry. There are suggestions throughout for combining dishes and for substituting better known or more widely available ingredients —also listed in the glossary. Throughout, the emphasis is on authentic-tasting, easily prepared dishes.

Equipment and Techniques

EQUIPMENT

The key piece of equipment is, of course, the cooking pan, and the most important feature is size: a good stir-fry pan must hold a large volume of ingredients, at the same time allowing sufficient room for stirring and turning them during cooking.

WOKS

A wok is the most suitable pan for the majority of stir-fry dishes, but there is a choice of types, from traditional wok pans to electric models.

CARBON STEEL WOK The traditional wok is made from thin, uncoated carbon steel. It is deeply curved, with a stout wooden handle, which is designed for lifting, tilting and shaking the pan in one hand, leaving the other hand free for using a scoop or spatula to stir the ingredients. The domed pan fits over a flaming brazier in Chinese restaurants, but at home a rack may be used to stabilize a wok on an electric hob or over a gas burner. However, depending on the pan stands on a gas hob, the rack may be redundant.

This type of wok conducts heat well, provides a large surface area for cooking, and is highly responsive to changes in heat. However, a carbon steel wok must be used regularly and kept oiled to prevent rusting between use. A new pan should be washed in hot soapy water to remove any protective coating, then tempered or seasoned. This is done by heating a small amount of oil in the wok, and rubbing it over the surface of the pan, until smoking hot but not burning. The pan should be wiped out with absorbent kitchen paper. The outside and any exposed metal around the edge of the handle must be oiled. Wipe with clean absorbent kitchen paper before storage and use. After each use, the pan must be wiped out and oiled before it is stored.

Depending on the food cooked, there are two ways of cleaning the pan. For most oil-based cooking, wipe it out with absorbent kitchen paper, then sprinkle in some salt and pour in a little oil. Heat this and remove the pan from the heat. Use a pad of absorbent kitchen paper to clean the wok—the salt acts as a scouring agent and removes food residues. Wipe out all the oil and salt, then heat the wok again with a little fresh oil before wiping it clean. If the food has left a cooked-on coating of sauce, the pan must be washed, dried and tempered.

Keep this kind of wok for vegetable stir-fries and dishes containing small amounts of meat and grains. The carbon steel pan is not suitable for stir-frying fruit.

STAINLESS STEEL AND NONSTICK PANS These pans are far easier to look after than the carbon steel versions. They can be washed in hot soapy water, dried and stored according to the manufacturer's instructions.

The quality of pans varies widely. In general, they are all slightly less responsive to changes in heat than carbon steel. Unlike carbon steel woks—when the cheapest can be excellent—price is often a good guide of quality in this group.

Consider the shape of the pan. Many are smaller than expected of a traditional wok, and they may have very flat bases, putting them more on a par with a frying pan than a wok. A pan with a small, quite flat base may not be the best buy, and a large, conventional frying pan with a deep sides may provide more surface area for cooking. Before you buy, check the instructions that go with the pan,

Two designs of wok. The brush can be used to oil woks, and the strainers are useful accessories.

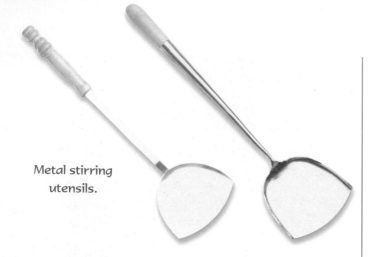

Metal stirring
utensils.

because some nonstick finishes are not ideal for the majority of stir-frying. Inexpensive nonstick finishes can deteriorate rapidly when used over a high heat and when the food is stirred constantly, even when the correct utensils are used.

FRYING PANS

A wok is not essential for stir-frying. If you use a frying pan it must be large, with deep sides. Ideally, choose a pan with slightly sloping sides and a curved edge around the base, which allows the food to be turned more easily.

A sauté pan is usually large with deep sides and, since sautéing is similar to stir-frying in that the food is cooked over high heat and stirred during cooking, this type of pan is suitable for stir-frying.

Heavy, nonstick, coated cast iron pans can be used for stir-frying, but they usually have to be heated slowly and kept over a medium rather than a high heat. The manufacturer may state that the pan should not be heated empty; therefore a coating of oil or fat should be added. The pan may be used for stir-frying once hot, but the heat is not as fierce and the pan is not as responsive, taking a long time to react to changes in temperature. These pans are suitable for stir-frying fruit or other ingredients that are not necessarily cooked over fierce heat.

CHOPPING BOARDS

Have a very large chopping board that can be scrubbed in hot soapy water. For the sake of food safety and hygiene, remember that wood is absorbent and easily damaged, allowing food particles to be trapped and bacteria to grow. If you do have a wooden board, scrub it in very hot water, using a mild solution of bleach or an abrasive cleaner. Rinse and

dry thoroughly after every use. Plastic-coated boards are non-absorbent and therefore less likely to be a food safety risk. However, these too must be scrubbed after each use to clean them.

KNIVES

Preparing much Asian food involves time-consuming chopping and slicing, so good quality, sharp knives are important. Never buy a knife by looks and technical information alone. Pick it up and feel it; hold it as if you were going to cut with it to feel if it is comfortable in your hand and if it is balanced.

A food processor, mandolin slicer or grater can be used and, for wafer-thin slices, a potato peeler is useful. A sharp knife is also needed for slicing and scoring meat and poultry.

CLEAVERS

These usually have wooden handles and come in three weights: light, medium and heavy. They are made of either tempered carbon steel or stainless steel. The former is preferable since it is harder and maintains a sharper cutting edge for longer. For all cutting and chopping, the sharper the cutting edge the better your results.

BAMBOO STEAMERS

The advantage of having bamboo steamers is that they can be stacked one on top of the other so that several dishes can be cooked at the same time. They are particularly useful for warming up leftovers.

RICE COOKER

Because of the amount of rice that is consumed in many Asian households, city dwellers now often use electric rice cookers to cook the rice perfectly every time and to keep it hot.

SHINSOLLO

In Korean cooking, a special bronze or brass pot is used for preparing the dish of the same name. The pot has a central funnel in which hot charcoal is placed to keep the food hot.

TABLE-TOP COOKER

Small table-top burners, fuelled by small butane gas canisters, are often used for both cooking and keeping dishes warm. Metal grids are used for cooking the food directly over the flame.

TECHNIQUES

The secret of success with most Asian dishes is in careful preparation, especially cutting and slicing the ingredients. Before you begin, make sure that all vegetables are clean before cutting and cooking. Drain them in a colander or sieve, and mop them on absorbent kitchen paper to prevent splitting.

PREPARATION AND CUTTING

Because most of the dishes are quickly cooked, all ingredients should be cut to cook evenly.

Slicing.

SLICES Whether the slices are thick or thin, which will depend on how much cooking is required and the finished texture, they must be even.

DIAGONAL SLICES Cut slices at an angle. For example, spring onions and celery sticks should have the end cut off at an angle, then all the slices should be cut at an angle to give evenly thick, slanting slices.

Diagonal slices.

Matchstick strips.

FINGERS OR STICKS Cut fairly thick slices, then cut these into fingers or sticks. Cucumbers and courgettes should be cut into lengths, then quartered lengthways.

THIN STICKS Finer than fingers, but not as delicate as matchstick strips, these are about 5 mm/¼ in thick.

MATCHSTICK STRIPS Literally the size of matchsticks, these should be fine and even. They cook very quickly and are useful for a garnish.

SHREDDED Cut into thin slices, then across into fine pieces. Firm cabbage and similar leaves can be shredded by cutting into chunks, then thinly slicing.

GRATED Use the coarse blade on a grater and discard the last, small chunk, which cannot be processed.

Shredding.

Chopping.

CHOPPED Cut slices, thin sticks, then cut across to chop the ingredient. Halve and slice an onion, then cut across the slices so that they fall into small, reasonably even pieces. This is not as even as dicing. The pieces should be small, unless roughly chopped, when they can be slightly larger and less even. Chop herbs by using a large, sharp knife and a guillotine action.

DICED Cut into small, even cubes, about 5 mm/¼ in or slightly larger.

CUBED Cut larger cubes than are required for dice, between 1 and 2.5 cm/½ and 1 in, but even in size.

CHUNKS Slightly larger than cubes and less even. There is no need to trim the food into neat squares.

Dicing.

EATING ASIAN STYLE

In most Far Eastern countries, including China, Thailand, Korea and Japan, people sit around a low table to eat. Every person has their own rice bowl—in Korea this is traditionally made of brass and lidded—and chopsticks are used for eating.

All the dishes for a meal are served at once and often, particularly for dinner, which is the main meal of the day, there will be quite a few. In Korea, for example, a simply family dinner might include about twenty side dishes (*panchan*), containing a tempting array of seasoned raw or lightly cooked vegetables (*namuls*), dishes containing dried vegetables or prawns, salted fish and roast seaweed (*nibles*), and dipping sauces and *kimchi*, of which there will be at least one and probably four or more. Soup is an essential element of every meal, and there will also probably be some flour- and egg-coated fried vegetables (*jon*). More substantial fish, meat and poultry dishes are served in what would be considered small amounts in the West, but with such variety on offer, large portions of any one dish are unnecessary.

Lunch is a lighter meal of noodles or rice mixed with vegetables, or another grain or beans for protein. Breakfast is traditionally almost as large a meal as dinner, although these days it tends to be lighter.

A similar arrangement occurs in Japan, where the concept of serving a succession of dishes, as happens in the West, is alien to traditional. All the dishes are served as a 'set', with the exception of the dessert, which is not regarded as an integral part of the meal, although fresh fruits are often provided at the end, together with green tea. A true Japanese meal always includes rice, a soup and a small dish of Japanese pickles, which are accompanied by a main dish of fish or meat together with a small side dish. A dinner party would be achieved by adding a second side dish and, perhaps, a second main dish. A thoughtful host will attempt to vary each of the dishes, so that the meal will combine as many different flavours, textures and types of preparation as possible.

If you are wondering how the cook manages to juggle the preparation and serving of so many dishes, remember that Japanese cooks make most of the dishes well in advance and re-heat them as necessary. Some are served warm rather than hot. Some dishes, such as *sukiyaki*, soups and noodles, are cooked at the table and should always be fresh and hot.

USING CHOPSTICKS

Using chopsticks is no more difficult than using a knife and fork, as long as they are held correctly. Think of your chopsticks as jaws that have been turned upside down. The lower chopstick, clamped between the tip of your ring finger, inner joint of your thumb, and the knuckle of your index finger, remains fixed in the same position during eating. The upper chopstick is held in the tips of the middle and index fingers and thumb, so that it can be opened and closed in relation to the lower chopstick.

There are several principles of etiquette that should be observed when eating with chopsticks, such as not passing food between chopsticks, and not using your chopsticks to pull a dish toward you or to push it away from you.

Position of lower chopstick.

Position of upper chopstick.

Using chopsticks.

LEFT Chopsticks and their accessories are always ornamental and decorative.

Starters

Asian cuisine as a whole includes an immense variety of dishes that can be served in small portions at the start of a meal as starters or as part of a buffet-style meal. Spring rolls, for example, are a perfect appetizer, or they can be served as part of a main meal or as a buffet dish. The great advantage of many of these dishes is that they are served cold, which means that they can be prepared and cooked in advance, leaving the cook free to concentrate on the other courses of the meal. They can also be served as snacks, to accompany drinks, in place of peanuts or crisps.

Fresh Spring Rolls

SERVES 4–6

Although they are rather time-consuming to prepare, the results are a nice change from the popular, fried spring rolls.

2 Chinese sweet sausages (combined weight 100 g/4 oz)

200 g/7 oz firm bean curd

225 g/8 oz crabmeat

2 tbsp peanut or corn oil

2 eggs, beaten lightly

100 g/4 oz cucumber

8–12 spring roll wrappers (or pancakes; add 1 tbsp cornflour to a standard recipe)

350 g/12 oz bean sprouts, blanched lightly

200 g/7 oz spring onions

FOR THE SPRING ROLL SAUCE

250 ml/8 fl oz chicken stock

50 g/2 oz palm sugar

50 ml/2 fl oz tamarind juice

1 tbsp cornflour

● Steam the Chinese sausages for about 8 minutes and then the bean curd for about 3 minutes. Remove and cut both into long pieces, about the width of a pencil and about 10 cm/4 in long. Steam the crabmeat for 5 minutes and set aside.

● Heat a non-stick, shallow pan over medium heat, add a drop of oil and just enough egg to cover the bottom—it should resemble a thin pancake. Cook for a minute on each side. Make 8–12 thin omelettes in the same way. Roll them up and slice them into lengths the same size as the sausage and bean curd. Cut the cucumber and spring onions into similar lengths too.

● Take each spring roll wrapper or pancake, lay it flat and place on a piece of bean curd, sausage, cucumber and spring onions. Add 1 teaspoon of crab, several strips of egg and some bean sprouts. Roll up carefully and cut each into 3 lengths.

● Place all the sauce ingredients, except the cornflour, in a pan, and boil for 5 minutes. Add the cornflour mixed with a drop of water, boil for 1 minute and take off the heat.

● Serve cold or steamed for 1–2 minutes. Sprinkle with more crab to serve, a teaspoon of spring roll sauce and extra chopped spring onion if liked. Serve the sauce alongside.

Vegetarian Spring Rolls

SERVES 4

These spring rolls are ideal for a buffet-style meal or as cocktail snacks.

1 pack of 20 frozen spring roll
  wrappers

225 g/8 oz fresh bean sprouts

225 g/8 oz young tender leeks
  or spring onions

100 g/4 oz carrots

100 g/4 oz white mushrooms

oil for deep-frying

1½ tsp salt

1 tsp sugar

1 tbsp light soy sauce

● Take the spring roll wrappers out of the packet and leave them to thaw thoroughly under a damp cloth.

● Wash and rinse the bean sprouts in a bowl of cold water and discard the husks and other bits and pieces that float to the surface. Drain.

● Cut the leeks or spring onions, carrots and mushrooms into thin shreds.

● Heat 3–4 tablespoons of oil in a preheated wok or frying pan and stir-fry all the vegetables for a few seconds. Add the salt, sugar and soy sauce and continue stirring for about 1–1½ minutes. Remove and leave to cool a little.

● Heat about 1.5 litres/2½ pt oil in a wok or deep fryer until it smokes. Reduce the heat or even turn it off for a few minutes to cool the oil a little before adding the spring rolls.

● Deep-fry 6–8 at a time for 3–4 minutes or until golden and crispy. Increase the heat to high again before frying each batch. As each batch is cooked, remove and drain it on absorbent kitchen paper.

● Serve hot with a dip sauce such as soy sauce, vinegar, chilli sauce or mustard.

Prawn Crystal Spring Rolls

SERVES 4

175 g/6 oz cooked crispy roast pork or 4 fresh boneless pork streaky rashers

3 tbsp clear honey

2 tbsp dry sherry

1 tsp chilli powder

225 g/8 oz rice vermicelli

450 g/1 lb fresh prawns, cooked and halved

175 g/6 oz cooked chicken, finely chopped

3 pickled onions, cut into fine strips

3 pickled gherkins, cut into fine strips

1 carrot, grated

1 packet of round Banh Trang rice paper

FOR THE DIPPING SAUCE

120 ml/4 fl oz fish sauce

1 red chilli, finely chopped

1 clove garlic, finely chopped

2–3 tbsp lemon juice

2 tsp wine vinegar

2 tsp ginger wine

1 tsp sugar

TO SERVE

1 Iceberg lettuce

sprigs of coriander

sprigs of mint

● To make the cold crispy pork, take the fresh pork. Mix the honey, dry sherry and chilli powder. Spread the mixture over the pork. Allow to rest for 1 hour. Grill the pork slices until really crisp. Turn often so that they are evenly cooked. Allow to cool and cut into thin strips.

● Make the dipping sauce by combining all the ingredients and mixing thoroughly.

● Soak the rice vermicelli in boiled water, slightly cooled. When soft, drain thoroughly and leave to cool.

● Place a clean tea towel on your working surface. Dip single sheets of Banh Trang into warm water and place on the tea towel. They should be pliable and soft. Place some cold vermicelli, some prawns, chicken, pork, pickled onion, gherkin and carrot near the centre of the Banh Trang but toward the bottom edge. Spread out the filling to a sausage shape. Roll up the bottom edge of the Banh Trang and tuck tightly under the mixture. Fold the left and right sides into the centre and continue rolling away from you. This roll will be transparent and allow you to see the mixture inside. Repeat for the remaining mixture.

● Place the cold, rolled, transparent spring rolls on a platter. Guests help themselves to lettuce leaves, one at a time. The roll is placed on the leaf and some mint and coriander are added: The whole is rolled up and dipped in the dipping sauce.

Prawns Fried with Garlic and Pepper

SERVES 4

approx 120 ml/4 fl oz peanut or corn oil for frying

325 g/11 oz large prawns, shelled

½ tbsp lightly chopped garlic

2 tbsp ground white pepper

1 tsp salt

● Heat the oil in a pan or wok, add the prawns and brown lightly for about 2 minutes.

● Remove all but a quarter of the oil and add the garlic, pepper and salt to the prawns in the pan. Fry lightly for 2 more minutes until brown.

● Drain off most of the remaining oil and serve immediately, accompanied by rice and sliced cucumber.

Prawn Crystal
Spring Rolls

Beef Crystal Spring Rolls

SERVES 4

FOR THE MARINADE

1 tsp lemon grass, finely chopped

1 tsp finely chopped garlic

1 tbsp ginger wine

225 g/8 oz steak, cut against the grain into pieces 2.5 mm/ ⅛ in thick and 5 cm/2 in long

175 g/6 oz rice vermicelli

2 pickled onions, finely cut

2 pickled gherkins, finely cut

1 carrot, grated

1 packet round Banh Trang rice paper

warmed water in a bowl on the table

FOR THE DIPPING SAUCE

4 tbsp fish sauce

1 red chilli, finely chopped

1 clove garlic, finely chopped

1 tbsp lime or lemon juice

1 tsp wine vinegar

1 tsp sugar

2 tsp dry sherry

TO SERVE

1 Iceberg or round lettuce

sprigs of coriander

● Combine the marinade ingredients together and marinate the beef slices. Leave for 2–3 hours. Soak the rice vermicelli. When soft, drain thoroughly. Toss the cold rice vermicelli, pickled onion, gherkin and carrot together and place on the table in a dish.

● Prepare the dipping sauce by mixing all the sauce ingredients together and stir well. Put the lettuce leaves in a dish, the coriander and mint on a flat plate, and place on the table. Put the Banh Trang on a plate and place on the table.

● Put warm water in a bowl that is large enough for the Banh Trang to be dipped in on the table. Put either a table-top barbecue or a fondue on the table and bring the marinated meat to the table. Guests should help themselves by dipping a Banh Trang into the warm water until it becomes soft and pliable. They then place some of the vermicelli and pickle, mint and coriander, and the cooked pieces of beef on the *Banh Trang*. The mixture is then rolled up and placed on a fresh piece of lettuce. The lettuce leaf is rolled around it and then dipped in the sauce.

Beef Satay

SERVES 4

2 cloves garlic, sliced

1 tsp fresh basil

1 red chilli, sliced

1 tbsp lime juice

1 tbsp sesame oil

1 tbsp fish sauce (optional)

225 g/8 oz steak, cubed

FOR THE DIPPING SAUCE

3 tbsp fish sauce

1 tbsp lime or lemon juice

1 pickled onion, thinly sliced

1 clove garlic, finely chopped

1 tbsp peanuts, finely chopped

● Mix the garlic, basil, chilli, lime juice, sesame oil and fish sauce, if using, together. Marinate the cubes of beef in this for at least 4 hours, turning frequently.

● Make the dipping sauce by mixing all the ingredients thoroughly. Place it in a bowl on the table.

● When the beef is ready, thread onto four skewers and place on the barbecue or under a preheated high grill until cooked, turning frequently. Baste equally frequently with the marinade.

Golden Baskets

SERVES 4–6

A classy opening dish, these crisp, deep-fried batter cases can also be offered as a delicate snack. The only problem can be finding a suitable metal mould; a tiny ladle might do, but the dimensions should be no more than about 5 cm/2 in across. The Thai moulds are made from brass. You can make these cases in advance; sealed in an airtight jar, they will keep for a long time.

FOR THE BATTER

50 g/2 oz rice flour

6 tbsp plain flour

4 tbsp thin coconut milk

2 tbsp tapioca flour

1 egg yolk

¼ tsp sugar

¼ tsp salt

¼ tsp bicarbonate of soda

approx. 1 litre/1¾ pt peanut or corn oil for deep-frying

FOR THE FILLING

2 tbsp peanut or corn oil

4 tbsp finely diced onion

225 g/8 oz pork or chicken, finely chopped

25 g/1 oz sweetcorn kernels

2 tsp finely diced raw potato

2 tbsp finely diced carrot

2 tbsp sugar

¼ tsp black soy sauce

½ tsp salt

½ tsp ground white pepper

FOR THE GARNISH

sprigs of coriander

1 fresh small red chilli, sliced finely into circles

● Mix all the batter ingredients together well in a bowl. Heat the oil in a pan or wok to about 180°C/350°F. Dip the moulds in the oil to heat up, remove and pat lightly with absorbent kitchen paper. Dip the outside of the moulds into the batter and quickly into the hot oil again. Fry until light brown, about 5–8 minutes, remove the cups from the moulds and place on absorbent kitchen paper to dry. Repeat to make 20–25 cups.

● Now make the filling. Put the 2 tablespoons oil in a hot wok or pan, add the onion and pork, and stir-fry for 2 minutes. Add the rest of the ingredients and fry until the vegetables are fairly soft, about 3 minutes. Take off the heat and allow to cool.

● Divide the filling among the batter cups. Garnish with coriander leaves and small pieces of fresh red chilli. Serve as an hors d'oeuvre or with cocktails.

Prawn and Minced Pork on Sugar Cane

SERVES 4

1 tbsp dried prawns or shrimps (optional)

225 g/8 oz peeled prawns

175 g/6 oz minced pork

1 small onion, finely chopped

2 tbsp coriander leaves, finely chopped

salt and pepper

1 tbsp fish sauce

1 egg, beaten

4 x 15 cm/6 in lengths of sugar cane or bamboo skewers

plain flour or cornflour (optional)

vegetable oil for deep-frying (optional)

webbs lettuce

● If using dried prawns or shrimps, soak for about 1 hour in warm water. Squeeze out excess water and chop finely. Wash the fresh prawns and chop finely.

● Put the minced pork into a large bowl. Add the onion, coriander, fresh prawns, dried shrimps, salt and pepper, and fish sauce.

● Pour the egg into the pork and prawn mixture, and mix well with your hand. The mixture should come together so that it can be moulded around the lengths of sugar cane or around bamboo skewers. If it is too runny, sift a little plain flour or cornflour into the mixture.

● Peel the sugar cane, leaving 2.5 cm/1 in of the green covering on at each end, or 5 cm/2 in at one end. Mould the mixture on to the peeled part of the sugar cane.

● Grill the sticks under a moderately hot grill, turning to ensure evenness in the cooking. Make sure that the sugar cane does not burn. Alternatively, deep-fry in hot oil for 4–5 minutes.

● Serve on a bed of lettuce. The sugar cane should be chewed or sucked as you eat the prawn and pork.

Prawns with Sesame Seeds on Toast

SERVES 4

4 tbsp white sesame seeds

½ tbsp dried prawns or shrimps (optional)

225 g/8 oz peeled prawns, finely chopped

2 cloves garlic, chopped

½ tsp fresh ginger, grated

1 small onion, grated

1 small egg, beaten

salt and black pepper

cornflour for dusting

1 thin French stick or 8 slices bread, crusts cut off

vegetable oil for deep-frying

● Toast the sesame seeds in a dry wok or frying pan until they begin to brown, shaking frequently to prevent them from burning.

● If using dried prawns or shrimps, soak in warm water until soft. Drain thoroughly and squeeze out excess water. Chop them finely.

● Combine the dried prawns or shrimps and fresh prawns, garlic, ginger, grated onion, egg, salt and black pepper, and knead together with your hands. The mixture should be stiff but not too stiff to spread. If it is too runny, dust with the cornflour.

● Cut the French bread into 1 cm/½ in slices or cut the slices of bread into triangles or shape using pastry cutters. Press the sesame seeds firmly into the prawn mixture, using the back of a wooden spoon so that the prawn mixture is also pressed firmly onto the bread. Refrigerate for 2 hours or longer if possible.

● Heat just enough oil to deep-fry the rounds, prawn side down, for 1 minute. Using a fish slice, turn carefully and fry the other side for a further minute. Drain on absorbent kitchen paper and serve hot.

Thai Hors d'oeuvre

SERVES 6–8

A hard-to-find treat in Thailand, but always enjoyed. The Thais use fresh tree and vine leaves, but lettuce does just as well.

5 tbsp unsweetened grated coconut, roasted in a 180°C/350°F/Gas Mark 4 oven until light brown

3 tbsp finely diced shallots

3 tbsp finely diced lime

3 tbsp diced ginger

3 tbsp dried prawns or shrimps, chopped

3 tbsp unsalted roasted peanuts

2 tsp fresh small green chillies, chopped

1 lettuce or bunch of edible vegetable leaves

FOR THE SAUCE

2 tbsp desiccated coconut

½ tbsp shrimp paste

½ tsp sliced galangal

½ tsp sliced shallot

3 tbsp unsalted peanuts, chopped

2 tbsp dried prawns or shrimps, chopped

1 tsp fresh sliced ginger

175 g/6 oz palm sugar

600 ml/1 pt water

● Make the sauce. Roast the coconut, shrimp paste, galangal and shallot in a 180°C/350°F/Gas Mark 4 oven for 5 minutes until fragrant, and cool. Place with the peanuts, dried prawns or shrimps, and ginger in a blender or food processor and finely chop.

● Transfer the mixture to a heavy-bottomed pan with the sugar and water, mix well and bring to the boil. Simmer until it is reduced to about 300 ml/½ pt. Remove from the heat and leave to cool.

● To serve, pour the sauce into a serving bowl and arrange all the ingredients in separate piles on a platter or in small bowls.

● To eat, take a lettuce leaf, place a small amount of each of the garnishes in the middle, top with a spoonful of sauce and fold up into a little package.

Scallops Grilled in Pork Fat with Fish Sauce

SERVES 4

4 scallops, cleaned

½ tsp salt

juice of 1 lime or lemon

1 piece fresh pork fat or rind of
   8 bacon rashers

4 tbsp fish sauce

● Cover the scallops with water and add the salt and lime or lemon juice. Simmer for 1–2 minutes (do not overcook). Remove the scallops from the liquid and drain them.

● Place each scallop in a shell or heatproof dish, place some pork or bacon rind on the scallops and put under a preheated high grill for at most 4 minutes. The pork fat should drip down on to the scallops, giving them a smokey pork flavour.

● Remove and serve with the fish sauce.

Crispy Anchovies

SERVES 4

The dried anchovies for this dish are about the size of whitebait and are deep-fried in the same way. They can be found in most Japanese food departments in supermarkets. If the anchovies are very salty, rub or rinse off excess salt before frying. Deep-fried anchovies mixed with a sweet/hot sauce which contrasts with their saltiness, are extremely moreish.

1 clove garlic, finely chopped

1 small onion, chopped

1 fresh red chilli, seeded

¾ tsp salt

1½ tsp sugar

2 tbsp vegetable oil, plus extra for deep-frying

about 100 g/4 oz dried anchovies, heads removed if liked, rinsed if necessary

FOR THE GARNISH

fresh coriander leaves

● Pound the garlic, onion and chilli to a paste with the salt. Mix in the sugar. Set aside.

● Heat the vegetable oil in a frying pan. Add the onion paste and cook, stirring occasionally, for 3–4 minutes.

● Meanwhile, half fill a deep-fat fryer with vegetable oil and heat to 180°C/350°F. Add the anchovies so the pan is not crowded (in batches if necessary), and fry for 20–30 seconds until very crisp and lightly coloured.

● Transfer the anchovies to absorbent kitchen paper to drain, then tip into the frying pan and heat through, shaking the pan. Pour into a serving bowl and garnish with coriander leaves.

Deep-fried Chicken Nuggets

SERVES 2

The mixture of garlic, ginger and soy sauce enhances the taste of the chicken, with the sliced lemon giving refreshing bite to these delicious nuggets.

2 boneless chicken breasts, cut into bite-sized cubes

FOR THE MARINADE

3 tbsp soy sauce

25 g/1 oz fresh ginger, peeled and grated

2 large cloves garlic, peeled and grated

salt and freshly ground black pepper

FOR THE COATING

2 tbsp cornflour

2 tbsp plain flour

vegetable oil, for deep frying

FOR THE GARNISH

2 slices lemon

● Marinate the chicken with the soy sauce, ginger, garlic, salt and pepper for 30 minutes.

● Mix the cornflour with the flour. Take each piece of chicken from the marinade and roll in the flour mixture until completely coated.

● Heat the oil to 180°C/350°F and deep-fry the chicken pieces for 4–5 minutes or until golden brown.

● Garnish with the sliced lemon and serve on a bed of salad leaves.

Chicken Satay

SERVES 4

2 tbsp creamed coconut or natural yogurt

1 clove garlic, crushed

1 tsp chilli powder

1 tsp ground cumin

1 tsp ground coriander

1 tbsp lemon juice

225 g/8 oz fresh chicken, cubed

FOR THE DIPPING SAUCE

2 tbsp coconut cream or natural yogurt

1 clove garlic, crushed

½ tsp ground cumin

1 tsp ground ginger

1 tsp ground coriander

1 tbsp lemon juice

1 tbsp chopped fresh mint

● Combine the creamed coconut or yogurt with the garlic, chilli powder, cumin, coriander and lemon juice. Marinate the chicken pieces in the mixture for at least 4 hours, turning frequently.

● Make the dipping sauce by mixing together all the ingredients except the mint. Leave to blend in a cool place.

● When the chicken is ready, thread it onto four skewers. Place on the barbecue or under a preheated high grill and cook until well done, basting frequently with the marinade and turning.

● Heat the dipping sauce and toss in the mint leaves. Serve separately.

Deep-fried Chicken Nuggets

Prawn and Scallop Satay

SERVES 4

Satay was probably introduced into Vietnam by traders from India. Bite-sized pieces of succulent meat, seafood, poultry or vegetables are seasoned and cooked over charcoal. A dipping sauce is always presented with the satay.

150 ml/¼ pt dry sherry or dry white wine

1 tbsp wine vinegar

1 tbsp chopped dill

salt to taste

12 large scallops, washed

12 large prawns in their shells

1 cucumber, cut into 1 cm/½ in slices

FOR THE DIPPING SAUCE

1 large onion, finely chopped

2 tbsp vegetable oil

2 cloves garlic, crushed

2 fresh red chillies, finely chopped

6 tomatoes, skinned

1 tbsp chopped sweet basil

● Place the sherry, vinegar, dill and salt in a pan and bring to the boil. Reduce the heat to simmer and add the scallops. Allow to simmer for 2 minutes. Remove the scallops and keep the liquid to use as the baste when barbecuing.

● Skewer the prawns, cucumber and scallops alternately so that each skewer has three prawns, three scallops and three pieces of cucumber. Leave, covered, in a refrigerator.

● Gently fry the onion in the oil for 3 minutes. Add the garlic and fry for a further minute. Add the chilli and tomatoes and fry for another 5 minutes. Add the basil leaves and stir. Remove from the heat and leave to cool.

● Place the satay on the barbecue or under a preheated high grill and cook for 3–4 minutes on each side. Baste with the reserved cooking liquid.

Mushroom Satay

SERVES 4

1 clove garlic, crushed

1 tsp minced fresh ginger

1 tsp minced fresh lemon grass
   or grated lemon rind

1 tbsp chopped fresh coriander

2 tbsp fish sauce (optional)

1 tbsp sesame oil

16 firm white mushrooms

**FOR THE DIPPING
SAUCE**

3 tbsp roasted peanuts or 3 tbsp
   crunchy peanut butter

1 red chilli, finely chopped

1 clove garlic, crushed

1 tbsp finely chopped mint

1 tbsp lime or lemon juice

3 tbsp fish sauce or 3 tbsp light
   soy sauce mixed with 1 tsp
   anchovy essence

2 tbsp sesame oil

120 ml/4 fl oz thin coconut
   milk

● Mix the garlic, ginger, lemon grass, coriander, fish sauce, if used, and sesame oil. Marinate the mushrooms in the mixture for 3–4 hours, turning frequently during this time.

● Make the dipping sauce by mixing together and pounding all the dipping sauce ingredients, except for the coconut milk, to make a rough paste. Stir in the coconut milk.

● Thread the mushrooms onto four skewers. Place on the barbecue or under a preheated high grill for about 3 minutes on either side, basting with the marinade. Serve hot with the dipping sauce.

Deep-fried Mackerel

SERVES 2

The mackerel is one of the mainstays of the Japanese diet and can be prepared in numerous ways. **Age-mono**, or deep-frying, locks in the mackerel's oils, and this gives its flesh a meat-like quality.

450 g/1 lb mackerel, head removed and gutted

1 tbsp soy sauce

½ tbsp sake

½ fresh chilli, seeded and finely chopped

1 cm/½ in cube fresh ginger, crushed

2–3 tbsp cornflour

vegetable oil for deep-frying

● Cut the mackerel in half, slicing close to one side of the backbone. Repeat on the other side to give two fillets separated from the backbone. Remove as many bones from the fillets as possible without spoiling the flesh (a pair of tweezers is helpful). Cut each fillet into three pieces.

● Put the soy sauce, sake, chilli and ginger into a dish and marinate the fish for 20 minutes.

● Dry the fish, using absorbent kitchen paper, then coat in the cornflour. Heat the oil to 180°C/350°F, then deep-fry the fish for about 4 minutes.

● Serve with stir-fried vegetables and sprinkle with soy sauce.

Spicy Squid

SERVES 4

When the pieces of squid are stir-fried they curl to expose the diamond cuts. The tentacles may be used or not as preferred. The choice of cooking oil is important in order to achieve a high temperature and satisfactorily crisp results.

12 squid, cleaned

juice of 1 lemon

1 green chilli, seeded and chopped

¼ tsp five-spice powder

2 cloves garlic, crushed

2 tsp sesame oil

5 tbsp peanut oil

1 red pepper, diced

4 spring onions, thinly sliced

5 tbsp soy sauce

● Slit the squid body sacs lengthways, then cut each into 2–3 pieces. Using a small, sharp pointed knife, score a zigzag pattern on the inside of the pieces of squid. Do not cut right through the squid since this will not achieve the desired effect—simply mark a trellis pattern in the flesh.

● Place the squid pieces in a basin. Add the lemon juice, chilli, five-spice powder, garlic and sesame oil, and mix well to coat all the pieces in seasoning. Cover and leave to marinate for at least an hour—if possible leave the squid for 3–4 hours.

● Heat the peanut oil until shimmering, then stir-fry the squid until browned. The pieces should curl to expose the attractive diamond cuts. Use a slotted spoon to remove the pieces from the pan and divide them between serving plates.

● Pour off any excess oil from the pan, if necessary, leaving just enough to cook the vegetables. Stir fry the pepper and spring onions for 1–2 minutes, then sprinkle in the soy sauce and stir for a few seconds.

● Spoon the vegetable mixture and juices over the squid and serve at once.

Nine-section Appetizer

SERVES 4–6

Traditionally in Korea, small pancakes are served in a pile surrounded by a ring of eight fillings, all in their own lacquered dish. Each person takes a pancake and fills it with whichever filling they like, then rolls it up with their fingers. The fillings should all look different and provide a variety of tastes and textures. This recipe may look complicated, but each of the fillings is very quick and easy to prepare.

100 g/4 oz plain flour

salt and freshly ground black
   pepper

vegetable oil for frying

CUCUMBER FILLING

½ cucumber, sliced into thin
   strips

salt

2 tsp sesame oil

MUSHROOM FILLING

6 shiitake mushrooms, sliced

2–3 tsp sesame oil

1 tsp soy sauce

freshly ground black pepper

MEAT FILLING

100 g/4 oz sirloin or rump
   steak, cut into very fine strips

1 small clove garlic, chopped

1 spring onion, white part and a
   little green part, finely
   chopped

1 tbsp soy sauce

1 tsp toasted sesame seeds

freshly ground black pepper

1½–2 tsp sesame oil

BAMBOO SHOOT FILLING

100 g/4 oz bamboo shoots, cut
   into fine strips

1 cm/½ in piece fresh ginger,
   cut into very fine strips

1½ tsp soy sauce

1 tsp sesame oil

EGG FILLING

2 eggs

salt and freshly ground black
   pepper

vegetable oil for frying

CARROT FILLING

1 carrot, cut into very fine strips

1 tsp rice vinegar

1 tsp sugar

PRAWN FILLING

175 g/6 oz prawns, chopped

1½ tsp rice vinegar

pinch of Korean chilli powder, or
   cayenne pepper mixed with
   paprika

salt

● To make the pancakes, sift the flour and seasoning into a bowl, then slowly pour in about 175 ml/6 fl oz water to make a smooth batter. Leave for 30 minutes.

● Heat a very shallow layer of oil in a frying pan. Add spoonfuls of the batter and spread out to form 7.5-cm/ 3-in diameter rounds. Fry until lightly browned on both sides. Stack in piles in a small, shallow serving dish.

● To make the cucumber filling, put the cucumber in a colander. Sprinkle with salt and leave for 30 minutes. Rinse well and squeeze out as much water as possible. Heat the sesame oil in a frying pan and fry the cucumber for 2–3 minutes. Transfer to a small, shallow serving dish.

● To make the mushroom filling, heat the oil in a frying pan. Add the mushrooms and stir-fry for 3–4 minutes. Toss with the soy sauce and transfer to a small serving dish.

● To make the meat filling, mix the beef with the garlic, spring onions, soy sauce, sesame seeds and pepper. Heat the sesame oil in a frying pan. Add the beef mixture and stir-fry for 4–5 minutes. Transfer to a small serving dish.

● To make the bamboo shoot filling, mix the bamboo shoots with the ginger and soy sauce. Heat the sesame oil in a frying pan and stir-fry the bamboo shoots for 2–3 minutes. Transfer to a small serving dish.

● To make the egg filling, lightly beat the yolks and the whites with the seasoning. Heat the oil in a frying pan. Fry the egg to make an 'omelette' and cut into strips. Transfer to a small serving dish.

● To make the carrot filling, mix all the ingredients together. Transfer to a small serving dish.

● To make the prawn filling, mix all the ingredients together. Transfer to a small serving dish.

● To assemble the starter, put the dish of pancakes in the centre and arrange the other dishes in a ring around it.

Banh Xeo Stuffed with Minced Pork and Bean Sprouts

SERVES 4

2 tbsp vegetable oil

1 clove garlic, finely chopped

1 small onion, finely chopped

175 g/6 oz minced pork

1 handful bean sprouts, washed and drained

3 eggs

1–2 tsp fish sauce (optional)

● Heat half the vegetable oil in an omelette pan or a wok. Quickly fry the garlic and onion until the aromas are released. Add the pork and stir-fry until brown.

● Toss in the bean sprouts and stir-fry for 2–3 minutes. Remove from the heat and keep warm.

● Beat the eggs with the fish sauce until light and fluffy. In an omelette pan, heat the remaining oil over a medium heat and pour in the egg and fish sauce. When the omelette begins to set, put the pork and bean sprout mixture into the centre and fold over the sides to form a square.

● To finish off the top and obtain a successful rise, finish off under a preheated high grill.

Eggstrip Bundles

SERVES 4–6

Egg strips are tied in bundles with 'strings' of blanched spring onion. In Korea the eggs are cooked in rectangular pans, but you can use an ordinary round crêpe pan or frying pan and trim the curves of the 'omelettes'. Serve with whichever dipping sauce you like, or even a selection of them.

5 eggs	12 spring onions, trimmed
salt and freshly ground black pepper	vegetable oil for frying
	dipping sauce of choice

● Lightly beat the eggs with the seasoning.

● Heat a very fine layer of oil in a 15-cm/6-in frying pan, preferably nonstick. Pour in half of the eggs. Cover and cook over a low heat for 5–6 minutes until the bottom of the 'omelette' is firm. Using a spatula, turn the 'omelette' over and cook for 2–3 minutes more until the second side is firm. Remove and leave to cool. Cook the remaining egg in the same way.

● Lower the spring onions, bulbs first, into a saucepan of boiling water, easing in the green parts as they soften. Cover and quickly return to the boil. Boil for 2 minutes, then drain and rinse under running cold water. Dry on absorbent kitchen paper. Split each spring onion lengthways into two or more strands by cutting through the bulb, then tearing upward.

● Trim the curves of the 'omelettes', then cut the 'omelettes' into strips about 6 cm x 5 mm/2½ x ¼ in wide. Make bundles of eight to ten egg strips each. Wrap a strip of spring onion around the centre of each bundle and tuck the end of the spring onion under the binding. Arrange the bundles on a serving plate and serve with a dipping sauce.

Scallops Stuffed with Shrimp Paste

SERVES 4

12 scallops, cleaned

vegetable oil for frying

FOR THE SHRIMP PASTE

1 tbsp dried shrimps, soaked in water until soft, drained and finely chopped, or 20 thawed frozen prawns or shrimps, finely chopped

2 small pieces of black wood ear fungus, soaked in warm water until soft, drained and finely chopped

100 g/4 oz sweet potato, boiled and mashed

1 tbsp fish sauce or 1 tbsp light soy sauce

● Make the shrimp paste stuffing by combining all the stuffing ingredients together.

● Steam the scallops until cooked—about 5 minutes in a bamboo steamer. Remove and leave to cool.

● Slit the scallops in their thickest part and spoon in the stuffing. Heat the oil until very hot. Gently lower the stuffed scallops in a basket and fry for 2 minutes.

Mung Bean Pancakes

MAKES ABOUT 8 PANCAKES

These pancakes are a popular street snack, but they are also made in restaurants and homes for celebratory occasions such as birthdays, weddings and New Year. The street versions are usually a thick round, approximately 18 cm/7 in across, but those cooked in restaurants or homes are thinner and smaller.

185 g/6½ oz whole mung beans, soaked for 10 hours

2 tbsp short-grain rice, washed and soaked

50 g/2 oz red pepper, diced

1 clove garlic, crushed

½ onion, diced

2 spring onions, white and some green parts sliced

1 tbsp crushed toasted sesame seeds

2 tsp sesame oil

1 tbsp soy sauce

175 g/6 oz mung bean sprouts

vegetable oil for frying

● Rub the beans, without draining them, between your palms to detach the skin. Pour off the water, which will take a lot of the skins with it. Repeat the process until all the skins have been removed. Put the beans into a blender or food processor.

● Drain the rice and add to the blender or food processor with 4 tablespoons water. Mix to a paste, then, with the motor running, slowly pour in 120 ml/4 fl oz water. Pour into a bowl and stir in the red pepper, garlic, onion, spring onions, sesame seeds, sesame oil and soy sauce.

● Add the mung bean sprouts to a saucepan of boiling water. Cover and quickly return to the boil. Boil for 2 minutes, then drain and squeeze out as much water as possible. Separate the bean sprouts and stir into the batter.

● Heat a little oil in a frying pan, preferably nonstick. Stir the batter and add a ladleful to the pan, spreading it out evenly with the back of the ladle. Trickle one teaspoon vegetable oil over the top of the pancake. Cover the pan and cook the pancake until brown, 2½–3 minutes.

● Turn the pancake over and cook, uncovered, for 2½–3 minutes more.

● Slide the pancake onto a warmed plate and cook the remaining batter in the same way.

Scallops Stuffed
with Shrimp Paste

Fried Mussel Pancakes

MAKES 8 PANCAKES

Mussels and pancakes may seem an unlikely combination, but here the batter is made from tapioca flour. This is market food—if you stroll through the night market of any provincial town in Thailand you can hear, and smell, the sizzling of this dish.

250 ml/8 fl oz peanut or corn oil for frying

350 g/12 oz raw mussel or oyster meat

8 eggs

325 g/11 oz large bean sprouts

3 tbsp finely sliced spring onions

2 tsp ground white pepper

FOR THE BATTER

475 ml/16 fl oz water

50 g/2 oz plain flour

100 g/4 oz tapioca flour or cornflour

2 tbsp baking powder

2 tbsp sugar

2 eggs, beaten

2 tsp salt

● Mix all the batter ingredients together thoroughly (alternatively, use shop-bought tempura batter). Heat a large, heavy frying pan, preferably cast iron, and add about 1 cm/½ in oil.

● Mix 40 g/1½ oz of the mussel meat and 50 ml/2 fl oz of the batter together and pour into the pan. Cook over medium heat for about 5 minutes until brown on the bottom, then break one egg on top of the mussel cake. Flip over carefully and fry until the egg is lightly browned, 3–5 minutes. Remove the mussel cake from the pan and drain well on absorbent kitchen paper. Repeat with the rest of the mussel and batter to make eight cakes.

● Add the bean sprouts to the pan and fry lightly. Place on a serving plate and arrange the mussel cakes on top. Sprinkle with the spring onion and white pepper before serving.

● Serve accompanied by Siricha chilli sauce or other thick chilli or hot sauce.

Spring Onion and Prawn Pancakes

SERVES 4–6

This is a more elaborate version of the previous recipe. Break and lightly beat the eggs as you need them.

100 g/4 oz plain flour

100 g/4 oz rice flour

salt and freshly ground black pepper

2 eggs

2 tsp sesame oil

dash of soy sauce

vegetable oil for frying

10 large spring onions, white and some green parts split lengthways and cut into strips

1 red pepper, cut into strips

1 courgette, cut into strips

175 g/6 oz peeled prawns

● Season the flours, then stir in the two eggs, the sesame oil and the soy sauce. Slowly pour in about 150 ml/¼ pt water, stirring, to make a medium-thick batter. Leave for 30 minutes.

● Heat a very fine layer of vegetable oil in a large frying pan, preferably nonstick. Pour in one-third of the batter. Scatter over one-third of the spring onions, pepper, courgette and prawns. Cook over a medium-hot heat for 5–7 minutes until set and browned underneath. Carefully turn over the pancake and cook for 5–7 minutes more.

Vegetable Snow Pancakes

SERVES 4

Light pancakes made from egg whites and flavoured with spring onions are the ideal base on which to serve mixed vegetables. Large white radish peps up the already delicious broccoli and mushroom mixture.

2 egg whites

2 tbsp cornflour

salt

2 spring onions, finely chopped

FOR THE STIR-FRIED VEGETABLES

5 cm/2 in piece white radish, peeled

225 g/8 oz broccoli

225 g/8 oz mushrooms, thinly sliced

3 tbsp soy sauce

1 tbsp caster sugar

1 tbsp rice vinegar or cider vinegar

oil for cooking

3 tbsp sesame seeds

● Lightly whisk the egg whites with 3 tablespoons water, adding the cornflour a teaspoonful at a time. Whisk in a little salt, then stir in the spring onions.

● Cut the white radish lengthways into thin slices, then cut the slices into fine strips. Place these in a bowl and set aside.

● Cut the broccoli into small pieces and mix them with the radish. Place the mushroom slices in a separate bowl and add the soy sauce, sugar and vinegar. Mix well but try not to break up the mushroom slices. Cover and set the mixture aside.

● The pancakes may be cooked individually in a wok or three to four at a time in a large frying pan. Heat a little oil, then lightly whisk the batter and pour a spoonful into the pan to make a thin round pancake. Cook until set and browned underneath, then turn and cook the second side until lightly browned. Drain the pancakes on absorbent kitchen paper and keep them hot. Make eight small pancakes.

● Heat a little oil, then use a draining spoon to add the mushrooms. Stir-fry over high heat for about 1 minute, until the mushrooms are browned. Add the radish and broccoli and continue cooking for about

3 minutes. Stir in the sesame seeds and cook for 1 minute, then pour in the juices from marinating the mushrooms.

● Arrange the pancakes on individual plates, then top each with a portion of the stir-fried vegetables. Serve at once.

Spring Onion Pancakes

SERVES 3–4

These delicious pancakes are one of Korea's national dishes. They are served straight from the sizzling pan and cut into squares so they can be picked up easily with chopsticks. For variety, add strips of pepper.

75 g/3 oz plain flour

75 g/3 oz rice flour

salt

1 size 1 large egg, beaten

1 tsp sesame oil

3 tbsp vegetable oil

6 spring onions, quartered lengthways, each length cut into 7.5-cm/3-in long strips

vinegar dipping sauce to serve

● Stir together the flours and salt. Stir in the egg, then slowly pour in 250 ml/8 fl oz water, stirring, to make a smooth batter. Stir in the sesame oil. Leave to stand for 30 minutes.

● Heat 1 tablespoon vegetable oil in a 20-cm/8-in nonstick frying pan over a medium-low heat. Sprinkle one third of the spring onions evenly over the bottom, then pour over one-third of the batter. Cover and cook for 5–6 minutes. Turn the pancake, cover again and cook for 3 minutes more. Remove the lid and cook for another 2 minutes.

● Transfer to a warm plate and repeat. Cut the pancakes into 5-cm/2-in squares and serve hot with vinegar dipping sauce.

Chicken Livers with Peppers in a Sweet Soy Sauce

SERVES 2

Chicken livers are widely eaten in Japan. Cooking in soy sauce and sugar disguises the smell of the liver, which some people find off-putting. It also softens the flesh.

300 g/10 oz chicken livers, cut into bite-sized pieces

1 tbsp vegetable oil

½ green pepper, seeded and thinly sliced lengthways

1½ tbsp soy sauce

1½ tbsp *mirin*

½ tbsp caster sugar

● Dip the livers into a bowl of boiling water until blanched, then drain.

● Heat the oil in a frying pan and fry the green pepper for about 3 minutes. Remove and set aside.

● Add the livers to the pan, frying over a medium heat for about 7 minutes. Sprinkle over the soy sauce, *mirin* and sugar, and continue to cook, stirring, for about 5 minutes.

● Return the green pepper to the pan and stir in lightly for a few minutes.

● Serve hot with rice and a vegetable dish.

Vietnamese Pancake

SERVES 2

The Vietnamese fried pancake or omelette reflects the Indian influence in Vietnamese cuisine. This omelette can be eaten on its own as part of a mixed array of starters, or left to cool, cut into strips, and placed as a garnish on noodles, salad or rice dishes.

3 eggs

1–2 tsp fish Nuoc Mam sauce (optional)

1 tbsp vegetable oil

1–2 tsp dried prawns or shrimps soaked in warm water until soft and drained, or 10 peeled prawns

1 tsp finely chopped fresh mint

1 tsp finely chopped coriander

● Beat the eggs and the fish sauce together until light and fluffy.

● In an omelette pan, heat the oil over a medium heat. Add the egg and fish sauce mixture. Before it sets, stir in the prawns, mint and coriander. Continue cooking until set.

● To finish off the top and obtain a successful rise, finish off under a preheated hot grill. Ease around with a wooden spatula and fold the omelette.

Soups

In the West soups provide additional bulk to the meal and are always served at the start of proceedings. In an Asian meal, however, soups are meant either to act as a lubricant to help wash down the bulky and savoury foods, in which case they are offered throughout the meal, or, on more formal occasions, a soup or soups are served between courses to refresh and cleanse the palate.

Hot and Sour Soup

SERVES 4

A little vinegar can be added to the soup if you find that the pickled vegetables do not give a sufficiently sour taste.

3 dried Chinese mushrooms, soaked in warm water for 30 minutes

2 cakes of bean curd

50 g/2 oz Szechwan preserved vegetables

50 g/2 oz pickled vegetables, such as cucumber, cabbage or green beans

2 slices fresh ginger, thinly shredded

2 spring onions

900 ml/1½ pt water

1 tsp salt

2 tbsp rice wine or sherry

1 tbsp soy sauce

freshly ground pepper to taste

1 tsp sesame seed oil

1 tsp cornflour with 2 tsp water

● Squeeze dry the mushrooms after soaking. Discard the hard stalks, and cut the mushrooms into thin shreds. Reserve the water for use later.

● Thinly shred the bean curd, Szechwan preserved vegetables, pickled vegetables and ginger. Finely chop the spring onions.

● In a wok or large pan, bring the water to the boil. Add all the ingredients and seasonings and simmer for 2 minutes. Add the sesame seed oil, and thicken the soup by stirring in the cornflour and water mixture. Serve hot.

Hot and Sour Prawn Soup

SERVES 4

750 ml/1¼ pt chicken stock

3 stalks of lemon grass, cut into 5 mm/¼ in slices

3 kaffir lime leaves

12 raw medium-sized or 6 large prawns, shelled but not deheaded

150 g/5 oz mushrooms, halved

5 fresh small whole green chillies

25 g/1 oz coriander leaves and stalks, sliced

3 tbsp lime juice, or to taste

½ tbsp fish sauce, or to taste

● Boil the stock in a pan, add the lemon grass and lime leaf, then the prawns and mushrooms. When the prawns are cooked, about 8–10 minutes, remove the pan from the heat and add the rest of the ingredients.

● Leave to stand for 5 minutes, then check the seasoning, adding more fish sauce or lime juice, or breaking up the chillies to release more heat as required—the soup should be spicy-sour and a little salty. Serve accompanied by rice.

Korean Chicken Stock

MAKES ABOUT 1.2 LITRES/2 PT

The garlic cloves can be left whole, cut into halves or chopped, according to how strong you want the flavour to be.

1 chicken carcass, preferably with skin, or 675–900 g/ 1½–2 lb raw or cooked chicken trimmings, bones, and skin

3 thin slices of fresh ginger

2 cloves garlic (optional)

2 spring onions, white and some green parts split lengthways

● Put the chicken into a large saucepan. Add 1.7 litres/3 pt water and bring slowly to the boil. Skim the scum from the surface. Add the garlic, ginger and split spring onions. Cover and simmer for about 3 hours.

● Drain through a strainer lined with muslin. Leave until cold, then put in the refrigerator until set. Remove the fat from the surface. Cover and keep in the refrigerator for up to 4 days; boil every other day.

Dried Bean Curd Skin and Vermicelli Soup

SERVES 4

15 g/½ oz dried bean curd skin

25 g/1 oz tiger lily buds

10 g/¼ oz black moss

50 g/2 oz bean thread vermicelli

900 ml/1½ pt water

1 tsp salt

2 tbsp light soy sauce

1 tbsp rice wine or dry sherry

1 tsp finely chopped fresh ginger

2 spring onions, finely chopped

2 tsp sesame seed oil

FOR THE GARNISH

fresh coriander

● Soak the bean curd skin in hot water for 30–35 minutes and then cut it into small pieces.

● Soak the lily buds and black moss in water separately for 20–25 minutes. Rinse the lily buds until clean. Loosen the black moss until it resembles hair.

● Cut the vermicelli into short lengths. Bring the water to the boil in a wok or large pan, and add all the ingredients, together with the seasonings. Stir until well blended.

● Cook the soup for 1–1½ minutes. Add the sesame seed oil and serve hot, garnished with coriander leaves.

Crab and Corn Porridge

SERVES 4

Corn is grown throughout Vietnam, and crabs are caught daily and sold cheaply in the market. If you want, fresh corn and crab can be used, but the recipe here saves time by using canned products. The result is just as good.

600 ml/1 pt basic chicken stock or 1 can condensed cream of chicken soup

325 g/11 oz can sweetcorn kernels

325 g/11 oz can creamed corn

325 g/11 oz can crabmeat, drained

1 egg

2 spring onions, cut into thin rings

● If using condensed soup, add 2 cans of water and milk mixed. Bring the stock or soup to just below boiling point.

● Roughly chop the sweetcorn kernels or leave whole. Add the corn and the creamed corn to the stock. Add the crabmeat and stir thoroughly.

● Beat the egg quickly and, holding a fork over the stock, pour the beaten egg along the back of the fork head, moving the fork in a circular motion at the same time. Remove from the heat and cover. Allow to set for about 40 seconds.

● Sprinkle with the spring onions, stir once and serve hot.

Stuffed Squid Soup

This is one of a range of clear, unspicy soups that are intended to accompany other dishes and serves as a contrast to dishes that are either spicy or have oil.

450 g/1 lb minced pork

½ tsp white soy sauce

¼ tsp ground white pepper

325 g/11 oz squid (body not tentacles), cleaned

1 litre/1¾ pt chicken stock

½ tbsp preserved cabbage, chopped roughly

7 white peppercorns, crushed

5 cloves garlic, crushed

1 tsp fish sauce

¼ tsp sugar

3 spring onions, cut into 1 cm/ ½ in pieces

2 tbsp coriander leaves and stalks, cut in 1 cm/½ in pieces

● Mix the pork, soy sauce and white pepper together well and use to stuff the squid. If there is any extra pork mixture, form it into small meatballs.

● Heat the chicken stock in a pan or wok, add the preserved cabbage, crushed peppercorns and garlic, and bring to the boil.

● Place the stuffed squid in the boiling stock, with meatballs if there are any, and then add the fish sauce and sugar. Boil until the stuffed squid is cooked, about 15 minutes or until it is no longer pink when cut into.

● Add the spring onion and coriander and remove from the heat immediately. Serve accompanied by rice.

Miso Stock

1 tbsp sesame oil

1 cm/½ in piece fresh ginger, peeled and finely chopped

1 clove garlic, finely chopped

1 spring onion, finely chopped

4 tbsp Chinese rice wine or Japanese *sake*

3 tbsp light soy sauce

2 tbsp sugar

8 tbsp red *miso* paste

2 tsp chilli oil

1.5 litres/2½ pt chicken stock

black pepper

● Heat the oil in a pan. Add the ginger, garlic and spring onion, then fry for 30 seconds.

● Add the wine first, then soy sauce, sugar, *miso* paste and chilli oil, and mix together. Add the chicken stock and bring to the boil.

● Remove from the heat, and the stock is now ready to use.

Miso Ramen with Shredded Leek

Noodles in **miso** *stock are one of the most popular noodle dishes served in Japan. It is essential to use a good quality* **miso** *paste, as this provides the crucial sweet and salty flavouring to the dish. The shredded leek should have a firm, supple texture, so if it has been prepared beforehand, soak it in a little water to prevent it from drying out.*

225 g/8 oz fresh spinach

450 g/1 lb *ramen* noodles, or 400 g/14 oz fresh or 350 g/12 oz dried egg noodles

1.5 litres/2½ pt *miso* stock

10 cm/4 in piece of leek, cut in 4 pieces and shredded

4 tbsp cooked dried bamboo shoots *(shinachiku)* (optional)

● Bring some water to the boil in a pan, and blanch the spinach for 1–2 minutes. Rinse, drain and divide into four equal portions.

● Bring more water to the boil in a large saucepan. Add the noodles and boil for 4 minutes. Drain and place into individual serving bowls.

● Heat the *miso* stock for 2–3 minutes. Pile the leek, spinach and bamboo shoots on top of the noodles. Add the *miso* stock and serve immediately.

Seafood Soup

SERVES 4–6

The seafood ingredients listed here are only suggestions. Use whatever is available at the fishmonger but try to assemble a variety of textures and flavours—the more the better.

1.5 litres/2½ pt chicken stock

150 g/5 oz sea bass or other firm fish, cleaned, gutted and cut into 6 pieces

5 large, raw prawns, shelled

1 blue crab, cleaned, shell removed, and chopped into 6 pieces

6 mussels in their shells, cleaned well

150 g/5 oz squid, body and tentacles, cleaned, gutted and cut into 2 cm/¾ in pieces

2 stalks of lemon grass, cut into 5 cm/2 in lengths and crushed

25 g/1 oz galangal, sliced

3 kaffir lime leaves, shredded

25 g/1 oz sweet basil leaves

8 fresh small green chillies, lightly crushed

5 dried red chillies, lightly fried

2½ tbsp fish sauce, or to taste

¼ tsp palm sugar

1 tbsp lime or lemon juice

● Pour the chicken stock into a wok or pan, bring to the boil, and add all the fish and seafood.

● Add the lemon grass, galangal and lime leaf. Boil, add all the rest of the ingredients, cook for 2 more minutes, and remove from the heat.

● Taste and add more fish sauce or lime juice as it pleases you.

● Serve in bowls accompanied by rice, fish sauce and lime or lemon juice.

Smoked Fish Soup

SERVES 4–6

1 litre/1¾ pt chicken stock

15 g/½ oz galangal, sliced

2 stalks of lemon grass, cut into 4 cm/1½ in pieces and crushed lightly

1 tsp shrimp paste

250 g/9 oz dried smoked fish (not salted), bones removed and broken into 3–4 pieces

1 oz shallot, crushed slightly

1½ tsp tamarind or lime juice, or to taste

25 g/1 oz sweet basil leaves

1 tbsp fish sauce, or to taste

½ tsp salt

5 dried whole red chillies, dry-fried for 3–5 minutes

● Pour the chicken stock into a pan, bring to the boil and add the galangal, lemon grass and shrimp paste. Boil again for 2 minutes and then add the dried fish pieces, shallot and tamarind juice.

● Bring back to the boil and simmer for 5 minutes, then remove from the heat and add the rest of the ingredients.

● Mix and season to taste with more tamarind, lime juice or fish sauce if you like. Stand for 10 minutes before serving, accompanied by rice.

Mussel and Pineapple Curry Soup

SERVES 4

1 litre/1¾ pt thin coconut milk

1 quantity chilli paste

200 g/7 oz cooked mussel meat (steam approx 675 g/ 1½ lb mussels in their shells and remove meat)

½ medium-sized pineapple, finely diced

1 kaffir lime leaf, torn into small pieces

2½ tbsp fish sauce

½ tbsp palm sugar

● Heat a quarter of the coconut milk in a pan, add the chilli paste and cook for 2 minutes.

● Add the mussels, mix well, then add the rest of the ingredients and boil for 1 minute.

● Remove from the heat and serve in bowls accompanied by rice.

Seaweed Soup

SERVES 6

Wrap the meat and put it in the freezer for about 35 minutes to make cutting it into strips easier. **Wakame is the Japanese name for a green type of seaweed, available dried in packets from healthfood and ethnic shops.**

100 g/4 oz dried *wakame*, soaked for 30 minutes

1.5 litres/2½ pt fish or beef stock

1 bunch spring onions, white and some green parts, chopped

1 tbsp sesame oil

1 clove garlic, finely chopped

175 g/6 oz lean tender beef, cut into fine strips

soy sauce

FOR THE GARNISH

toasted sesame seeds

● Drain the *wakame* and cut it into strips.

● Pour the stock into a saucepan. Add the spring onions and bring to the boil. Lower the heat so the stock simmers slowly.

● Heat the oil in a frying pan. Add the garlic and beef and stir-fry for about 2 minutes. Add to the stock together with the *wakame*. Add soy sauce to taste and heat through.

● Serve garnished with toasted sesame seeds.

White Radish Soup

SERVES 4–6

This warming, soothing soup is usually served for breakfast in Korea.

16 dried Chinese mushrooms, soaked in hot water for 30 minutes

1.5 litres/2½ pt chicken stock

450 g/1 lb white radish, diced

300 g/10 oz mung bean sprouts

1 tsp soy sauce

½ tsp sugar

freshly ground black pepper

● Remove the mushrooms from the soaking water. Drain and reserve the water.

● Remove and discard the stalks from the mushrooms. Thinly slice the caps and put into a large saucepan with the stock. Bring to the boil and add the white radish. Cover the saucepan and simmer slowly for about 10 minutes until the white radish is tender.

● Add the bean sprouts, return to the boil. Cover again and simmer for 3–4 minutes more. Add the soy sauce, sugar and pepper.

Malaysian Sour Noodle Soup

SERVES 4

This is a version of **laksa lemak** *from Penang. The stock is made from fish, and coconut milk is not used. The soup has a spicy, sour taste.*

450 g/1 lb cod

1.6 litres/2¾ pt water

4 shallots, sliced

2 cloves garlic, sliced

5 cm/2 in piece galangal or 2.5 cm/1 in fresh ginger, chopped

3 small red chillies, chopped

5 cm/2 in stalk lemon grass

2 tbsp vegetable oil

2 tsp ground turmeric

2 tsp dried shrimp paste (optional)

4 tbsp tamarind pulp

2 tsp salt

2 tsp sugar

225 g/8 oz rice vermicelli

FOR THE GARNISH

75 g/3 oz bean sprouts

2 rings canned pineapple, chopped

5 cm/2 in piece cucumber, shredded

3 fresh kaffir lime leaves, sliced

mint leaves, sliced

1 large red chilli, sliced

● Put the cod and water in a saucepan, bring to the boil, and simmer for 15–20 minutes. Meanwhile, blend the shallots, garlic, galangal, small red chillies, and lemon grass in a mixer or food processor.

● When the fish stock is ready, take out the fish, remove the skin and flake the meat. Heat the oil in a saucepan, then fry the shallot mixture together with the ground turmeric and dried shrimp paste for 3–4 minutes.

● Soak the tamarind pieces in warm water for 5 minutes, then sieve to squeeze and extract the juice. Add the fish stock, fish flakes, salt, sugar and tamarind juice to the fried spice mixture in the pan, and simmer for 3–4 minutes.

● Soak the rice vermicelli in warm water for 3 minutes, rinse and drain. Put into four bowls. Blanch the bean sprouts in boiling water for 1 minute.

● Pour the fish soup into serving bowls. Garnish with the bean sprouts, pineapple, cucumber, lime leaves, mint leaves and red chilli. Serve at once.

White Radish Soup

Sour Curry Soup

SERVES 4

This delicious soup includes lots of vegetables.
The bones are cooked with the fish for more flavour.

425 g/15 oz whole freshwater
fish, cleaned and gutted

1.2 litres/2 pt water

50 g/2 oz cucumber, quartered
and sliced lengthways

50 g/2 oz green beans, cut into
5 cm/2 in pieces

50 g/2 oz morning glory, cut
into 5 cm/2 in pieces

50 g/2 oz Chinese cabbage, cut
into 5 cm/2 in pieces

3 tbsp tamarind juice

2 tbsp fish sauce

2 tsp lemon juice

1 tsp palm sugar

FOR THE CHILLI PASTE

8 dried red chillies, chopped

50 g/2 oz shallots, chopped

1 tbsp chopped *krachai*

1 tbsp salt

½ tsp shrimp paste

● Cut the fish into 4 cm/1½ inch long pieces. Boil 150 g/5 oz of it in water until cooked, then remove with a slotted spoon (discard the water) and allow to cool. Remove all the bones, but retain the skin.

● Pound all the chilli paste ingredients together well with a pestle and mortar or in a blender. Mix in the cooked fish pieces and pound or process again.

● Place the fish–chilli paste mixture in a pan or wok large enough to hold all the ingredients, add the 1.2 litres/2 pt water and bring to the boil.

● Add the rest of the fish, boil again for 2 minutes, then add the cucumber, beans, morning glory and Chinese cabbage. Bring back to the boil, add the rest of the ingredients and simmer for 10 minutes.

● Serve accompanied by rice, sun-dried beef or dry salted fish, and pickled vegetables as condiments.

Prawn Pho

SERVES 4

Prawn Pho is a very light soup. It is simple yet delicious and unusual. As a variation, and to make it a little more substantial, you could add prawn balls.

2 pieces black wood ear fungus or 8 button mushrooms

900 ml/1½ pt fish stock or use a good-quality vegetable, fish or chicken stock cube

2 cucumber, peeled

175 g/6 oz bean thread vermicelli or spaghetti

225 g/8 oz prawns, cooked and peeled

150 ml/¼ pt Nuoc Nam fish sauce

4 large, cooked, unpeeled prawns, to garnish

● Soak the black wood ear fungus for 10 minutes or until soft in nearly boiling water. When soft, slice thinly and place in the stock. Add the mushrooms to the stock if using those instead. Put into a dish and place on the table.

● Slice the cucumber into thin rounds or cut into fine matchsticks. Place in a dish and put on the table.

● Soak the vermicelli in water that has been boiled and allowed to cool slightly (about 5 minutes). Drain and place in four bowls.

● Place the prawns in a bowl and put on the table. Meanwhile boil and simmer the stock.

● The guests garnish their bowls with the ingredients in the dishes placed on the table, then pour the hot stock over the whole. The fish sauce is added to taste and the soup bowls are garnished with the unpeeled prawns.

Prawn Balls

SERVES 4

175 g/6 oz prawns, minced

1 small hard-boiled egg, finely minced

1 small onion, finely minced

1 egg, beaten

salt and pepper

● Mix all the ingredients using your hand, then shape into small balls. Drop into the simmering stock to cook.

Spicy Vegetable Soup with Prawns

SERVES 4–6

1.8 litres/3¼ pt chicken stock

200 g/7 oz pumpkin flesh, diced

150 g/5 oz banana flower (if available)

100 g/4 oz young butternut squash, cut into wedges (with seeds)

100 g/4 oz green beans, cut into 2.5 cm/1 in pieces

½ tbsp fish sauce

200 g/7 oz large, raw prawns, peeled

60 g/2½ oz lemon basil leaves

FOR THE CHILLI PASTE

100 g/4 oz shallots, sliced

10 white peppercorns

25 g/1 oz dried shrimps, chopped

3 fresh small green chillies, chopped

½ tbsp shrimp paste

● Pound the chilli paste ingredients together with a pestle and mortar or in a blender.

● Place the stock in a pan, add the chilli paste and bring to the boil. Add the vegetables and boil for 10 minutes. Add the fish sauce, then add the prawns and lemon basil. Cook for 3–5 minutes.

● Serve accompanied by rice.

Chicken Pho

SERVES 4

Traditionally, **pho** *is made only with beef, but it is now being made with chicken and prawns.*

3 celery sticks, finely chopped

3 spring onions, chopped into rings (use green tops as well)

300 g/10 oz cooked chicken, finely shredded

225 g/8 oz flour sticks or spaghetti noodles

750 ml/1¼ pt chicken stock

2 pieces light wood ear fungus or 8 white button mushrooms, finely sliced

● Place the celery and spring onions in a bowl and put on the table. Place the cooked shredded chicken in a separate bowl and put that on the table, too.

● Follow the instructions on the flour sticks pack, or boil the spaghetti until just soft. Drain and rinse with some boiling water. Place in four bowls.

● Boil up the chicken stock until simmering, then add the light wood ear fungus or the mushrooms. Place in a bowl and put on the table.

● The guests should put a mixture of celery, spring onion and shredded chicken onto the noodles then ladle the hot chicken stock into the bowls.

Indonesian Chicken Soup with Rice Vermicelli

SERVES 4

This Indonesian soup dish has a spicy, sour, and nutty flavour. **Sambal oelek** *provides the spice in this soup. If you like a hotter taste, simply add more.*

2 tbsp vegetable oil

4 shallots, sliced

3 cloves garlic, sliced

5 cm/2 in piece galangal, or 2.5 cm/1 in fresh ginger, sliced

1 tsp ground coriander

3 tbsp macadamia nuts

1.5 litres/2½ pt light chicken stock

2 tsp salt

400 g/14 oz cooked chicken meat, shredded

225 g/8 oz rice vermicelli

FOR THE TOPPING

2 tsp salt

75 g/3 oz bean sprouts, blanched

2 spring onions, chopped

1 celery stick, sliced

2 tbsp ready-made crispy onions

4 lime wedges

2 tsp Indonesian chilli paste (*sambal oelek*) or chilli sauce

● Heat the oil in a frying pan. Fry the shallots, garlic, *galangal* or ginger and the ground coriander, then add the nuts. Blend to a paste with 3 tablespoons chicken stock in a mixer or food processor.

● Put the paste and chicken stock in a pan, and simmer for 5 minutes. Add the chicken meat and salt, and simmer for 2–3 minutes. Meanwhile, soak the rice vermicelli in warm water for 3 minutes. Rinse, drain and divide into four bowls.

● Put the bean sprouts, spring onions and celery on top of the noodles. Pour in the soup and sprinkle with the crispy onions. Garnish with lime wedges and ½ teaspoon of chilli sauce to each bowl. Serve immediately while still hot.

Pork and Spinach Curry Soup

SERVES 4–6

750 ml/1¼ pt water

450 g/1 lb pork spare ribs, cut into 3 cm/1¼ in pieces

½ tbsp tamarind juice

½ tbsp fish sauce

2 tsp chopped anchovies or dried salted fish

325 g/11 oz fresh spinach leaves

2 tsp sliced garlic

2 tsp sliced shallot

2 tbsp peanut or corn oil

4 whole dried red chillies

● Boil the water in a pan, add the pork and bring back to the boil. Cook until the pork is tender, about 20–25 minutes.

● Add the tamarind juice, fish sauce and anchovy. Bring back to the boil, simmer for 5 minutes, add the spinach and remove from the heat after 1 minute. Transfer to a bowl.

● Fry the garlic, shallot and chillies in the oil in a frying pan until tan-coloured. Sprinkle over the soup with the oil. Serve accompanied by rice.

Chicken Porridge

SERVES 4–6

65 g/2½ oz long- or short-
  grained rice

1.2 litres/2 pt water

225 g/8 oz corn-fed chicken
  breast, boned and slivered

FOR THE MARINADE

2 tbsp fish sauce

1 tsp cornflour dissolved in
  2 tbsp water

2 tsp dry sherry

salt

FOR THE GARNISH

1 large spring onion, finely
  chopped

salt and black pepper

fresh coriander, chopped

● Rinse and drain the rice. Add the water and bring
to the boil over high heat. Turn the heat to medium
low, partially cover the pan and let the rice bubble for
5 minutes. This loosens the starch and blends the
water and rice. Give the rice a stir and turn the heat as
low as possible, cover and simmer for about 1 hour.

● Place the chicken in the marinade for 30 minutes.
Add the chicken to the porridge and stir gently.
Continue until all the pink in the chicken has
disappeared. Turn off the heat, cover and serve in a
couple of minutes.

● Garnish with coriander for more flavour, and
spring onion and salt and pepper to taste.

Corn and Asparagus Soup

SERVES 4

175 g/6 oz white asparagus

1 egg white

1 tbsp cornflour

2 tbsp water

600 ml/1 pt water

1 tsp salt

100 g/4 oz sweetcorn kernels

FOR THE GARNISH

1 spring onion, finely chopped

● Cut the asparagus spears into small cubes.

● Beat the egg white lightly. Mix the cornflour with the water to make a smooth paste.

● Bring the water to a rolling boil. Add the salt, sweetcorn, and asparagus. When the water starts to

boil again, add the cornflour and water mixture, stirring constantly.

● Add the egg white very slowly and stir. Serve hot, garnished with finely chopped spring onion.

Dashi

MAKES ABOUT 1.5 LITRES/2½ PT

10 cm/4 in piece dried kelp, wiped with a damp cloth

1.5 litres/2½ pt water

40 g/1½ oz bonito flakes

● Make two or three cuts, about 2.5 cm/1 in long, in the kelp to help release the flavour. Put the water and kelp in a saucepan and heat on a low flame. Remove the kelp just before the water begins to boil.

● Add the bonito flakes when the liquid comes back to a boil, and turn off the heat. Leave the liquid to stand until all of the flakes have sunk to the bottom of the pan.

● Sieve the liquid through a muslin or paper filter. Retain the bonito flakes and kelp to make a less strong *dashi*.

Dashi Stock

MAKES ABOUT 1.5 LITRES/2½ PT

2 tbsp *mirin*

1.5 litres/2½ pt *dashi*

100 ml/3½ fl oz Japanese soy sauce

3 tbsp sugar

● Put the *mirin* in a saucepan and bring to the boil.

● Add the *dashi*, soy sauce and sugar. Simmer for 3–4 minutes. It is now ready to use.

Miso Soup with Wakame Seaweed and Onion

SERVES 2

In Japan this soup is served at breakfast, lunch or dinner, when it is accompanied by a main dish and a bowl of rice. Unlike Western soups, Japanese soup is sipped from the bowl, with any pieces of vegetable or tofu being eaten with chopsticks.

500 ml/18 fl oz *dashi* stock

½ medium onion, sliced

2 tsp dried *wakame* seaweed

2 tbsp *miso* paste

● Put the *dashi* stock and onion in a pan, bring to a boil and simmer until the onion becomes transparent.

● Add the *wakame* and continue to simmer until it has expanded. (This takes only a couple of minutes.)

● Add the *miso* paste and stir using a small whisk, until dissolved. Heat for a few more minutes until the soup starts to boil. Do not boil for more than 1–2 minutes or the soup will be too salty. Serve immediately while still hot.

Miso Soup with Silken Bean Curd and Spring Onions

SERVES 2

Two types of bean curd are widely used in Japanese cookery, **kinu,** *or silken bean curd, and* **momen,** *or cotton bean curd. As the names suggest,* **kinu dofu** *has a very smooth, silky texture, whereas* **momen dofu** *is characterised by its more solid, coarser appearance and feel. It is* **kinu dofu** *that is usually used in miso soups.*

500 ml/18 fl oz *dashi* stock

100 g/4 oz silken bean curd cut into 1 cm/½ in cubes

3 spring onions, chopped

2 tbsp *miso* paste

● Put the *dashi* stock and bean curd in a pan, bring to the boil and simmer for 4–5 minutes.

● Add the spring onion and simmer for a further minute. Stir the *miso* paste into the soup using a mini whisk until it is completely dissolved.

● Simmer again until the soup just returns to the boil. Serve immediately.

Chinese Cabbage Soup

SERVES 4

250 g/9 oz Chinese cabbage

3–4 dried Chinese mushrooms, soaked in warm water for 30 minutes

2 tbsp oil

2 tsp salt

1 tbsp rice wine or dry sherry

900 ml/1½ pt water

1 tsp sesame seed oil

● Wash the cabbage and cut it into thin slices. Squeeze dry the soaked mushrooms. Discard the hard stalks and cut the mushrooms into small pieces. Reserve the water in which the mushrooms have been soaked for use later.

● Heat a wok or large pan until hot, add oil and wait for it to smoke. Add the cabbage and mushrooms. Stir a few times and then add the salt, wine, water and the water in which the mushrooms had been soaked. Bring to the boil, add the sesame seed oil and serve.

Egg and Leek Consommé

SERVES 2

Tomato and Egg Flower Soup

SERVES 4

This clear soup is usually eaten with **sushi** *dishes and has a subtle flavour. The use of shiitake mushrooms adds extra taste. Do not boil the leek for too long as it needs to retain some of its texture.*

500 ml/18 fl oz *dashi* stock	½ tsp salt
2.5 cm/1 in leek, halved and sliced very finely	dash of soy sauce
	1 egg, beaten
3 shiitake mushrooms, sliced	

● In a pan bring the *dashi* stock to the boil then add the leek, mushrooms, salt and soy sauce. Simmer the liquid for 3–4 minutes.

● Gradually add the beaten egg to the pan, whisking continuously to stop it from forming into lumps. Serve immediately.

250 g/9 oz tomatoes, skinned	1 litre/1¾ pt water
1 egg	2 tbsp light soy sauce
2 spring onions, finely chopped	1 tsp cornflour mixed with 2 tsp water
1 tbsp oil	

● Skin the tomatoes by dipping them in boiling water for a minute or so and then peel them. Cut them into thick slices.

● Beat the egg. Finely chop the spring onions.

● Heat a wok or pan over a high heat. Add the oil and wait for it to smoke. Add the spring onions to flavour the oil and then pour in the water.

● Drop in the tomatoes and bring to the boil. Add the soy sauce and slowly pour in the beaten egg. Add the cornflour and water mixture. Stir and serve.

Chinese Mushroom Soup

SERVES 4

6 dried Chinese mushrooms

2 tsp cornflour

1 tbsp cold water

3 egg whites

2 tsp salt

600 ml/1 pt water

1 spring onion, finely chopped

● Soak the dried mushrooms in warm water for 25–30 minutes. Squeeze them dry, discard the hard stalks and cut each mushroom into thin slices. Reserve the water in which the mushrooms were soaked for use later.

● Mix the cornflour with the water to make a smooth paste. Comb the egg whites with your fingers to loosen them.

● Mix the water and the mushroom-soaking water in a pan and bring to the boil. Add the mushrooms and cook for about 1 minute. Now add the cornsflour and water mixture, stir and add the salt.

● Pour the egg whites very slowly into the soup, stirring constantly.

● Garnish the soup with the finely chopped spring onion and serve hot.

Ramen with Stir-fried Vegetables

SERVES 4

Ramen *noodles topped with a blend of fresh and flash-fried vegetables—deliciously simple and simply delicious!*

450 g/1 lb *ramen* noodles or 400 g/14 oz fresh or 350 g/ 12 oz dried thin egg noodles

1.5 litres/2½ pt soy sauce stock

FOR THE TOPPING

2 tbsp vegetable oil

1 tbsp sesame oil

1 small onion, sliced

75 g/3 oz mange tout, cut in half diagonally

2–3 small carrots, cut into long matchsticks

150 g/5 oz bean sprouts

225 g/8 oz Chinese cabbage, chopped

2 dried wood ear fungus or dried *shiitake* mushrooms, soaked in water, rinsed and chopped

salt and pepper

● Make the topping. Heat the oils in a wok or frying pan until very hot. Stir-fry the onion, mange tout and carrots for 2 minutes, then add the bean sprouts, Chinese cabbage, wood ear or shiitake mushrooms, and stir-fry for another 3–4 minutes. Season.

● Boil plenty of water in a large pan and add the noodles. Cook for 3 minutes before draining well. Put the noodles into four bowls.

● Heat the soy sauce stock. Pile the stir-fried vegetables onto the noodles, and pour the stock over the top.

Ramen with Garlic

SERVES 4

Do not be surprised at the amount of garlic used in this recipe. The key point of this dish is the strong garlic flavouring, which makes it a warming dish for a cold winter's day.

1 tbsp sesame oil

16 cloves garlic, sliced

450 g/1 lb *ramen* noodles or 400 g/14 oz fresh or 350 g/12 oz dried thin egg noodles

4 cloves garlic, crushed

1.5 litres/2½ pt soy sauce stock

4 tbsp cooked dried bamboo shoots (*shinachiku*) (optional)

2 spring onions, chopped

● Heat the sesame oil in a frying pan. Fry the garlic for 2–3 minutes or until turned golden brown. Set aside.

● Boil plenty of water in a pan and add the noodles. Cook for 3 minutes, then drain. Place the noodles in individual bowls.

● Put the crushed garlic and soy sauce stock in a pan. Bring to the boil, and simmer for 2–3 minutes.

● Put a quarter of the fried garlic, bamboo shoots and spring onions onto each serving of noodles. Pour the stock over the top, and serve immediately.

Ramen with Stir-fried Vegetables

Coconut and Galangal Soup

SERVES 4–6

This creamy soup has become one of the favourites on Thai restaurant menus, not least for the delicate aroma and flavour given by the galangal.

1.2 litres/2 pt thin coconut milk

25 g/1 oz shallot, finely chopped

15 g/½ oz galangal, thinly sliced

2 stalks lemon grass, cut into 2 cm/¾ in pieces

6 fresh small whole red chillies

3 kaffir lime leaves, torn into small pieces

1 tsp salt

325 g/11 oz boneless skinned chicken breasts, cut across into 5 mm/¼ in thick slices

200 g/7 oz fresh mushrooms (oyster if available)

2 tbsp lime or lemon juice

½ tbsp fish sauce

3 tbsp coriander leaves and stalks cut into 2 cm/¾ in pieces

● Pour the coconut milk into a pan and bring to the boil. Add the shallot, galangal, lemon grass, chilli, lime leaf and salt.

● Boil, add the chicken and bring to the boil again, then add the mushrooms and bring back to the boil for 2 minutes.

● Remove from the heat and stir in the lime juice, fish sauce and coriander.

● Serve in bowls accompanied by rice, lime quarters and fish sauce with chillies.

Soy Sauce Stock

MAKES 1.5 LITRES/2½ PT

1.5 litres/2½ pt chicken stock

2 tsp salt

4 tsp Chinese rice wine or Japanese *sake*

2 tsp white fat

4 tbsp light soy sauce

4 tsp dark soy sauce

black pepper

● Put the stock, salt, wine and fat in a pan. Bring to the boil, and simmer for 2–3 minutes.

● Turn off the heat, add the light and dark soy sauce, pepper and stir. The stock is now ready to use.

Cucumber Soup

SERVES 4

½ cucumber

50 g/2 oz black field mushrooms

600 ml/1 pt water

1½ tsp salt

1 tsp sesame seed oil

1 spring onion, finely chopped

● Split the cucumber in half lengthways and slice it thinly, but do not peel.

● Wash and slice the mushrooms, but do not peel.

● Bring the water to the boil in a wok or large pan. Add the cucumber and mushroom slices and salt. Boil for about 1 minute.

● Add the sesame seed oil and finely chopped spring onion. Stir and serve hot.

Deep-fried Bean Curd and Wood Ear Soup

SERVES 4

50 g/2 oz deep-fried bean
curd, or 1 cake fresh bean
curd

15 g/½ oz wood ear fungus

600 ml/1 pt water

1 tsp salt

1 tbsp light soy sauce

FOR THE GARNISH

1 spring onion, finely chopped

1 tsp sesame seed oil

● Use either two packets of ready-made deep-fried bean curd (there are about 10 to each 25 g/1 oz packet), or cut a cake of fresh bean curd into about 20 small cubes and deep-fry them in very hot vegetable oil until they are puffed up and golden. Cut them in half.

● Soak the wood ears in water until soft (this will take 20–25 minutes) and rinse until clean.

● Bring the water to the boil in a wok or large pan. Add the bean curd, wood ears and the salt.

● When the soup starts to boil again, add the soy sauce and cook for about 1 minute. Garnish with finely chopped spring onion and sesame seed oil. Serve hot.

Ramen with Pork and Bean Curd

SERVES 4

Pork and bean curd, called **Ma Po's Tofu** *in China, is a popular family dish throughout east Asia. It is commonly served with rice. However, this spicy sauce with pork and bean curd really goes down just as well piled onto a bowl of hot noodles.*

450 g/1 lb *ramen* noodles, or 400 g/14 oz fresh or 350 g/ 12 oz dried medium egg noodles

1.5 litres/2½ pt soy sauce stock

2 spring onions, chopped

FOR THE TOPPING

1 tbsp vegetable oil

1 clove garlic, finely chopped

1 cm/½ in piece fresh ginger, peeled and finely chopped

175 g/6 oz minced pork

½ leek, finely sliced

300 ml/½ pt chicken stock

1 tbsp chilli bean sauce *(toban djan)*

2 tsp sugar

1 tsp light soy sauce

1 tbsp Chinese rice wine or dry sherry

1 tsp tomato purée

400 g/14 oz bean curd, diced

2 tbsp cornflour mixed with 2 tbsp water

● To make the pork with bean curd, heat the oil in a wok or frying pan until very hot. Fry the garlic and ginger for 1 minute. Then add the pork and stir-fry for 3–4 minutes.

● Add the leek and stir-fry for another minute. Then add the chicken stock, chilli bean sauce, sugar, soy sauce, wine and tomato purée, and bring to the boil.

● Add the bean curd and simmer for about 5–7 minutes. Next, add the cornflour paste and stir to thicken.

● Boil plenty of water in a pan and add the noodles. Cook for 3 minutes, then drain. Place the noodles in individual bowls. Heat the soy stock.

● Put a quarter of the bean curd mixture and spring onions onto each serving of noodles. Gently pour the soy stock over the top, and serve at once.

Northern Thai Soup

SERVES 4–6

1 litre/1¾ pt water

175 g/6 oz boneless skinned chicken breasts

350 g/12 oz minced pork

1 tbsp preserved cabbage

50 g/2 oz onion, sliced

2 tbsp fish sauce

15 g/½ oz dried large shrimps, soaked in cold water for 5 minutes

15 g/½ oz spinach leaf

2 tbsp tamarind juice

● Boil the water in a pan, add the chicken and cook for 7–10 minutes until well cooked. Remove and cut across into thin slices.

● Using the same cooking water, add the pork, preserved cabbage, onion and fish sauce. Boil and then add the rest of the ingredients.

● Boil again before pouring into bowls. Serve accompanied by rice.

Chicken Soup with Clams and Spinach

SERVES 4

Shellfish and poultry have a natural affinity. Here, chicken and clams are combined with great success, and the union is enhanced by spinach.

16 clams

1 tbsp vegetable oil

2 cloves garlic, crushed

1½–2 tsp fresh ginger, finely chopped

3 spring onions, white and some green parts, chopped

1 chicken breast, cut into very fine strips

900 ml/1½ pt chicken stock

350 g/12 oz fresh spinach, chopped

1½ tsp sesame oil

salt and freshly ground black pepper

● Scrub the clams and rinse them under running cold water.

● Heat the vegetable oil in a saucepan. Add the garlic, ginger, spring onions and chicken, and stir-fry for 30 seconds. Add the chicken stock and bring to the boil. Simmer for 5 minutes.

● Add the clams. Return to the boil and simmer for 3–5 minutes until the clam shells open; discard any that remain closed.

● Stir in the spinach. Simmer for 1–2 minutes, then remove the pan from the heat. Add the sesame oil and season to taste.

Boiled Rice Soup with Chicken

SERVES 4

This tasty and nourishing soup is the traditional and universal Thai breakfast. It is also made with minced pork, and an optional extra is an egg cracked straight into the dish just before serving; it partly poaches in the hot stock.

1.5 litres/2½ pt chicken stock

325 g/11 oz boneless skinned chicken breasts, cut across into thin slices

550 g/1¼ lb cooked rice

1 tbsp chopped pickled cabbage

1 tsp salt

1 tsp ground white pepper

100 g/4 oz celery, finely sliced

2 spring onions, sliced

25 g/1 oz cloves garlic, unpeeled and fried until soft

50 g/2 oz *phrik dong* (sliced red chilli with vinegar)

2 tbsp fish sauce

● Boil the chicken stock in a pan. Add the chicken, rice, cabbage, salt and pepper. Boil the chicken until cooked, about 8–10 minutes.

● Add the celery and spring onions, and remove from the heat immediately.

● Pour into bowls and sprinkle with the fried garlic. Serve the soup with the *phrik dong* and fish sauce in separate bowls.

Ramen with Wakame

SERVES 4

Wakame *seaweed is sold either dried or salted. The dried variety is more easily preserved and handled. Wakame is very nutritious, full of minerals and trace elements, and virtually calorie-free! It makes a healthy hot noodle soup dish.*

450 g/1 lb *ramen* noodles or 400 g/14 oz fresh or 350 g/ 12 oz dried medium egg noodles

1.5 litres/2½ pt soy sauce broth

FOR THE TOPPING

2½ tbsp dried *wakame* seaweed, soaked in hot water and then drained

4 tbsp cooked dried bamboo shoots *(shinachiku)* (optional)

2 spring onions, chopped

2 hard-boiled eggs, cut in half

● Boil plenty of water in a pan. Add the noodles and cook for 4 minutes. Drain and put into four bowls.

● Heat the soy sauce stock. Place the *wakame*, bamboo shoots (if used), spring onions and eggs on the noodles. Pour the soy sauce stock gently into the bowls. Serve immediately.

Ramen Noodles in Miso Soup

SERVES 2

Ramen *is Japanese fast-food. In this variation, the flavour of fried garlic and sesame oil complements the* **miso** *and chilli. It is difficult not to make a noise when you eat Japanese noodles. In fact, the more you slurp, the better you will enjoy the meal, or so it is*

250 g/9 oz fresh *ramen* noodles

475 ml/16 fl oz *ramen* stock

½ tsp salt

freshly ground black pepper

2 tsp sesame oil

2 tsp toasted sesame seeds

3 tbsp *miso* paste

FOR THE COATING

1 tbsp sesame oil

175 g/6 oz bean sprouts

1 large clove garlic, sliced

½ red pepper, thinly sliced

pinch of chilli powder

pinch of salt

● Cook the noodles for about 2–2½ minutes in boiling water. Drain and put into the individual bowls.

● Heat the stock with the salt and pepper in a pan. When it boils, add the sesame oil and sesame seeds and stir in the *miso* paste until it has dissolved.

● Meanwhile, heat the oil in a frying pan. Stir-fry the bean sprouts, garlic and red pepper. Sprinkle in the pinch of chilli powder and salt. Place the vegetables on top of the noodles. Pour over the *miso* soup, serve and eat immediately.

Bamboo Shoot Soup

SERVES 4

600 ml/1 pt water

3 tbsp dried salted mackerel or anchovies, chopped

1 stalk of lemon grass, cut into 2 cm/¾ in pieces and crushed lightly

3 kaffir lime leaves, torn into small pieces

65 g/2½ oz pumpkin flesh, cut into 2cm/¾ in pieces

65 g/2½ oz bamboo shoots, sliced

25 g/1 oz green beans, cut into 2 cm/¾ in pieces

3 small white aubergines, quartered

3 fresh large green chillies, cut into thirds

1 tbsp fish sauce

25 g/1 oz lemon basil leaves

● Boil the water in a pan or wok and add the dried fish, lemon grass and lime leaf. Boil for 1 minute.

● Add the rest of the ingredients, except the lemon basil, and simmer for 7–10 minutes or until the pumpkin is soft.

● Stir in the basil and remove from the heat immediately. Serve accompanied by rice.

Creamy Coconut Noodle Soup

SERVES 4

This famous Malaysian dish **laksa lemak,** *reflects the multicultural nature of that country and its people. It has a smooth texture and silky hot taste!*

8 shallots, sliced

3 cloves garlic, sliced

5 cm/2 in piece galangal or 2.5 cm/1 in fresh ginger, peeled and sliced

4 small red chillies, sliced

1 tbsp chopped fresh lemon grass

5 tbsp vegetable oil

2 tsp ground turmeric

1 tsp ground coriander

2 tsp dried shrimp paste (optional)

100 g/4 oz bean curd, diced

600 ml/1 pt light chicken stock

475 ml/16 fl oz coconut milk

2 tsp sugar

2 tsp salt

2 fish balls or 2 golfball-sized chunks imitation crabmeat, sliced

225 g/8 oz rice vermicelli

12 large prawns, peeled and deveined

FOR THE GARNISH

cooked chicken from the light chicken stock, shredded

75 g/3 oz bean sprouts

5 cm/2 in piece cucumber, shredded

1 large red chilli, sliced

2 spring onions, chopped

● Blend the shallots, garlic, galangal, red chilli and lemon grass in a food processor. Heat 3 tablespoons of the oil in a saucepan, and stir-fry the shallot mixture with the turmeric, coriander seeds and dried shrimp paste over a low heat for 3–4 minutes.

● Heat the remaining oil in a frying pan and fry the bean curd until lightly browned. Add the chicken stock, coconut milk, sugar, salt and fish balls or imitation crabmeat, bring to the boil, and simmer for 2–3 minutes.

● Meanwhile, blanch the bean sprouts in boiling water for 1 minute.

● Soak the vermicelli in warm water for 3 minutes, rinse and drain well. Divide the vermicelli equally into four bowls.

● Add the prawns to the soup and simmer for 2 minutes. Pour the soup into the bowls; garnish with shredded chicken, bean sprouts, cucumber, sliced chilli and spring onions. Serve immediately.

Noodles in Soy Sauce Soup

SERVES 2

FOR THE BASIC *RAMEN* BROTH

MAKES 1.15 LITRES/2 PT

300 g/10 oz chicken carcass, roughly chopped

2 pork bones

½ leek

2.5 cm/1 in piece fresh ginger, peeled and cut in half

1 large clove garlic, cut in half

1.8 litres/3¼ pt water

FOR THE *SHOYU RAMEN*

250 g/9 oz fresh *ramen* noodles

475 ml/16 fl oz *ramen* stock

3 tbsp soy sauce

½ tsp salt

pinch of freshly ground black pepper

FOR THE TOPPING

8 tbsp sweetcorn kernels

3 spring onions, chopped

20 g/¾ oz butter, cut in half

● To make the *ramen* stock, blanch the chicken and pork bones. Then put the water, bones, leek, ginger and garlic into a large pan. Bring to the boil and simmer for 1 hour, occasionally skimming off the scum. Strain the stock through muslin. Adjust the heat to prevent the stock from boiling again (this will make the liquid cloudy).

● Boil the noodles for about 2–2½ minutes. Drain and put them in individual bowls.

● Heat the 475 ml/16 fl oz stock, soy sauce, salt and pepper in a pan. When it boils, pour the soup into the bowls.

● Put the sweetcorn kernels on top of the noodles, sprinkle with the chopped spring onion, then top with the butter. Eat as soon as possible or the noodles will absorb the soup and become soggy.

Cold Buckwheat Noodle Soup

SERVES 4

This soup is almost a meal in itself. Because of the number of elements that have to be prepared separately, it may appear to be a complicated recipe, but, in fact, each vegetable is simple to prepare and all of them can be done ahead.

225 g/8 oz buckwheat noodles

1.2 litres/2 pt chicken stock

1 tsp sesame oil

½ cucumber, thinly sliced

salt

1½ tsp rice vinegar

pinch of sugar

pinch of Korean chilli powder or cayenne pepper mixed with paprika

2 hard-boiled eggs, shelled and thinly sliced

8 pieces of white radish, cut into thin strips

½ Korean pear, peeled, cored and thinly sliced

250 ml/8 fl oz liquid from white radish

selection of dipping sauces to serve

● Cook the noodles according to the instructions on the packet. Drain and rinse under running cold water. Drain well, then put into a bowl and toss with 120 ml/ 4 fl oz of the stock and the sesame oil.

● Put the cucumber slices in a colander and toss with salt. Leave for 1 hour. Rinse the cucumber well, drain and dry thoroughly on absorbent kitchen paper. Mix with the rice vinegar, sugar and chilli powder or cayenne pepper mixed with paprika.

● Divide the noodles among four dishes. Pour one-quarter of the remaining stock into each dish. Arrange a few neatly overlapping slices of egg around the top of each pile of noodles. Surround with slightly overlapping vegetable and pear slices.

Hot and Sour Noodle Soup with Prawns

SERVES 4

This is one of the representative dishes of Thai cuisine. The soup is a myriad of flavours: the sour element of lime leaves and lemon grass combined with the hot chilli and fish sauce, with its strong aroma.

1 tbsp vegetable oil

2 cloves garlic, grated

2 shallots, grated

2.5 cm/1 in piece galangal or 1 cm/½ in fresh ginger, thinly sliced

4–5 small red chillies, chopped

1.5 litres/2½ pt light chicken stock

3 kaffir lime leaves, sliced

10 cm/4 in piece lemon grass, chopped

225 g/8 oz rice vermicelli

20 large, peeled prawns

6 tbsp fish sauce

6 tbsp fresh lemon or lime juice

2 tbsp palm or brown sugar

16 canned straw mushrooms

coriander leaves

● Heat the oil in a saucepan, then stir-fry the garlic, shallots, galangal, and chilli for about 1 minute. Put in the chicken stock, add the lime leaves and lemon grass, bring to the boil and simmer for 5 minutes.

● Meanwhile, soak the rice vermicelli for 3 minutes, rinse, drain and divide equally among four bowls. Add the prawns, fish sauce, lemon or lime juice, sugar and straw mushrooms to the soup, then simmer for 2–3 minutes.

● Pour the soup into the bowls and sprinkle with the coriander leaves. Serve immediately.

Spinach Soup

SERVES 3–4

This is a favourite soup throughout South Korea.

150 g/5 oz chicken breast, thinly sliced and cut into 2.5 cm/1 in cubes

3 spring onions, finely chopped

2 cloves garlic, chopped

2 tbsp soy sauce

1½ tsp sesame seeds

freshly ground black pepper

1½ tbsp vegetable oil

1.25 litres/2¼ pt chicken stock

350 g/12 oz fresh spinach, trimmed and shredded

sesame oil for sprinkling

● Mix the chicken with the spring onions, garlic, soy sauce, sesame seeds and plenty of pepper. Leave for 30 minutes.

● Heat the vegetable oil in a saucepan. Add the chicken mixture and fry until browned. Add the stock and heat until simmering. Simmer very slowly for about 25 minutes until the chicken is tender.

● Add the spinach and cook for 2–5 minutes more until the spinach is tender. Adjust the seasonings; if the liquid has reduced too much, add hot water.

● Serve sprinkled with sesame oil.

Hot and Sour Noodle Soup
with Prawns

Dumpling Soup

SERVES 6

Korean dumpling soup is nothing like a European soup with dumplings. Instead, it contains small dumplings filled with water chestnuts, pork and chicken, like Chinese dim sum.

1 carrot, chopped

1 onion, chopped

1 clove garlic, chopped

6 water chestnuts, chopped

100 g/4 oz lean pork

100 g/4 oz chicken

175 g/6 oz cooked, peeled prawns

2 tbsp soy sauce

1 tbsp sesame oil

pinch of Korean chilli powder or cayenne pepper mixed with paprika

30 wonton wrappers

1.7 litres/3 pt chicken stock

FOR THE GARNISH

spring onions, chopped

● Put the vegetables and three-quarters of the pork, chicken and prawns in a food processor. Dice the remaining pork, chicken and prawns. Add the soy sauce, sesame oil and a pinch of Korean chilli powder, or cayenne pepper mixed with paprika, to the food processor, and mix to a smooth paste.

● Spoon a little of the vegetable mixture into each wonton wrapper. Wet the edges and draw together to make a neat bundle. Pinch the edges together to seal.

● Bring the stock to the boil in a saucepan. Add the dumplings and diced pork, chicken and prawns. Simmer for 8–10 minutes. Garnish with spring onions before serving.

Spinach and Bean Curd Soup

SERVES 4

225 g/8 oz fresh spinach

2 cakes bean curd

2 tbsp oil

2 tsp salt

600 ml/1 pt water

2 tbsp soy sauce

1 tsp sesame seed oil

● Wash the spinach well, discarding the tough and discoloured leaves. Shake off the excess water and cut the leaves into small pieces.

● Cut the bean curd into about 14 pieces.

● In a wok or large pan, heat the oil until hot. Stir-fry the spinach until soft. Add the salt and water, and bring to the boil.

● Add the bean curd and soy sauce and cook for 1½–2 minutes. Add the sesame seed oil just before serving the soup.

Issaan-style Soup

SERVES 4–6

100 g/4 oz each of calf's heart, liver, lung, kidney and small intestines, cleaned and prepared

1.2 litres/2 pt water

25 g/1 oz galangal, sliced

3 stalks of lemon grass, cut into 3 cm/1¼ in pieces and crushed

5 kaffir lime leaves, shredded

1½ tbsp fish sauce

1 tbsp lemon juice

2 dried red chillies, crushed

½ tsp salt

1 spring onion, cut into 1 cm/½ in pieces

● Boil all the offal together in a pan of water until tender, about 30–40 minutes. Rinse well in cold water and slice everything up fairly small.

● Place the cooked offal in a pan with the water, bring to the boil, and add all the remaining ingredients, except the spring onion. Bring back to the boil for 2 minutes, add the spring onion, and remove from the heat.

● Serve immediately accompanied by sticky or steamed rice.

Bean Sprout Soup

SERVES 4

225 g/8 oz fresh bean sprouts

1 small red pepper, cored and
    seeded

2 tbsp oil

2 tsp salt

600 ml/1 pt water

1 spring onion, finely chopped

● Wash the bean sprouts in cold water, discarding the
husks and other bits and pieces that float to the
surface. It is not necessary to trim each sprout.

● Thinly shred the red pepper.

● Heat a wok or large pan, add the oil and wait for it
to smoke. Add the bean sprouts and red pepper and
stir a few times. Add the salt and water.

● When the soup starts to boil, garnish with finely
chopped spring onion and serve hot.

Fish and Shellfish Main Dishes

Almost everything that the sea has to offer, from squid to seaweed, can be found in Eastern cuisine. The dishes in this section use all kinds of fish and seafood, most well known but a few less often found in Western shops. There are dishes for every type of meal, from simple grilled fish to stir-fried squid, and from barbecued fish garnished with ginger sauce to lobster and sweet potato curry.

Steamed Fish with Lemon and Chilli

SERVES 4

The combination of lemon or lime juice and fresh chillies in the topping gives this dish a refreshing spicy tartness.

500 g/1 lb 2 oz whole sea bass or perch, cleaned and gutted

120 ml/4 fl oz lemon or lime juice

2 tbsp small, fresh green chillies, lightly chopped

2 tbsp chopped garlic

2 tbsp fish sauce

½ tbsp salt

1 tsp sugar

10 g/¼ oz coriander leaves and stalks, cut into 1 cm/½ in pieces

● Steam the fish whole for 15 minutes until tender but firm.

● Meanwhile, mix all the remaining ingredients, except the coriander, together. When the fish is cooked, place it on a serving platter and spread the lemon juice mixture all over (the fish must be very hot when the sauce is poured over).

● Sprinkle with the coriander and serve accompanied by rice.

Fish with Black Beans

SERVES 4

Serve this flavoursome fish dish with plain cooked rice. If it is included along with several other dishes as part of an extensive menu, the quantity of fish may be reduced by half.

900 g/2 lb plaice or whiting, skinned

3 tbsp salted black beans

5 tbsp dry sherry

3 tbsp light soy sauce

1 tsp sesame oil

25 g/1 oz cornflour

3 tbsp oil

5 cm/2 in piece fresh ginger, peeled and cut in fine strips

1 green chilli, seeded and cut into rings

1 clove garlic, crushed

1 piece lemon grass or strip of lemon rind

1 bunch spring onions, cut diagonally into strips

● Cut the fish across into 1 cm/½ in wide strips and place these in a large shallow dish. Sprinkle the salted black beans, sherry, soy sauce and sesame oil over the fish. Cover the dish and leave the strips to marinate for 2–3 hours.

● When you are ready to cook the fish, drain the strips well, reserving all the juices. Toss the strips in the cornflour.

● Heat the oil, then stir fry the ginger, chilli, garlic and lemon grass or rind over medium heat for 4–5 minutes, to extract their flavour. Add the fish strips to the pan and stir fry them carefully, avoiding breaking the strips, until they are lightly browned.

● Add all the spring onions and continue to stir fry for 2 minutes, until the onions are cooked. Add 5 tbsp water to the reserved marinating juices and pour them into the pan. Bring to the boil, reduce the heat and stir fry for 1 minute. Serve at once.

Fried Fish Strips

SERVES 3–4

*These strips are similar to French **goujons**, but they are lighter to eat as they are coated in just egg and flour, rather than batter, and then shallow- rather than deep-fried.*

550 kg/1¼ lb white fish fillets, such as cod or plaice

1 plump clove garlic, halved lengthways

seasoned plain flour for coating

1–2 eggs, beaten

oil for frying

seasoned dipping sauce to serve

● Rub the fish with the cut side of the garlic halves, then thinly slice the fish diagonally.

● Coat the fish in seasoned flour, then dip in beaten egg and let the excess egg drain off.

● Heat a shallow layer of oil in a frying pan. Add the fish strips, in batches if necessary so they are not crowded, and fry for about 5 minutes, depending on thickness. Transfer to absorbent kitchen paper to drain, then serve hot with seasoned dipping sauce.

Lemon Fish Strips with Courgettes

SERVES 4

225 g/8 oz firm white fish
   fillets, skinned

salt and freshly ground black
   pepper

25 g/1 oz plain flour

grated rindJ of 1 lemon

5 tbsp oil

½ small onion, thinly sliced and
   separated into strips

1 red pepper, cut in thin strips

225 g/8 oz small courgettes,
   halved lengthways and cut in
   5 cm/2 in long sticks

40 g/½ oz snipped spring
   onions

FOR THE GARNISH

lemon wedges

● Cut the fish fillets across into 1-cm/½-in wide strips. Place them in a dish, then sprinkle with the seasoning, flour and lemon rind. Mix well to coat evenly.

● Heat the oil, then stir-fry the onion and pepper for 3 minutes, until lightly cooked, before adding the fish. Carefully stir-fry the fish, taking care not to break the strips, for 4–5 minutes, until lightly browned. Use a slotted spoon to transfer the fish mixture to a heated serving dish.

● Add the courgettes to the oil remaining in the pan (there should be just enough to keep the pan greased) and stir-fry them over high heat for about 2 minutes, so that they are hot and slightly tender.

● Stir in the spring onions, then arrange the courgettes around the fish. Garnish with lemon wedges and serve at once. The juice from the lemon should be squeezed over the fish before the fish is eaten.

Fried Fish Topped with Chilli Sauce

SERVES 4–6

The scoring makes small trenches in the flesh for the sauce, which is not intended to surround the fish, but to be poured on top at the last minute.

8 cloves garlic

5 fresh yellow chillies

1 kg/2¼ lb whole perch or sea bass, cleaned and gutted

750 ml/1¼ pt peanut or corn oil for frying

½ tsp each salt and ground white pepper

plain flour for dusting

120 ml/4 fl oz chicken stock

2 fresh red chillies, quartered lengthways

1 tbsp tamarind juice or vinegar

2 tsp sugar

1 tsp fish sauce

15 g/½ oz sweet basil leaves, fried in oil for 1 minute until crisp

● Pound the garlic and chilli together lightly with a pestle and mortar or in a blender.

● Score the fish on both sides five or six times, sprinkle on the salt and pepper and dust with flour. Heat the oil to 180°C/350°F in a pan or wok and fry the fish well, until crisp but tender inside, about 7–10 minutes. Remove and drain the fish and put in a serving dish.

● Take out all except about 3 tablespoons of the oil. Then, cook the garlic and chilli mixture, add the rest of the ingredients, except for the basil, and boil lightly for about 5 minutes until slightly thick. Pour on top of the fish and sprinkle over the fried basil to garnish. Serve accompanied by rice.

Grilled Salted Trout

SERVES 2

Grilling is a very simple way of cooking fish. The trout need to be fresh to make the most of this dish.

2 medium trout, gutted

1 tsp salt

soy sauce, to serve

● Make 3 cuts on each side of the fish, place them on a wire tray, and sprinkle both sides with salt.

● Grill for 5–6 minutes or until lightly browned, then turn and Grill for a further 5–6 minutes. (Remember the cooking time will vary depending on the size of the fish.)

● When the fish is ready, transfer to a plate and drizzle with soy sauce. Serve with rice.

Chilled Egg Noodles with Tuna, Prawns, Wakame and Sesame Sauce

SERVES 4

450 g/1 lb fresh thin egg noodles

2 tsp sesame oil

FOR THE DRESSING

4 tbsp sesame sauce

4 tbsp sugar

4 tbsp vinegar

4 tbsp Japanese soy sauce

4 tbsp chicken stock

1 cm/½ in piece fresh ginger

FOR THE TOPPING

4 tsp dried *wakame* seaweed, soaked in hot water, than drained

225 g/8 oz tuna (in water)

50 g/2 oz canned sweetcorn

8 tbsp cooked prawns

generous handful alfalfa sprouts

● Bring a large pan of water to the boil. Cook the noodles for 3 minutes, then rinse and drain. Toss them in the sesame oil, then place onto four serving plates.

● Mix the sesame sauce, sugar, vinegar, soy sauce and chicken stock well. Extract the juice from the ginger by grating it, then squeezing out the juice. Add it to the mixture, and mix again. Refrigerate.

● Divide the seaweed, tuna, sweetcorn, prawns and sprouts among each serving of the noodles.

● Pour the sesame dressing over each serving, and serve immediately.

Chilled Egg Noodles with Mackerel and Prawns

SERVES 4

This recipe is just perfect for one of those summer's days when you are hungry but can't face the thought of eating anything hot.

450 g/1 lb fresh or 350 g/ 12 oz dried thin egg noodles

FOR THE SAUCE

generous 250 ml/8 fl oz chicken stock

120 ml/4 fl oz light soy sauce

4 tbsp sugar

120 ml/4 fl oz vinegar

4 tsp sesame oil

2 tbsp juice of squeezed ginger

FOR THE TOPPING

75 g/3 oz bean sprouts

100 g/4 oz mange tout

1 large fillet smoked mackerel, flaked

100 g/4 oz cooked prawns

handful alfalfa sprouts

1 medium-sized tomato, sliced

● Boil plenty of water in a pan, add the noodles and cook for 3 minutes. Rinse under water, drain and arrange on four shallow dishes.

● Heat the chicken stock, soy sauce and sugar in a pan, and simmer for 3 minutes. Add the vinegar, sesame oil and ginger juice, and mix well. Chill in the refrigerator.

● Blanch the bean sprouts and mange tout for 1 minute in boiling water. Remove and cut the mange tout into long matchsticks. Now arrange the mackerel flakes, prawns, bean sprouts, mange tout, alfalfa sprouts and tomato on the noodles. Pour the chilled sauce over and serve at once.

Chilled Egg Noodles with Tuna, Prawns,
Wakame and Sesame Sauce

Fried Fish with Pork and Ginger

SERVES 4

A relatively simple dish to prepare, the fish acquires considerable flavour from the pork fat, but is quite mild.

325 g/11 oz whole flat fish, cleaned and gutted

½ tsp salt

100 g/4 oz belly of pork, finely sliced

2 salted preserved plums or 1 tbsp pickled lemon juice

25 g/1 oz fresh ginger, sliced

10 small cloves garlic, crushed

50 g/2 oz celery with its leaves, cut into 2.5 cm/1 in pieces

4 spring onions, cut into 2.5 cm/1 in pieces

2 fresh red chillies, cut into lengthways strips

● Wash and dry the fish and rub it inside and out with the salt.

● Place half the pork fat on a heatproof plate that fits a steamer, put the fish on top and cover with the rest of the pork fat. Roughly chop the salted plum and sprinkle it (or the juice) over the top together with the ginger and garlic.

● Steam for 15 minutes, then add the celery, spring onion, and chilli, and steam for 5 more minutes, until the fish is firm but tender.

● Serve accompanied by rice.

Steamed Fish Curry

SERVES 6–8

Although curry is the closest English description, the final mixture is quite thick and sets quite firmly in the steaming. The banana leaf wrapping not only makes the presentation attractive, but adds some flavour.

325 g/11 oz fish fillets, skinned and cut into slices

600 ml/1 pt thin coconut milk

2 eggs, beaten

3 tbsp fish sauce

25 g/1 oz sweet basil leaves

100 g/4 oz cabbage, finely sliced

6 squares of banana leaf (optional)

1½ tbsp cornflour

2 kaffir lime leaves, torn into small pieces

1 fresh red chilli, seeded and cut into strips

FOR THE PASTE

10 small cloves garlic, chopped lightly

5 dried red chillies, chopped lightly

5 white peppercorns

3 shallots, chopped lightly

2 coriander roots, sliced

1 tsp galangal, sliced

1 tsp lemon grass, chopped

½ tsp kaffir lime rind, finely chopped

½ tsp salt

● Pound together all the ingredients for the paste with a pestle and mortar or in a blender until fine. Put in a bowl, stir in the fish pieces and 450 ml/¾ pt of the coconut milk. Break in the eggs and mix well. Stir in the fish sauce.

● Divide the basil and cabbage among the banana leaf squares or into six to eight ovenproof ramekins or cups. Top with the fish mixture and wrap up. Cook in a pressure cooker, or bake in a 180°C/350°F/Gas Mark 4 oven, covered in a pan half-filled with hot water, for 10 minutes.

● Meanwhile, boil the remaining 150 ml/¼ pt of coconut milk in a pan, and add the cornflour to thicken slightly.

● After the fish mixture has cooked for 10 minutes, spoon the thickened coconut milk over the tops and sprinkle with the lime leaf and chilli. Pressure-cook or bake again for 5 more minutes. Leave to stand for 5 minutes before serving, accompanied by rice.

Soba with Simmered Herring

SERVES 4

In Japan, this dish requires the use of a kind of smoked herring not usually available overseas. Kippers make an excellent substitute.

400 g/14 oz dried soba

1.5 litres/2½ pt *dashi* stock

FOR THE TOPPING

4 kipper fillets

2 tbsp soy sauce

2 tbsp *mirin*

2 tbsp sugar

120 ml/4 fl oz water

3 spring onions, chopped

seven-flavour chilli powder (optional)

● Rinse the kippers in hot water. Put them, together with the soy sauce, *mirin*, sugar and water, into a pan and simmer for about 20 minutes, or until the sauce has thickened.

● Bring plenty of water to the boil in a pan and add the *soba*. Cook for 5–6 minutes. Drain and rinse well under cold water. Drain again. Divide into serving bowls.

● Heat the *dashi* stock.

● Place a kipper fillet onto each serving of soba and sprinkle with chopped spring onion. Pour the stock over the top, sprinkle with seven-flavour chilli powder and serve immediately.

Deep Fried Fish Cakes

SERVES 4

In Vietnam a milkfish or pomfret might be used for this recipe. Frozen cod fillets are a perfectly adequate substitute.

300 g/10 oz white fish

150 ml/¼ pt coconut milk or cow's milk

225 g/8 oz sweet potatoes, boiled and mashed

2 tomatoes, skinned and chopped

2 tbsp chopped fresh coriander

2 tbsp fish sauce or 2 tbsp light soy sauce mixed with 1 tsp anchovy essence

2 eggs, lightly beaten

rice flour or plain flour

vegetable oil for deep-frying

FOR THE GARNISH

lettuce leaves

sprigs of mint

● Cover the fish with the coconut milk. (If there is not sufficient, add a little water or cow's milk.) Bring the milk to the boil and simmer for 10 minutes or until the fish is tender. Remove any skin or bones and flake the fish.

● Place the fish, potato, tomatoes and coriander in a bowl and mix well.

● Combine the fish sauce and egg. Add half this mixture slowly to the fish mixture so that it retains its shape. Add some flour if the mixture is too runny.

● Shape the mixture into small balls. Dip each ball into the remaining egg and fish sauce mixture, and roll into the rice flour.

● Heat the oil until it is smoking and deep-fry until the balls are golden brown.

● Serve hot, garnished with the lettuce and a few sprigs of mint.

Mackerel Cooked in a Pot Lined with Pork

SERVES 4

2 large mackerel, cleaned

2 pieces bean curd

salt

salt and pepper for seasoning

3 tbsp vegetable oil

100 g/4 oz belly of pork, cut into threads

100 g/4 oz black Chinese mushrooms, soaked in warm water, cut into threads

100 g/4 oz bamboo shoots, sliced

1 red chilli, chopped

2 slices fresh ginger, chopped

1 tbsp dark soy sauce

1 tbsp fish sauce

½ tbsp wine

600 ml/1 pt water

2 spring onions, chopped

● Chop the mackerel into slices about 2.5 cm/1 in thick. Wash the bean curd gently with water, salt lightly to absorb the water and season. Cut the bean curd in half and then cut the pieces into cubes.

● Heat a wok and pour in 1 tablespoon oil to fry the bean curd cubes. Set aside. Heat 1 tablespoon oil and fry the mackerel until both sides turn golden brown.

● Add the remaining oil. Add the pork, black mushrooms, bamboo shoots, chilli, ginger, soy sauce, fish sauce, wine and sugar, and stir-fry.

● Pour the contents of the wok into an earthenware pot or heavy pan, add the water and bring to the boil over a high heat. Reduce the heat to low and braise for 20 minutes. Taste and add the spring onions. Serve in the pot when cooked.

Simmered Mackerel in Miso Sauce

SERVES 2

This Japanese dish is a particular favourite in autumn, when the mackerel is reputed to be at its best. The fish is cooked unboned to give extra flavour.

450 g/1 lb mackerel, head removed and gutted

FOR THE SAUCE

120 ml/4 fl oz water

2 tbsp caster sugar

1 tbsp *sake*

50 g/2 oz *miso*

1 thin slice peeled fresh ginger

2 spring onions, cut in half

● Cut the mackerel in half, close to one side of the backbone, to make two pieces of fish, one with the backbone attached and one without. Cut each piece in half again.

● Put the water, sugar, *sake* and *miso* in a pan, then heat until the liquid is simmering. Add the fish and ginger and continue to simmer, covered, for 7–8 minutes with a lid, slightly smaller than the pan and placed directly onto the fish. Use foil if you do not have a lid.

● Add the spring onions and simmer for a further 5–10 minutes. Serve immediately with rice.

Golden Fish with Potatoes

SERVES 4

40 g/1½ oz plain flour

½ tsp turmeric

salt and freshly ground white
pepper

grated rind of 1 lemon

450 g/1 lb monkfish, thick cod
fillet or other firm white fish,
skinned and cubed

4 tbsp oil

2 celery sticks, thinly sliced

1 small onion, finely chopped

225 g/8 oz fine green beans,
blanched in boiling water for
1 minute and drained

675 g/1½ lb baby potatoes,
scraped and cooked

● Mix the flour, turmeric, seasoning and lemon rind,
then toss the fish cubes in this mixture to coat them
completely.

● Heat the oil, then stir-fry the celery and onion until
slightly softened, about 7 minutes. Add the beans and
potatoes, and continue to stir fry for 5–7 minutes,
until all the vegetables are hot and tender.

● Push the vegetables to one side of the pan and add
the fish. Stir-fry the cubes over medium to high heat,
taking care not to break them, until golden brown.
Gently mix the ingredients and serve at once.

Stir-fried Rice Vermicelli with Barbecued Pork and Prawns

SERVES 4–6

This Chinese noodle dish uses barbecued pork to provide extra flavour. If you do not have time to make **cha siu**, *you can use sliced lean pork instead.*

225 g/8 oz rice vermicelli

4 tbsp vegetable oil

2.5 cm/1 in piece fresh ginger, peeled and finely chopped

2 cloves garlic, finely chopped

225 g/8 oz Chinese barbecued pork (*cha siu*), diced

100 g/4 oz peeled prawns

150 g/5 oz bean sprouts

8 water chestnuts, sliced

6 spring onions, chopped

100 g/4 oz spinach, chopped

2 tbsp Chinese rice wine or dry sherry

4 tbsp light soy sauce

1½ tbsp dark soy sauce

6 tbsp chicken stock

black pepper and salt

● Soak the vermicelli in warm water for 3 minutes, or according to the instructions on the packet. Rinse under running water and drain.

● Heat 3 tablespoons of the oil in a wok or large frying pan until very hot. Stir-fry the ginger and garlic for 30 seconds. Add the pork, prawns, bean sprouts, water chestnuts, spring onions, and spinach, and stir-fry for 2–3 minutes.

● Add the remaining tablespoon of oil and the vermicelli, stir quickly, then add the rice wine, soy sauce and chicken stock. Keep stirring until the sauce is absorbed. Sprinkle with black pepper and salt to taste. Serve immediately.

Prawns in Jackets

SERVES 4

When raw, tiger prawns are dark greyish-brown with darker rings, but the shells turn rosy pink and the flesh pale pinkish-white when they are cooked. They are quite expensive, but they are large and meaty—they can range from 7.5 cm/3 in up to enormous specimens of 25 cm/10 in—so three tiger prawns of about 7.5–10 cm/3–4 in are enough for one portion.

75 g/3 oz plain flour

2 tsp black sesame seeds

salt and freshly ground black pepper

1 egg, beaten

1–2 tsp sesame oil

12 raw tiger prawns in their shells, about 7.5 cm/3 in long

vegetable oil for deep-frying

vinegar dipping sauce to serve

● Stir together the flour, sesame seeds and seasoning. Stir in the egg and sesame oil, then add enough water (about 120 ml/4 fl oz) to make a light coating batter. Set aside.

● Remove the heads and fine legs from the prawns, leaving the tails intact. With a fine knife-point, slit along the back of each prawn and remove the dark thread.

● Half fill a deep-fat fryer with vegetable oil and heat to 180°C/350°F.

● Stir the batter, then dip the prawns into it. Let the excess batter drain off the prawns, then deep-fry in batches for about 3–4 minutes until crisp and brown. Transfer to absorbent kitchen paper to drain. Keep warm while frying the remaining prawns. Serve hot with vinegar dipping sauce.

Prawns with Lemon and Coconut

SERVES 4–6

The lemon, coconut and prawns combination is wonderful. This is a good cocktail snack, too.

500 g/1 lb 2 oz large raw prawns, shelled

250 ml/8 fl oz thin coconut milk

2 tbsp lemon juice

¼ tsp fish sauce

¼ tsp sugar

¼ tsp salt

2 tbsp diced shallots

5 fresh small green chillies, sliced into thin circles

● To butterfly the prawns, cut them lengthways almost all the way through and splay them out.

● Boil the coconut milk in a pan, add the prawns, cook for 1 minute and remove the pan from the heat. Allow to stand for about 1 minute—until the prawns are just cooked—then remove them with a slotted spoon and place on a serving plate.

● Add the lemon juice, fish sauce, sugar and salt to the coconut milk in the pan, stir well for 1 minute, and then spoon this sauce over the prawns. Sprinkle over the shallot and chilli, and serve with rice.

Prawns in Jackets

Egg-fried Rice with Prawns

SERVES 4

Crunchy water chestnuts add a pleasing contrast in texture to this favourite rice dish. The rice should be freshly cooked.

4 tbsp oil

1 tsp sesame oil

1 bunch spring onions, shredded diagonally

200 g/7 oz can water chestnuts, drained and sliced

100 g/4 oz frozen peas

350 g/12 oz cooked prawns, peeled

3 eggs, beaten

200 g/7 oz long-grain rice, cooked

4 tbsp light soy sauce

whole cooked prawns to garnish

● Heat the oils together, then stir-fry the onions, water chestnuts and peas for 3–5 minutes, until the peas are thawed and hot. Add the prawns and stir-fry for another minute.

● Lower the heat, pour the eggs into the pan and cook until they are half-set. They should be thickened, but not scrambled—if they are too thin, they coat the rice grains too freely and give the finished rice an inferior texture. If the eggs are allowed to set before the rice is added, they tend to be overcooked.

● Tip all the rice into the pan and turn it over in the egg mixture to combine all the ingredients evenly. The eggs should finish cooking almost immediately.

● Sprinkle in the soy sauce and serve at once, garnished with the whole prawns, if liked.

Casseroled Prawns with Cellophane Noodles

SERVES 6

The size of the prawns is unimportant; you could use small prawns or lobster tails, or even crab claws.

2 bacon rashers, cut into
    2.5 cm/1 in pieces

6 large prawns, shelled

2 coriander roots, cut in half

25 g/1 oz fresh ginger,
    pounded or finely chopped

25 g/1 oz garlic, chopped

1 tbsp white peppercorns,
    crushed

450 g/1 lb cellophane or glass
    noodles, soaked in cold water
    for 10 minutes

1 tsp butter

3 tbsp black soy sauce

10 g/¼ oz roughly chopped
    coriander leaves and stalks

FOR THE STOCK

475 ml/16 fl oz chicken stock

2 tbsp oyster sauce

2 tbsp black soy sauce

½ tbsp sesame seed oil

1 tsp brandy or whisky

½ tsp sugar

● Place all the stock ingredients in a pan, bring to the boil, and simmer for 5 minutes. Leave to cool.

● Take a heatproof casserole dish or heavy-bottomed pan and place the bacon over the base. Put in the prawns, coriander root, ginger, garlic and peppercorns. Place the noodles over the top, then add the butter, soy sauce and stock.

● Place on the heat, cover, bring to the boil and simmer for 5 minutes. Mix well, add the coriander, cover and cook again until the prawns are cooked, about 5 minutes more. Remove excess stock liquid before serving.

Deep Fried Squid with Plantain Fritters

SERVES 4

450 g/1 lb fresh squid, cleaned and prepared

2 large cloves garlic, finely chopped

2 tsp fish sauce (optional)

2 tbsp chopped fresh dill

black pepper

cornflour

vegetable oil for deep-frying

NUOC CHAM SAUCE

2 small cloves garlic, crushed

1 small fresh red chilli, seeded and finely chopped

25 g/1 oz sugar

2 tbsp fresh lime or lemon juice

3 tbsp cider vinegar or wine vinegar

3 tbsp fish sauce

1 tbsp water

PLANTAIN FRITTERS

1 egg

2 tbsp caster sugar

1 whole ripe plantain, peeled and mashed

50 g/2 oz plain flour

1 tsp baking powder

vegetable oil for frying

FOR THE BATTER

100 g/4 oz plain flour

pinch of salt

pinch of ground cinnamon

1 egg, beaten

150 ml/¼ pt milk

● Make the fritters first. Make the batter by mixing the flour and salt. Stir the cinnamon, egg and milk together and add to the flour and salt mixture. Mix thoroughly using a wire whisk. Place on a low shelf in the refrigerator for at least 30 minutes.

● Add the egg and then 2 tablespoons sugar to the plantain, beating continuously. Mix the flour and baking powder, stir into the plantain mixture and blend thoroughly. Coat the mixture, a tablespoon at a time, with the batter. Heat the oil and fry these one at a time. Set the fritters aside.

● Make the *nuoc cham* sauce. Place the garlic, chilli, sugar, lime or lemon juice, vinegar, fish sauce and water in a blender or food processor and blend for 30 seconds or until the sugar dissolves. Set aside.

● Separate the head and body of the squid by pulling it apart gently. Cut off and chop up the tentacles; discard the head. Peel off the membrane from the body. Wash the squid under cold water and cut the body into rings.

● Combine the squid, tentacles, garlic, fish sauce (if used), dill and black pepper. Allow to marinate for 30 minutes. Coat the rings and tentacles in cornflour, shaking off any excess.

● Heat the oil until it starts to smoke. Drop in the squid pieces a few at a time and deep-fry for about 1 minute or until golden brown. Remove and drain on absorbent kitchen paper.

● On a serving plate, make a ring with the plantain fritters and heap the deep-fried squid in the middle. Serve hot with the *nuoc cham* sauce in a small bowl.

Deep Fried Squid
with Plantain Fritters

Grilled Scallop Kebabs

SERVES 2–4

Rice vinegar begins to 'cook' the scallops in the same way that lime juice 'cooks' fish when making Mexican **ceviche,** *so the scallops need only brief cooking under the grill if they are not to become overcooked.*

12 large scallops

1 clove garlic, finely chopped

1 tbsp finely chopped spring onions, green part

2 tbsp soy sauce

2 tsp rice vinegar

1 tbsp sesame oil

1 cm/½ in piece fresh ginger, grated

2 tsp crushed toasted sesame seeds

pinch of chilli powder

● Cut each scallop in half horizontally. Thread the scallops onto skewers and lay them in a shallow, non-metallic dish.

● Mix together the remaining ingredients and pour over the scallops. Turn the skewers over and leave for 15–30 minutes, turning occasionally.

● Preheat the grill.

● Lift the skewers from the marinade and cook under the grill for about 4 minutes, turning occasionally and brushing with the marinade.

Simmered Squid with White Radish

SERVES 2

*The flavour of this dish comes from the subtle taste of the squid combined with the fresh white radish which is easier to cook than Japanese **daikon**, because of its higher water content.*

300 g/10 oz squid

300 g/10 oz white radish, peeled, cut in half lengthways and cut into 1 cm/½ in widths

3 tbsp *sake*

2½ tbsp soy sauce

120 ml/4 fl oz water

● Pull the head and tentacles from the squid, then remove the transparent centre bone and wash the body cavity. Take off the skin, then cut the head from the tentacles.

● Cut the body and legs of the squid into 1 cm/½ in widths and blanch in boiling water. Put the radish in a pan and cover with cold water. Bring to the boil and simmer for about 6 minutes until the radish has become almost transparent, then drain.

● Heat the *sake* in a pan with the soy sauce. When it boils, add the squid and simmer for about 4 minutes. Remove the squid with a slotted spoon and set aside.

● Add the water and drained radish to the pan, simmer, covered, for about 7 minutes. Put the squid in the pan with the radish and simmer for 3–4 minutes. Serve with rice and a vegetable dish.

Stir-fried Squid with Chillies and Vegetables

SERVES 3–4

Both the hot, fermented bean paste, **kochujang,** *and Korea's excellent coarsely pounded red chilli powder, are used in this spicy dish. The Korean chilli powder adds a characteristic bright, carmine pink colour. If necessary, you can always use cayenne pepper mixed with paprika to obtain the same result. Chilli bean paste can also be substituted for the* **kochuchang.**

550 g/1¼ lb cleaned squid

3 tbsp vegetable oil

1 onion, thinly sliced

2 cloves garlic, crushed

1 carrot, thinly sliced lengthways

1 courgette, thinly sliced lengthways

2–3 long fresh red chillies, thinly sliced lengthways

2 long, fresh green chillies, thinly sliced lengthways

1 tbsp chilli bean paste

about ½ tsp Korean chilli powder, or cayenne pepper mixed with paprika

1 tsp sugar

salt and freshly ground black pepper

2 spring onions, white and green parts sliced diagonally

2 tsp sesame oil

toasted sesame seeds to garnish

● Cut open each squid body so that it lies flat, then cut across into 6 x 1-cm/2½ x ½-in pieces. Cut the tentacles into 6 cm/2½ in lengths.

● Bring a large saucepan of water to the boil. Add all the squid simultaneously and remove from the heat. Stir immediately and continue to stir until the squid turns white, about 40 seconds. Drain well and discard the water.

● Heat the oil in a large frying pan over a moderate heat. Add the onion, garlic and carrot. Stir for 30–40 seconds, then add the courgette, chillies and 2 teaspoons *kochujang* or chilli bean paste, half the chilli powder or cayenne and paprika. Stir for 30 seconds. Stir in the squid, the remaining *kochujang* and chilli powder or cayenne and paprika, sugar and salt and pepper. Cook slowly for 2 minutes, then add the spring onions and sesame oil. Tip into a warm serving dish and garnish with toasted sesame seeds.

Thai-style Scallops

SERVES 4

A great favourite and an especially tasty alternative to normally bland treatments for this shellfish.

16 medium-sized scallops, with 4 shells if available

3 tbsp melted butter

2 tbsp lime juice

1 tbsp chopped garlic

1 tbsp chopped shallot

1 tbsp chopped fresh ginger

1 tbsp chopped coriander leaf

salt and ground white pepper to taste

● Mix the scallops with all the other ingredients in a bowl, and season. If you have the scallop shells, place 4 scallops with mixture in each shell; otherwise put all in a heatproof dish.

● Bake in a 180°C/350°F/Gas Mark 4 oven or grill under medium heat until just cooked, about 10 minutes. Do not overcook. Serve with other dishes or double the recipe and serve with rice.

Stir-Fried Squid with Chillies
and Vegetables

Lobster and Sweet Potato Curry

SERVES 4–6

25 g/1 oz unsalted butter

450 g/1 lb sweet potatoes, peeled and cut into 2.5 cm/ 1 in cubes

1 tbsp *sake* or dry sherry

1 whole lobster, chopped into 2.5 cm/1 in cubes

FOR THE CURRY SAUCE

1 tbsp vegetable oil

50 g/2 oz onion, chopped

1 tbsp finely chopped garlic

2 tsp shrimp paste

1 dried chilli, seeds removed, crushed

2 tsp cumin seeds

1 tbsp coriander seeds

1 tsp dried lemon grass, sliced

1 tsp galangal, ground

2 tsp finely chopped lemon rind

2 tbsp chopped fresh coriander

1 tsp salt

1 tsp ground turmeric

2 tsp sweet paprika

● Make the curry sauce by heating the oil over medium-high heat. Add the onion and garlic, and cook for 5 minutes or until soft. Add the shrimp paste and stir thoroughly, pressing the paste to blend it well. Cook for a further 3 or so minutes and remove from the heat.

● Pound the chilli, cumin seeds, coriander seeds and lemon grass until powdery.

● Place the onion mixture in a blender or food processor and blend until very smooth. Add the ground spices, galangal, lemon rind, fresh coriander, salt, turmeric and paprika. Blend until the mixture becomes a smooth paste. This makes about 4 tbsp curry sauce.

● Melt the butter over medium heat and add the sweet potatoes. Cook for 15 minutes, taking care the potato does not burn.

● Stir in the curry sauce and *sake* together until the curry mixture is dissolved. Add the lobster cubes and cook for 2–3 more minutes.

Baby Clams with Chilli and Basil

SERVES 4

120 ml/4 fl oz peanut or corn oil for frying

600 g/1 lb 6 oz fresh baby clams in their shells, cleaned well

1½ tbsp chopped garlic

5 fresh red chillies, sliced lengthways

2 tbsp red chilli paste

2 tsp white soy sauce

120 ml/4 fl oz chicken stock

40 g/1½ oz sweet basil leaves

● Heat the oil in a pan or wok until quite hot, about 190°C/375°F. Add the clams and garlic, and cook until the clams open slightly, 2–3 minutes.

● Add the fresh chillies, chilli paste and soy sauce, mix well, then pour in the chicken stock. Bring to the boil, cook for 2 minutes, stir in the basil and serve immediately accompanied by rice.

Poultry
Main Dishes

The everyday main meals in this and the following section are suitable for family meals or for informal lunches and suppers with friends. They are inexpensive, easy and satisfying. Many of the recipes in this section can be adapted to seafood- or vegetable-based dishes and vice versa.

Stir-fried Chicken

SERVES 4

Prepare the vegetables while the chicken is marinating; then, when you start cooking, the dish is soon ready to serve.

450 g/1 lb skinned, boneless chicken breasts, cut into strips

2 tbsp soy sauce

1 tbsp sugar

2 spring onions, white and some green parts, finely chopped

2.5 cm/1 in piece fresh ginger, finely chopped

1½ tsp crushed toasted sesame seeds

freshly ground black pepper

1 small carrot, thinly sliced diagonally

3 dried Chinese black mushrooms, soaked for 30 minutes in hot water

1½ tbsp sesame oil

1 red pepper, seeded and cut into thin strips

● Put the chicken into a bowl.

● Mix together the soy sauce, sugar, spring onions, ginger, sesame seeds and plenty of pepper. Pour the mixture over the chicken. Turn the chicken over and leave for 30 minutes. Remove from the marinade; reserve the marinade.

● Meanwhile, blanch the carrot in boiling water for 5 minutes. Drain and set aside.

● Drain the mushrooms, cut out and discard any hard patches and the stalks. Slice the mushroom caps.

● Heat the sesame oil in a frying pan. Add the chicken and stir-fry for 2–3 minutes. Remove from the pan and set aside. Add the mushrooms and carrots, and stir-fry for a further 2 minutes. Add the pepper and stir-fry for another minute.

● Return the chicken to the pan. Add the reserved marinade and bring to the boil. Stir and cook for 1 minute, then serve garnished with egg strips.

Boiled Chicken with Fish Sauce

SERVES 6

1 large chicken, either corn-fed or free-range

about 2.25 litres/4 pt water

2 x 2.5 cm/1 in sliced peeled fresh ginger, about 3 mm/ ⅛ in thick

2 tbsp fish sauce or light soy sauce and 1 tsp anchovy essence

2 dried black Chinese mushrooms

1 tbsp dry sherry

salt

FOR THE INDIVIDUAL DIPS

1 tbsp light soy sauce

1 tbsp sesame seed oil

1 tbsp fish sauce

● Tear off the fat from the chicken cavity and discard. Cut off the tail end and rinse the chicken in cold water. Bring a large pan of water to the boil over high heat and plunge in the chicken. When the water comes to the boil again, let the chicken cook for 1 minute to firm the skin. Remove it and rinse it briefly with running warm water to get rid of any scum.

● Bring the measured amount of water to the boil with the ginger slices and fish sauce in a deep pan into which the chicken will fit snugly. Add the chicken and, when the water boils again, turn the heat down to a simmer. Cover and simmer for 1½ hours, turning the chicken from time to time to ensure that it cooks evenly all over.

● In the meantime, soak the black mushrooms in some warm water for about 20 minutes. Squeeze them dry and rinse in cold water, repeating this a couple of times. Cut off and discard the stalks, and add the mushrooms to the soup about 30 minutes into the cooking time. Add the sherry when the chicken is cooked and season with salt to taste.

● Serve the chicken whole in the soup and the dips in individual saucers. Guests tear off pieces of the meat with a fork or chopsticks and put it in their bowls with a little stock and mushrooms. Leftover chicken can be used for a variety of dishes.

Chicken with Broccoli and Cashew Nuts

SERVES 4

1 tbsp cornflour

5 tbsp dry sherry

5 tbsp soy sauce

120 ml/4 fl oz chicken stock

1 tsp sesame oil

3 tbsp sunflower or peanut oil

2 large boneless chicken breasts, skinned and cut into thin strips

40 g/1½ oz unsalted cashew nuts

50 g/2 oz broccoli florets, broken into small pieces

200 g/7 oz can bamboo shoots, drained and sliced

6 spring onions, sliced diagonally

● Blend the cornflour to a smooth, thin paste with the sherry, soy sauce and stock, then set the mixture aside until needed.

● Heat the sesame oil and sunflower or peanut oil, then stir-fry the chicken and cashew nuts until the chicken has become golden and cooked, and the nuts have been lightly browned.

● Add the broccoli, bamboo shoots and spring onions, and continue to stir fry for 3–4 minutes, until the broccoli is lightly cooked.

● Give the cornflour mixture a stir, then pour it into the pan and stir over medium heat, until the sauce boils. Allow the mixture to boil for a minute or so, stirring all the time, so that all the ingredients are coated in a lightly thickened sauce. Serve at once, while still hot.

Chicken with Mango

SERVES 4

450 g/1 lb corn-fed chicken, cubed

1 large carrot

½ red pepper

½ green pepper

100 g/4 oz bamboo shoots

1 large mango, just ripe and firm, cut into chunks

4 tbsp vegetable oil

FOR THE MARINADE

½ tsp bicarbonate of soda

1 tbsp sugar

1 egg white, lightly beaten

1 tbsp cornflour or potato flour

salt

water

FOR THE SAUCE

1 tsp sugar

1 tbsp light soy sauce

1 tbsp oyster sauce

1 tbsp sesame seed oil

1 tbsp rice wine

½ tbsp cornflour or potato flour, mixed with a little water

● Mix the marinade ingredients thoroughly and combine well with the chicken pieces. Leave to marinate for 30 minutes.

● Trim and peel the carrot; cut into matchstick strips a little less than 2.5 cm/1 in long. Cut the peppers and bamboo shoots into strips to match the carrots. Cut the mango flesh into small, fairly thin pieces as neatly as possible.

● Heat the oil in a wok and fry the chicken pieces for about 2 minutes. Remove from the oil and drain well. Add the carrot, peppers, mango and bamboo shoots to the hot oil and fry in batches. Remove and drain.

● Rinse and dry the wok, add the chicken and vegetables and stir in all the sauce ingredients, except the cornflour. Stir-fry briefly and add the cornflour to the sauce to thicken.

Chicken with Broccoli
and Cashew Nuts

Chicken Fried with Cashew Nuts

SERVES 4

A delicious dish, of Chinese origin, which is very easy to make and looks impressive.

325 g/11 oz boneless skinned chicken breasts, cut into slices

plain flour for coating

250 ml/8 fl oz peanut or corn oil

4 dried red chillies, fried and cut into 1 cm/½ in pieces

1 tbsp chopped garlic

10 spring onions, white parts, cut into 5 cm/2 in pieces

40 g/1½ oz unsalted roasted cashew nuts

75 g/3 oz onion, sliced

2 tbsp oyster sauce

1 tbsp light soy sauce

1 tbsp sugar

⅛ tsp dark soy sauce

● Coat the chicken lightly with flour. Heat the oil in a frying pan or wok and fry the chicken for about 5 minutes until light brown. Remove almost all of the oil from the frying pan.

● Add the chilli and garlic to the chicken in the pan and fry for 1 minute. Add all the remaining ingredients; fry until cooked, about 3 more minutes. Serve accompanied by rice.

Fresh Chicken with Lemon Grass and Cashew Nuts

SERVES 4

vegetable oil

2 small dried chillies

1 clove garlic, chopped

450 g/1 lb lean, corn-fed chicken, sliced

½ tsp sugar

1 tbsp oyster sauce

1 tbsp fish sauce or light soy sauce

3 tbsp chicken stock or water

50 g/2 oz roasted, unsalted cashew nuts

1 tbsp chopped lemon grass

2 shallots, cut in quarters

● With a drop or two of oil, stir-fry the chillies until cooked evenly but not burnt. Set aside.

● Stir-fry the garlic with a few more drops of oil until golden. Add the chicken slices, sugar and oyster and fish sauces and stir-fry until the chicken is golden in colour. Lower the heat and add the stock. Cook for a few more minutes, stirring occasionally.

● When the chicken is thoroughly cooked, add the cashew nuts, lemon grass, shallots and chillies, and stir several times, being careful not to break the chillies. Remove from the heat and serve.

Chicken and Spring Onion Kebabs

SERVES 4

As good as the kebabs are when grilled, they are even better when cooked on a barbecue.

about 675 g/1½ lb skinned, boneless chicken thighs

1–2 bunches plump spring onions, white parts only

4 tbsp soy sauce

1 tbsp sesame oil

2 tsp sugar

2 cloves garlic, finely chopped

2 cm/¾ in piece fresh ginger, grated

1 tbsp crushed toasted sesame seeds

diagonally sliced pale green parts of spring onion for garnish

toasted sesame seeds for garnish

● Cut each chicken thigh into three lengths. Thread pieces of chicken and spring onions alternately onto short skewers. Lay the skewers in a large, shallow dish.

● Mix together the remaining ingredients, except the garnishes, and pour over the skewers. Turn to coat with the sauce, then leave for 3–4 hours, turning two or three times.

● Preheat the grill or barbecue.

● Lift the skewers from the marinade and grill or barbecue for about 10–15 minutes, turning occasionally and brushing with the remaining marinade. Serve garnished with spring onions and toasted sesame seeds.

Chicken Fried Rice

SERVES 4

One of the basic standard Thai dishes, this always tastes best with rice from the day before—and is easier to cook if the rice has been chilled in the refrigerator for a while. In place of chicken, pork or prawns are also commonly used.

3 tbsp peanut or corn oil

200 g/7 oz boneless skinned chicken breasts, cut lengthways into 1 cm/½ in thick slices

1 tbsp chopped garlic

1 medium-sized onion, sliced

2 eggs

550 g/1¼ lb cooked rice

1 tomato, cut into 8 wedges

1 spring onion, chopped

2 tsp light soy sauce

1 tsp fish sauce

1 tsp sugar

1 tsp ground white pepper

● Heat the oil in a wok or pan, add the chicken and garlic and mix well over the heat for 1 minute. Add the onion and cook for 1 minute, break in the eggs, mix very well and then stir in the rice and the rest of the ingredients. Stir well. Cook for 2 minutes and serve immediately.

● Serve accompanied by cucumber slices, whole spring onions, and fish sauce with chillies.

Chicken and Egg on Rice

SERVES 2

165 g/5½ oz short-grain rice

150 ml/¼ pt *dashi* stock

1 tbsp caster sugar

1 tbsp *mirin*

3 tbsp soy sauce

2 boneless chicken breasts, diced

1 medium onion, sliced

1 egg, beaten

FOR THE GARNISH

watercress

● Rinse and boil the rice according to the instructions on the packet.

● Bring the *dashi* stock, sugar, *mirin* and soy sauce to the boil in a frying pan. Add the chicken and onion. Simmer for about 8 minutes or until the chicken is cooked through.

● Pour over the egg, letting it set on top of the chicken without stirring. When the egg has set, sprinkle on some watercress as a garnish. Serve the mixture on top of the serving of rice.

Chicken Fried with Green Pepper

SERVES 4

4 tbsp peanut or corn oil

1 tbsp chopped garlic

325 g/11 oz boneless skinned chicken breasts, cut lengthways into 1 cm/½ in thick slices

100 g/4 oz green pepper, sliced

5 fresh red chiles, sliced lengthways

50 g/2 oz onion, thickly sliced

1 tbsp oyster sauce

½ tbsp light soy sauce

1 tsp fish sauce

¼ tsp dark soy sauce

15 g/½ oz sweet basil leaves

● Heat the oil in a wok or pan, add the garlic and chicken and fry well for a minute. Add the green pepper and chilli, mix, then add the onion and cook for 1 minute.

● One by one stir in the rest of the ingredients, cooking for about 30 seconds after each addition. Remove from the heat immediately after stirring in the basil. Serve accompanied by rice.

Chicken Fried with Ginger

SERVES 4

5 tbsp peanut or corn oil

1 tbsp chopped garlic

325 g/11 oz boneless skinned chicken breasts, cut into 5 mm/¼ in thick slices

25 g/1 oz wood ear fungus or fresh button mushrooms, sliced

4 spring onions, cut into 2.5 cm/1 in pieces

50 g/2 oz onion, sliced

25 g/1 oz fresh ginger, cut into small matchsticks

3 fresh red chillies, each sliced into 6 strips lengthways

1 tbsp light soy sauce

2 tsp brandy

½ tsp sugar

¼ tsp salt

● Heat the oil in a wok or pan, add the garlic and stir-fry, mixing well.

● Add the chicken, mix well for 1 minute, and then add the mushrooms. Stir for a minute and add all the rest of the ingredients. Stir-fry well until the chicken is cooked, about 8–10 minutes.

● Serve accompanied by rice and phrik nam plaa.

Thai Sweet and Sour Chicken

SERVES 4 – 6

A dish that is popular with most people. It is not spicy, but a spoonful of fish sauce will add zest.

1 litre/1¾ pt peanut or corn oil

425 g/15 oz boneless skinned chicken breasts, cut across into 5 mm/¼ in slices

plain flour for coating

1 medium-sized onion, sliced

1 medium-sized green pepper, sliced

100 g/4 oz tomato ketchup

50 g/2 oz tomato quarters

50 g/2 oz pineapple, diced

120 ml/4 fl oz chicken stock

2 tsp light soy sauce

1 tsp sugar

1 tsp white vinegar

● Heat the oil in a wok or pan, coat the chicken lightly with flour and fry it until it is light brown, about 5 minutes. Remove and drain on absorbent kitchen paper.

● Remove all the oil except for about 5 tablespoons. Add the onion and pepper, cook for 1 minute, mix in the ketchup, and then add the remaining ingredients. Stir-fry for 1 minute, add the chicken and continue to cook until the onion is tender, about 2 minutes.

● Serve accompanied by rice and fish sauce with fresh chillies.

Caramelized Chicken Wings with an Orange Sauce

SERVES 4

This dish should have a slightly nutty, burnt flavour, but be careful not to burn the sugar.

8 chicken wings	4 tbsp vegetable oil
salt and pepper	2 tbsp caster sugar
2 tbsp sesame oil	grated rind and juice of
4 tbsp clear honey	1 orange

● Season the chicken wings with salt and pepper. Mix the sesame oil and honey, and spread this over the wings.

● Heat the oil in a heavy-based pan and cook the chicken wings for about 4 minutes on each side or until just done. Remove the pan and keep warm. Reserve the pan juices.

● Add the sugar to the pan and heat without stirring until it caramelizes. Remove from the heat.

● Add the orange juice and reserved pan juices. Stir over a low heat until a smooth sauce forms, adding a little water or orange juice if it becomes too thick. Add half the orange rind and continue to cook over a very low heat.

● Place the chicken wings on to a warmed dish. Pour the caramel sauce over them and garnish with the leftover strips of orange.

Stuffed Chicken Wings
SERVES 4

This is a delicious and economical dish, which looks very impressive.

8 chicken wings

FOR THE STUFFING

100 g/4 oz bean thread vermicelli

3 pieces wood ear fungus

300 g/10 oz minced pork

1 small onion, finely grated

1 small carrot, finely grated

1 egg, beaten

1 tbsp fish sauce or light soy sauce

salt and black pepper

● Bone the chicken wings by cutting around the bone with a sharp knife. Holding the wingtip, gently ease the bone away to leave the skin and a thin layer of chicken.

● Soak the vermicelli in warm water for 10 minutes, then drain thoroughly and cut into short strands. Soak the wood ear fungus in warm water for 10 minutes, then squeeze dry and chop into thin slices.

● Mix all the stuffing ingredients together. The mixture should be firm. Mould the stuffing into a ball and insert it into the bag of flesh and skin of the chicken wings.

● Preheat the oven to 200°C/400°F/Gas Mark 6. Steam the stuffed wings for 10–15 minutes. (If you want to make a large quantity, multiply the measures accordingly and freeze after the steam stage.)

● After steaming, place in a lightly oiled roasting tin and roast in the oven for 30 minutes. Serve on a bed of lettuce as a starter or with rice and a beef stir-fried dish for a main course.

Spiced Minced Chicken

SERVES 6

One of the special characteristics of the northeastern Thai version of this meat dish is the addition of uncooked sticky rice, which is first roasted (either in an oven or in a dry wok) until golden and then pounded in a mortar. It adds a slightly nutty flavour and gives the dish more body.

450 g/1 lb finely minced chicken

25 g/1 oz shallots, sliced

10 g/¼ oz coriander leaves

4 tbsp sticky rice, dry-fried for 8–10 minutes until brown and finely pounded

4 tbsp lemon juice, or to taste

3 tbsp fish sauce, or to taste

1 tbsp chopped dried red chilli, or to taste

½ tsp sugar

FOR THE GARNISH

fresh mint leaves

● Cook the chicken in a nonstick pan over low heat for 10 minutes—do not add water or oil. When cooked, transfer to a bowl and mix in well all the remaining ingredients except the mint.

● Check the seasoning, and add more lemon juice, fish sauce or chilli if necessary. Sprinkle the mint over the top to garnish.

● Serve accompanied by raw cabbage leaves, spring onions and raw green beans.

Korean Braised Chicken Thighs

SERVES 4

Chicken thighs become richly flavoured and very tender and succulent when steeped in a tasty marinade, then fried and braised in it.

8 chicken thighs

4 spring onions, white parts only, very finely chopped

2.5 cm/1 in piece fresh ginger, grated

2 cloves garlic, crushed

4 tbsp soy sauce

1 tbsp sesame oil

1½ tbsp crushed toasted sesame seeds

2 tsp sugar

vegetable oil for frying

1 red pepper, seeded and diced

2 spring onions, white and pale green parts sliced diagonally

● Slash each chicken thigh three times and place in a shallow dish.

● Mix together the finely chopped spring onions, ginger, garlic, soy sauce, sesame oil, sesame seeds and sugar. Pour over the chicken. Turn to coat with the sauce and leave in a cool place for about 4 hours, turning occasionally.

● Heat a little vegetable oil in a heavy flameproof casserole. Lift the chicken thighs from the marinade, add to the casserole and brown evenly. Pour in the marinade and enough water just to cover the chicken. Bring barely to simmering point. Cover the casserole and leave to cook gently for about 30–35 minutes, turning the chicken occasionally, until very tender.

● Add the red pepper and sliced spring onions about 5 minutes before the end of cooking.

Yellow Chicken Curry

SERVES 6

An Indian-influenced curry dish, which is very popular in Thailand.

1.2 litres/2 pt thin coconut milk

450 g/1 lb chicken, cut into medium-sized pieces

200 g/7 oz potatoes, peeled and cut into 1 cm/½ in cubes

2 tsp salt

3 tbsp sliced shallots, fried until light brown

FOR THE YELLOW CURRY PASTE

5 dried red chillies, chopped

10 small cloves garlic, chopped

½ stalk of lemon grass, sliced

½ tbsp sliced shallot

2 tsp curry powder

1 tsp sliced fresh ginger

1 tsp sliced galangal

1 tsp shrimp paste

1 tsp salt

½ tsp coriander seeds

½ tsp fennel seeds

● Pound all the curry paste ingredients together with a pestle and mortar or in a blender until a fine paste is formed.

● Heat 250 ml/8 fl oz of the coconut milk in a wok or pan and cook the curry paste for 5 minutes. Add the rest of the coconut milk, bring to the boil, add the chicken and cook until tender, about 10 minutes.

● Add the potato and salt, and cook until the potatoes are done, about 10 minutes. Pour into soup bowls and sprinkle with the fried shallots.

● Serve accompanied by ajaad salad, sliced pickled ginger and rice.

Red Chicken Curry

SERVES 6

1.2 litres/2 pt thin coconut milk

1 quantity chilli paste

10 white peppercorns, crushed

325 g/11 oz boneless skinned chicken breasts, cut across into 5 mm/¼ in thick slices

3 tbsp fish sauce

½ tbsp palm sugar

7 small white aubergines, quartered

3 fresh red chillies, quartered lengthways

2 kaffir lime leaves, torn into small pieces

15 g/½ oz sweet basil leaves

● Heat 250 ml/8 fl oz of the coconut milk in a pan, stir in the chilli paste and white peppercorns, and cook for 2 minutes.

● Add the chicken slices, mix well and add the rest of the coconut milk. Bring to the boil, then add the fish sauce and palm sugar. Boil for 1 minute and then add the aubergines, chillies and lime leaf. Bring back to the boil, cook for 3 minutes, add the basil, remove from the heat and serve.

● Serve in bowls accompanied by rice, sun-dried beef and salted preserved eggs.

Northern Thai Chicken Curry

SERVES 4–6

A spicy chicken curry with no curry powder—chopped red chillies add the fire to this dish.

4 tbsp peanut or corn oil

450 g/1 lb chicken (with skin and bone), cut into small pieces through the bones

1.5 litres/2½ pt water

4 kaffir lime leaves, quartered

2 stalks of lemon grass, halved

1 tbsp fish sauce

FOR THE CHILLI PASTE

10 dried red chillies, roughly chopped

2 tbsp finely sliced lemon grass

2 tbsp sliced shallots

½ tbsp sliced garlic

1 tsp galangal

1 tsp chopped coriander leaf

1 tsp shrimp paste

¼ tsp turmeric

● Pound all the chilli paste ingredients to a fine paste with a pestle and mortar or in a blender.

● Heat the oil in a pan, add the chilli paste and fry over medium heat for 1 minute. Add the chicken pieces, fry, then add the water and all the rest of the ingredients.

● Boil until the chicken is tender and the curry reduced to about half its original volume, about 20 minutes. Serve accompanied by rice.

Red Chicken Curry

Turkey with Chestnuts and Sprouts

SERVES 4

Chestnuts canned in brine may be substituted for the fresh ones in this recipe.

450 g/1 lb chestnuts

675 g/1½ lb Brussels sprouts

450 g/1 lb skinned fillet of turkey breast, cubed

25 g/1 oz plain flour

salt and pepper

3 tbsp oil

1 onion, chopped

2 large sprigs of sage

1 sprig of thyme

250 ml/8 fl oz chicken or turkey stock

120 ml/4 fl oz medium cider

● Wash the chestnuts, then use a pointed knife to make a slit in each one. Place in a saucepan, cover with water and bring to the boil. Reduce the heat and simmer for 15 minutes. Remove the shells.

● Halve any large Brussels sprouts, then blanch the vegetables in boiling water for 2 minutes. Drain.

● Toss the turkey with the flour and seasoning. Heat the oil, then stir fry the onion, sage and thyme for about 7 minutes, until the onion is softened. Add the turkey and fry until all pieces are cooked.

● Stir in the chestnuts and sprouts. Cook for 5 minutes before pouring in the stock and cider.

● Stir the mixture until it boils, then stir over medium heat for 2 minutes, until the juices are thickened. Taste for seasoning before serving.

Turkey Nests

SERVES 4

You need to have two fine metal strainers or a special frying basket to make the nests in which to serve this stir fry. If you do not want to go to all the trouble of making the nests, the stir fry may also be served in crispy baked potato nests, pastry cases or pancakes.

175–225 g/6–8 oz Chinese egg noodles

oil for deep frying

100 g/4 oz cream cheese

3 tbsp chopped fresh parsley

1 tsp chopped fresh thyme

1 tsp grated lemon rind

3 tbsp olive oil

450 g/1 lb boneless turkey breast, finely shredded

1 red pepper, seeded and finely shredded

salt and freshly ground black pepper

100 g/4 oz fine green beans, blanched in boiling water for 1 minute

100 g/4 oz lean ham, shredded

● Add the noodles to boiling water and bring back to the boil. Drain and rinse under cold water. Drain well.

● Grease two metal strainers: one measuring about 7.5 cm/3 in, the other 10 cm/4 in. Heat the oil for deep frying. Line the larger strainer with a layer of noodles and press the smaller one on top. Deep fry the noodles until golden, then drain on absorbent kitchen paper. Make eight nests.

● Mix the cream cheese, parsley, thyme and lemon rind, then shape into eight small pats and chill them.

● Heat the oil, then stir fry the turkey and pepper, adding seasoning, until the turkey is lightly browned and the pepper tender. Stir in the beans and continue cooking for 3 minutes to heat them through. Lastly, add the ham and cook for a minute or so.

● Divide the stir-fried mixture between the nests and top each with a pat of flavoured cream cheese.

Red Duck Curry

SERVES 6

1.6 litres/2¾ pt thin coconut milk

1 roasted duck, boned with skin left on, cut into 1 cm/ ½ in slices

15 cherry tomatoes

5 fresh large red chillies, sliced lengthways

25 g/1 oz sweet basil leaves

3 kaffir lime leaves, chopped

3 tbsp sugar

2 tbsp fish sauce

1 tsp salt

FOR THE PASTE

3 stalks of lemon grass, sliced thinly

25 g/1 oz galangal, chopped

7 dried red chillies, roughly chopped

3 tbsp chopped garlic

1 tbsp shrimp paste

1 tsp chopped kaffir lime leaf

1 tsp chopped coriander root

1 tsp white peppercorns

½ tsp coriander seeds

● Pound all the curry paste ingredients together with a pestle and mortar or in a blender to a fine paste.

● Heat 475 ml/16 fl oz of the coconut milk in a wok or pan, add the chilli paste mixture and cook together for 5 minutes.

● Add the rest of the coconut milk, bring to the boil, then add the duck, cherry tomatoes and red chilli. Bring back to the boil and then add the rest of the ingredients. Boil all together for 5 minutes, and remove from the heat.

● Serve accompanied by rice, salted eggs and sun-dried beef.

Duck with Ginger Sauce

SERVES 4

450 g/1 lb Ho Chi Minh duck (see recipe)

vegetable oil for frying

12 thin slices fresh ginger, peeled and shredded

1½ tbsp hot soy paste

1½ tbsp sweet soy paste or hoisin sauce

1½ tsp rice wine

1½ tbsp fish sauce (optional)

1 tsp finely chopped garlic

1 tbsp chilli oil

1 tsp sugar

salt

250 ml/8 fl oz chicken stock

1 spring onion, shredded

1 red chilli (fresh, shredded, or dried, crumbled)

2 tsp cornflour mixed with a little water

FOR THE HO CHI MINH DUCK

salt

pinch of five-spice powder

½ tsp finely chopped fresh ginger

½ tsp finely chopped garlic

½ tsp hot soy paste

1 oven-ready duck (about 1.75 kg/4–4½ lb)

120 ml/4 fl oz hot water

3 tbsp wine vinegar

20 g/¾ oz sugar

red food colouring

● Make the Ho Chi Minh duck by mixing the salt, five-spice powder, ginger, garlic and soy paste. Put the mixture inside the duck's cavity and sew up both ends. Mix the remaining ingredients well and brush over the entire surface with a pastry brush. Leave to dry on a rack with the breast uppermost for 7 hours in a cool, dry place.

● Preheat the oven to 200°C/400°F/Gas Mark 6. Put the rack together with the duck on a roasting tin and roast for 1 hour. Reduce the heat if the skin begins to burn. (Ideally, the duck should be roasted upright in the Oriental style but most household ovens cannot accommodate an upright duck.)

● Take the cooked duck meat off the bone in as large pieces as possible and cut these into neat pieces about 1 x 2.5 cm/½ x 1 in. Heat the oil in a wok until it starts smoking and stir-fry the duck pieces for a few minutes. Set these aside making sure to drain well.

● Empty and wipe the wok, heat some more oil in it and stir-fry the ginger very briskly; add the soy bean pastes, return the duck to the wok and stir in the rice wine, fish sauce, if used, garlic, chilli oil, sugar and salt. Stir-fry for a few more minutes.

● Add the chicken stock to the wok. As soon as it comes to the boil, reduce the heat and simmer, uncovered, for 5 minutes. Increase the heat, add the spring onion and chilli and cook fast for 1 minute, then stir in the cornflour.

Duck with Ginger Sauce

Garlic Roasted Duck

SERVES 4

1 tbsp fish sauce or light soy
    sauce

120 ml/4 fl oz red wine
    vinegar

1 onion, chopped

12 juniper berries, crushed

2 tsp fennel seeds

1 clove garlic, crushed

4 duck breast and wing portions

150 ml/¼ pt natural yogurt

salt and black pepper

FOR THE GARNISH

watercress

● Mix the fish sauce, vinegar, onion, juniper berries, fennel seeds and garlic thoroughly in a large bowl and rub well into the duck portions. Cover the bowl with some cling film and leave in a refrigerator for 8 hours, turning occasionally.

● Preheat the oven to 220°C/425°F/Gas Mark 7. Drain and reserve the marinade. Place the duck portions, skin side down, in an ovenproof dish. Put in the oven for 30 minutes, basting at least once. Turn the duck portions over, baste, and cook for a further 30 minutes, basting at least once. Switch off the oven but leave the duck in it until ready to serve.

● Spoon 250 ml/8 fl oz of the marinade into a hot pan, cover and allow to simmer for at least 5 minutes. Strain, whisk in the yogurt, and season with salt and black pepper to taste.

● Serve the duck on a dish garnished with the watercress. The sauce is served in a bowl. If guests are not proficient with chopsticks, the duck should be chopped into bite-sized pieces.

Duck with Rice

SERVES 4

A very popular dish, of Chinese origin, with two contrasting sauces.

1 roasted duck (rub with red food colouring before roasting), boned and cut into 6 x 1 cm/ 2½ x ½ in slices

550 g/1¼ lb cooked rice

4 tbsp thinly sliced pickled ginger

4 tbsp thinly sliced pickled gherkins

FOR THE COOKED SAUCE

475 ml/16 fl oz chicken stock

1 tbsp sugar

½ tbsp light soy sauce

¼ tbsp dark soy sauce

1 tsp flour

FOR THE SOY CHILLI SAUCE

120 ml/4 fl oz dark soy sauce

3 fresh red chillies, sliced thinly into circles

1 tbsp sugar

½ tbsp vinegar

● Heat the ingredients for the cooked sauce together in a pan and boil for 1 minute. Mix the ingredients for the raw sauce in a bowl and put to one side.

● Warm the duck and rice in a 180°C/350°F/Gas Mark 4 oven for 5 minutes. Divide the rice between 4 serving plates, and arrange the duck meat over the top. Spoon the cooked sauce on top of each, and place ginger and gherkins around the edges. Serve with the raw sauce.

Meat Main Dishes

The recipes in this section use pork, lamb and beef in dishes drawn from all over the Far East. Beef, for example, is a great favourite in Korean cuisine, while many Vietnamese dishes use pork. Many of the dishes are subtly flavoured with oriental spices, while others are recognizably 'Eastern' by virtue only of the method of preparation.

Lamb in a Hot Garlic Sauce

SERVES 4

225 g/8 oz spinach or any
   green vegetable

2 tbsp vegetable oil

225 g/8 oz lean lamb, thinly
   sliced

4 cloves garlic, finely chopped

freshly ground white pepper

½ tsp sugar

1 tbsp fish sauce or 1 tbsp light
   soy sauce and 1 tsp anchovy
   essence

1 tbsp oyster sauce

fresh sprigs of mint and/or
   coriander to garnish

● Blanch the greens in boiling water for 1 minute.
Drain and place on a serving dish.

● Heat the oil in a wok and stir-fry the lamb until
nearly cooked. This should not take more than 2
minutes. Add the garlic, pepper, sugar, fish sauce and
oyster sauce, and stir-fry until the lamb is completely
cooked and tender.

● Pour the lamb and sauce over the greens. Garnish
with mint and/or coriander sprigs.

Lamb Liver with Ginger and Coriander

SERVES 4

450 g/1 lb lamb's liver, cut into 4 cm/1½ in wide strips and cut again crossways into strips 3 mm/⅛ in thick

2 tbsp vegetable oil

1 large onion, cut into wedges about 4 cm/1½ in wide

2 medium green peppers, halved

salt

1 tbsp sesame oil

FOR THE SAUCE

2 tbsp fish sauce or light soy sauce

2 tbsp rice wine or dry sherry

2 tsp sugar

2 large cloves garlic, coarsely chopped

1 tbsp fermented black beans, rinsed and coarsely chopped

2 x 2.5 cm/1 in slices fresh ginger, peeled and ground

1 tbsp chopped fresh coriander

1 spring onion, coarsely chopped

2 tsp cornflour mixed with 2 tbsp water

● Bring a large saucepan half full of water to the boil. Put in the liver slices and stir until the water begins to puff into a boil again. Drain the liver and hold under running cold water to stop the cooking. Drain.

● Combine the fish sauce, rice wine and sugar, and stir until the sugar dissolves.

● Heat a wok over high heat and add 1 tablespoon oil. Scatter in the onion and peppers, and stir and toss vigorously until they are shining. Sprinkle in some salt and stir for about 1 minute until the onions are translucent. Transfer to a dish.

● Wipe the wok, add the remaining oil and put in the garlic, black beans, ginger, coriander and spring onions, and stir for about 30 seconds to sear them. Add the liver and stir for a further 30 seconds.

● Add the fish sauce mixture and toss and turn the meat. Add the cooked vegetables and stir them around so they integrate with the meat. Add the cornflour to the wok, a little at a time, stirring constantly. Sprinkle in the sesame oil, toss a couple of times, and ladle out on a hot serving dish.

Stir-fried Lamb with Mint and Chilli

SERVES 4

1½ tbsp vegetable oil

225 g/8 oz lean lamb, cut in fine strips

1 clove garlic, finely chopped

1 tbsp oyster sauce

1 tbsp fish sauce

pinch of sugar

1 tbsp finely sliced red fresh chilli

5 tbsp fresh mint leaves, sliced if large

● Heat the oil in a wok and stir-fry the lamb for several minutes until almost cooked. Add the garlic, oyster sauce, fish sauce, sugar and chilli, and stir-fry for another 2 minutes or so. Taste to see if extra seasoning is necessary and adjust.

● When the meat is cooked and tender, stir the mint leaves through, remove and serve on a dish.

Sautéed Lamb with Aubergine in a Sauce

SERVES 4

2 large aubergines, ends cut off, thickly sliced

3 tbsp olive oil

8 lamb cutlets, trimmed

2 cloves garlic, crushed

6 large tomatoes, blanched, skinned and thickly sliced

salt and freshly ground black pepper

FOR THE SAUCE

2 tbsp chopped fresh mint

750 ml/1¼ pt natural yogurt

freshly ground black pepper

FOR THE GARNISH

1 lemon, sliced

sprigs of mint

● Sprinkle salt over the aubergine and leave for 20 minutes. Rinse and dry with absorbent kitchen paper.

● Heat 2 tablespoons olive oil in a wok over a very high heat and add the lamb cutlets. When brown, lower the heat and continue cooking until the meat is tender—about 5 minutes on each side. Remove from the wok, drain on absorbent kitchen paper and keep warm.

● Add the remaining oil to the wok and fry the aubergine slices with the garlic until they are lightly browned on both sides. (If the oil dries out, add a little more.) When they are cooked, push them up the side of the wok and add the tomato slices. Stir-fry for a few moments and season with salt and pepper.

● Place the vegetables on a dish and arrange the cutlets over the vegetables. Garnish with lemon slices and sprigs of mint.

● Prepare the sauce by stirring the mint into the yogurt. Grind some black pepper over it and serve in a small bowl.

Stir-fried Lamb with Ginger

SERVES 4

4 tbsp chicken stock

1 medium carrot, diced into 1 cm/½ in cubes

1 tbsp butter

150 g/5 oz green peas

1 tbsp vegetable oil

2 slices fresh ginger, finely chopped

450 g/1 lb lean lamb, chopped into 1 cm/½ in cubes

1 tbsp fish sauce

1 tsp sugar

½ tbsp hoisin sauce

salt

2 tsp cornflour mixed with a little water

● Heat the stock in a wok over a medium heat. Add the carrot and cook until the liquid has nearly disappeared. Add the butter and peas, and leave to cook for a further 2 minutes, stirring occasionally. Scoop out and leave in a bowl.

● Heat the oil in the wok on a high heat and add the ginger and lamb. Stir quickly for about 1 minute and then add the fish sauce, sugar, hoisin sauce and salt. Stirring for 1 minute, and then stir in the cornflour.

● When the cornflour thickens, it will give the lamb a beautiful gloss. At this stage add the carrots and peas. Stir and mix for 30 seconds and serve.

Sautéed Lamb with Aubergine
in a Sauce

Ramen with Barbecued Pork

SERVES 4

Cha siu *is a spicy Chinese marinade, and* **cha siu** *pork is widely eaten all over southeast Asia.* **Cha siu** *pork is roasted for a comparatively short time compared with roast pork dishes prepared in the West, leaving the inner part of the meat nearly rare.* **Cha siu** *sauce is available from Oriental or Chinese food shops.*

450 g/1 lb *ramen* noodles or 400 g/14 oz fresh or 350 g/12 oz dried thin egg noodles

1.5 litres/2½ pt soy sauce stock

FOR THE TOPPING

12 large slices Chinese-style barbecued pork

4 tbsp cooked dried bamboo shoots (optional)

3 spring onions, chopped

● Boil plenty of water in a pan, and cook the noodles for 3 minutes. Drain and divide into four bowls. Heat the soy sauce stock.

● Put three slices of *cha siu* into each bowl of noodles. Garnish with the bamboo shoots and spring onions. Pour the soy sauce stock over the top just before serving.

Pork Satay

SERVES 4–6

Now popular all over Thailand, and a speciality of market food stalls, satay arrived in the south from Indonesia, via Malaysia. The dish can be made with pork, chicken or beef; serve all together for variety.

450 g/1 lb pork loin, cut into 7.5 x 2 x 0.5 cm/3 x ¾ x ¼ in long slices

350 ml/12 fl oz thin coconut milk

5 kaffir lime leaves, roughly chopped

5 coriander roots, crushed

2 stalks of lemon grass, roughly chopped

1 tbsp curry powder

1 tsp palm sugar

½ tsp salt

FOR THE SATAY SAUCE

50 g/2 oz dried yellow mung beans

1.2 litres/2 pt thin coconut milk

100 g/4 oz unsalted roasted peanuts, very finely chopped

100 g/4 oz chilli paste

50 g/2 oz curry paste (see Red Duck Curry page 137)

3 tbsp palm sugar

2 tsp tamarind juice

1 tsp salt

FOR THE AJAAD SALAD

475 ml/16 fl oz white vinegar

60 g/2½ oz sugar

1 tsp salt

1 small cucumber, quartered and sliced lengthways

25 g/1 oz shallots, sliced

2 fresh red chillies, sliced thinly into circles

● Mix the pork with all the other ingredients in a bowl and leave to marinate for 3–4 hours. Then skewer the meat onto wood or metal skewers and grill, preferably over charcoal.

● While the pork is marinating, soak the mung beans in water for 1 hour, then drain and steam them for 20 minutes or until soft. Purée in a food processor.

● Next, make the satay sauce. Mix all the ingredients together and boil in a pan or wok for 5 minutes. Remove from the heat and leave to cool.

● To make the ajaad salad, boil the vinegar, sugar and salt together in a pan until reduced to about 250 ml/ 8 fl oz. Take off the heat, cool and mix with the cucumber, shallots and chillies.

● Serve the kebabs with the satay sauce and ajaad salad, with pieces of toasted bread.

Satay-flavour Pork

SERVES 4

450 g/1 lb lean boneless pork, cut in thin strips

3 tbsp lime or lemon juice

3 tbsp ground coriander

1 tsp ground ginger

1 clove garlic, crushed

salt and freshly ground black pepper

1 tsp sesame oil

5 tbsp peanut oil

1 bunch spring onions, shredded

FOR THE SAUCE

1 small onion, chopped

2 cloves garlic, crushed

juice of 1 lime or lemon

½ tsp chilli powder

60 g/2½ oz tahini

60 g/2½ oz crunchy peanut butter

3 tbsp soy sauce

FOR THE SALAD

½ Iceberg lettuce, shredded

½ cucumber, halved and thinly sliced

FOR THE GARNISH

spring onion curls

lime or lemon wedges

● Place the pork in a bowl. Add the lime or lemon juice, coriander, ginger, garlic, seasoning and sesame oil. Stir well so that all the pieces of meat are coated in the marinade. Cover and leave to marinate for several hours or overnight.

● To make the sauce, blend the onion, garlic, lime or lemon juice, chilli and tahini to a paste in a liquidizer or food processor. Stir 4–5 tablespoons boiling water into the peanut butter to soften it to a paste, then stir in the blended mixture and the soy sauce. Add a little extra boiling water if necessary to thin the sauce.

● Arrange the lettuce and cucumber on a platter or individual plates. Add the spring onion curls. Heat the peanut oil and stir-fry the pork until browned and cooked through. Add the spring onions and stir-fry for another minute. Arrange the meat on the salad base.

● Spoon a little peanut sauce over the meat and spring onions, then serve the rest separately. Add lime wedges to garnish and serve at once.

Stir-fried Pork Slices and Celery

SERVES 4

2 tbsp vegetable oil

450 g/1 lb lean pork, sliced
   thinly and cut in 1 cm/ ½ in
   pieces

1 tsp soy sauce

1 tsp sugar

225 g/8 oz button mushrooms

225 g/8 oz spring cabbage, cut
   in 5 cm/2 in slices, with
   tougher stalks discarded

4 celery sticks, sliced thinly

1 tbsp fish sauce (optional)

3 tbsp chicken stock

cornflour

salt

● Heat 1 tablespoon oil in the wok, add the pork and stir-fry over highest heat for 2½ minutes or longer if the pork needs more cooking. Add the soy sauce and sugar, and stir with the pork for a further 2 minutes. Scoop into a bowl and keep in a warm oven.

● Wipe the wok and pour in the remaining oil. Add the mushrooms, cabbage and celery, and stir-fry for 1½ minutes. Add the fish sauce, if using, and stock and stir-fry for another minute. Cover and leave to cook for a further 2 minutes.

● Add the cooked sliced pork with the cornflour and salt to taste. Stir and mix thoroughly for a minute or so and serve immediately with rice or noodles.

Red Pork with Rice

SERVES 6

The marinade soaks a little way into the meat from the surface. When it is sliced, the red edges of the pork makes this a decorative as well as tasty dish.

325 g/11 oz pork loin

1 litre/1¾ pt water

50 g/2 oz tomato purée

3 tbsp light soy sauce

3 tbsp sugar

3 drops of red food colouring (optional)

1½ tbsp cornflour

300 g/10 oz cooked rice, heated

FOR THE *NAM CHIM* SAUCE

4 tbsp white vinegar

2 tbsp dark soy sauce

1 fresh red chilli, sliced thinly

¼ tsp sugar

● Mix together the pork, water, tomato purée, soy sauce, sugar and food colouring in a bowl and leave to marinate for 1 hour.

● Put the pork mixture with its marinade in a pan, bring to the boil and simmer for 30 minutes. Remove the pork and place in an ovenproof pan; roast it in a preheated 180°C/350°FGas Mark 4 oven for 10 minutes until lightly browned. Reserve the liquid.

● Mix a little of the cooking liquid with the cornflour, and then stir in 475 ml/16 fl oz more liquid. Bring to the boil in a small pan to thicken, then remove from the heat.

● Mix together the ingredients for the *nam chim* sauce. Slice the pork and place on serving plates (on top of the hot rice). Spoon the cornflour sauce over the top, and serve with the *nam chim* sauce.

● Serve accompanied by sliced cucumber, spring onions, hard-boiled eggs, and pieces of deep-fried belly of pork slices.

Stir-fried Pork in Ginger with Onion

SERVES 2

The sweet, tangy flavours of the soy sauce and ginger marinade are enriched and enhanced by the pork. Like most other Japanese dishes, this is easy to prepare and can be made in no time at all.

225 g/8 oz thinly sliced pork, cut into 5 cm/2 in lengths

1 tbsp vegetable oil

1 medium sized onion, peeled and sliced

FOR THE MARINADE

25 g/1 oz fresh ginger, peeled, grated and squeezed

1½ tbsp soy sauce

1 tbsp *sake*

● To make the marinade, mix together the juice of the ginger, the soy sauce and the *sake* in a bowl.

● Add the pork and marinate for 30 minutes. Heat the oil in a frying pan and fry the onion until it is transparent. Remove and set aside.

● Add the meat to the frying pan and fry for 5 minutes or until cooked.

● Return the onion to the frying pan and stir-fry for a further 1–2 minutes.

● Add the remaining marinade and stir-fry again for 1–2 minutes. Serve with a bowl of hot, plain rice.

Grilled Pork Belly

SERVES 6

*These pork slices are rather like a Korean version of Spanish **tapas** because they are served to customers in city **suljip** (or drinking houses) in order to increase thirst and therefore drink sales.*

450 g/1 lb belly of pork, thinly sliced

about 4 tbsp sesame oil

2 tsp sea salt

● Preheat the grill or barbecue, or use a table-top burner. Stir together the sesame oil and salt in a small serving bowl.

● Cook the pork slices until crisp and slightly charred. Drain quickly on absorbent kitchen paper and serve hot with the dip. Don't forget to offer plenty of paper napkins.

Steamed Minced Pork and Aubergine

SERVES 4

1 aubergine, about 350 g/
   12 oz

salt and freshly ground black
   pepper

½ tsp vegetable oil

1 small onion, thinly sliced and
   then coarsely chopped

1 egg, lightly beaten

450 g/1 lb minced pork

1 tbsp chopped pickled gherkin

1 tsp sugar

2 tbsp fish sauce or light soy
   sauce

1 tbsp cornflour

1 tbsp rice wine or dry sherry

● Peel the aubergine, slice it into pieces about 1 cm/ ½ in thick and then chop into 2.5 cm/1 in pieces. Sprinkle and rub with salt and pepper, and a little oil.

● Mix the onion, egg, pork, gherkin, sugar, fish sauce, cornflour, rice wine and a little salt. Mix with a wooden spoon until the ingredients are thoroughly mixed.

● Place the aubergine pieces at the bottom of a bowl and pack the pork mixture on top of the aubergine so that no vegetable shows above the surface.

● Place the bowl in a steamer over the wok and steam vigorously for 45 minutes. If you do not have a steamer, use the largest pan you have. Turn a fair-sized bowl upside down and place it in the bottom. Put the bowl containing the pork and aubergine on top of this and add water to halfway up the bowl containing the pork and aubergine. Serve hot. A stir-fried dish is an ideal accompaniment.

Pork Fried with Garlic and Peppercorns

SERVES 4–6

750 ml/1¼ pt peanut or corn
   oil for frying

325 g/11 oz pork loin, sliced
   into 2 x 2.5 cm/¾ x 1 in
   rectangles, 5mm/¼ in thick

2 tbsp chopped garlic

2 tsp black peppercorns, lightly
   crushed

1 tsp light soy sauce

1 tsp salt

10 g/¼ oz coriander leaves,
   chopped

2 fresh red chillies, cut into
   lengthways strips

● Heat the oil in a wok or pan to 180°C/350°F. Fry the pork until light brown, about 8–10 minutes. Take out all but the meat and 120 ml/4 fl oz of the oil, then add the garlic, peppercorns, soy sauce and salt. Stir-fry for 2 minutes or until the garlic is light brown.

● Remove the pork mixture from the pan with a slotted spoon, drain well and place on a serving plate. Sprinkle with the coriander and chilli to garnish.

● Serve accompanied by rice and sliced cucumber.

Steamed Minced Pork
and Aubergine

Spicy Grilled Pork on a Bed of Vermicelli

SERVES 4

225 g/8 oz rice vermicelli

450 g/1 lb belly of pork with
skin, cut against the grain
into 5 mm/¼ in strips, about
5 cm/2 in long

450 g/1 lb beef, minced

8 cloves garlic, finely chopped

**FOR THE CARAMEL
SAUCE**

100 g/4 oz sugar

4 tbsp fish sauce

4 thinly sliced spring onions

freshly ground black pepper

● Soak the vermicelli in warm water until soft. Drain
and set aside.

● Make the caramel sauce by swirling the sugar
gently in a wok over a hot heat. Be careful not to let
the sugar blacken but ignore the smoke. Remove from
the heat and add the fish sauce. Return to a low heat
and gently boil until the sugar dissolves. Add the
spring onions and pepper and stir.

● Put 24 bamboo skewers into water and allow to
soak for at least 30 minutes.

● Meanwhile, put the pork and beef into two
separate bowls. Put the garlic and half of the caramel
sauce onto the beef. Put the remainder of the caramel
sauce onto the pork. Blend both with the hand and
allow to stand for 30 minutes. Make 24 meatballs out
of the beef.

● Skewer the beef balls and pork slices and cook
under a hot grill for 15–20 minutes, turning
frequently. Place on the bed of vermicelli. Serve with
a selection of fresh vegetables.

Deep-fried Pork Steak in Breadcrumbs

SERVES 2

This is one of the most popular dishes in modern Japanese cuisine. It is usually served with shredded cabbage and garnished with tomato ketchup, brown sauce and/or mustard.

2 x 150–200 g/5–7 oz
  boneless pork loin steaks

2 tbsp plain flour

1 egg, beaten

2–3 tbsp dry white
  breadcrumbs

vegetable oil, for deep-frying

● Beat the meat gently with a steak hammer or rolling pin to tenderize it. Dust with the flour, then dip into the beaten egg.

● Coat the steaks with the breadcrumbs.

● Heat the oil to 170°C/330°F, and then deep fry the steaks until cooked through, about 6 minutes, depending on the thickness of the steaks.

● Serve garnished with lettuce, sliced tomato and cucumber, adding tomato ketchup, brown sauce and mustard if you wish.

Roasted Spareribs with Lemon Grass and Chilli

SERVES 4

12 pork spareribs

2 tbsp clear honey

1 tsp five-spice powder

2 cloves garlic, crushed

3 tbsp dry sherry or rice wine

3 tbsp fish sauce or 3 tbsp light
soy sauce mixed with 1 tsp
anchovy essence

2 stalks fresh lemon grass,
sliced thinly, or grated rind of
1 lemon

2 fresh red chillies, finely
chopped

● Wash and dry the spareribs and place them in a
large bowl.

● In another bowl, combine the honey, five-spice
powder, garlic, dry sherry, fish sauce, lemon grass and
chilli. Mix well. Spread the honey mixture over the
spareribs and leave to marinate for 4 hours.

● The ribs can be cooked over a barbecue, turning
frequently and basting with the marinade; or baked in
the oven at 190°C/375°F/Gas Mark 5, basting with the
marinade; or grilled under a moderately hot grill,
basting with the marinade.

Beef and Bean Curd Patties

SERVES 4–6

These light patties, **gogijon,** *are served as simple everyday fare in most Korean homes. The patties are usually small so that they can be lifted with the slim Korean chopsticks.*

225 g/8 oz medium-firm bean curd

675 g/1½ lb minced lean beef

2 cloves garlic, crushed

2 spring onions, white and green parts, very finely chopped

1 tbsp sesame oil

2 tsp soy sauce

4 tsp crushed toasted sesame seeds

plain flour for coating

2 eggs, beaten

vegetable oil for frying

● Put the bean curd in a piece of muslin and squeeze out as much water as possible. Press the bean curd through a strainer, then mix with the beef, garlic, spring onions, sesame oil, soy sauce and sesame seeds. Form into patties about 4 cm/1½ in in diameter and just under 1 cm/½ in thick.

● Toss the patties in plain flour to coat evenly, then dip in beaten egg.

● Heat a thin layer of vegetable oil in a large frying pan. Add some of the patties to make a single layer and fry slowly for 2½–3 minutes on each side or until golden. Using a slotted spoon, transfer the patties to absorbent kitchen paper to drain while frying the remaining patties.

● Serve with rice sticks and pickled cabbage.

Beef in Coconut Milk

SERVES 4

2 tbsp vegetable oil

1 clove garlic, crushed

225 g/8 oz topside of beef,
   thinly sliced

1 small onion, thinly sliced

pinch of turmeric

½ green chilli

1 cm/½ in lemon grass, cut
   from the bottom, thinly sliced

1 tbsp canned coconut milk

FOR THE GARNISH

1 tbsp peanuts, crushed

handful of fresh coriander,
   chopped

● Heat the oil until very hot. Add the garlic. When the smell is released, add everything except the coconut milk. Stir-fry for about 3 minutes or until the meat is cooked.

● Add the coconut milk and stir once. Serve garnished with crushed peanuts and chopped coriander.

Korean 'Hot Meat'

SERVES 4–6

The beef is served cold with its own spicy jelly as a side dish, and is eaten in small amounts. Because the jelly is an integral part of the dish, it is important to use a gelatinous cut of beef, such as shin. Adjust the number of chillies so suit your taste for 'hot' foods.

900 g/2 lb shin of beef

3 tbsp sesame oil

6 tbsp Japanese soy sauce

about 8 fresh red or green chillies, halved and seeded

1 red pepper, seeded and quite thinly sliced

● Put the meat into a saucepan. Add enough water just to cover it and bring to the boil. Skim the scum from the surface, then add the remaining ingredients.

● Cover the pan and simmer very slowly for 2–3 hours until the meat is so tender it is beginning to fall apart. Keep an eye on the water level to make sure the pan does not become dry, but do not drown the meat. At the end of the cooking, it should be surrounded by a thick sauce.

● Remove from the heat and let the meat cool in the liquid. Break the meat apart with a fork and serve with the jelly, chillies, and sliced red pepper.

Beef with Lemon Grass and Mushrooms

SERVES 4

450 g/1 lb fillet steak, sliced very thinly across the grain and cut into 5 x 7.5 cm/ 2 x 3 in pieces

2 stalks fresh lemon grass, sliced paper-thin and finely chopped

2 fresh red chillies, finely chopped

6 cloves garlic, finely chopped

3 tbsp fish sauce or light soy sauce

1 tsp cornflour

freshly ground black pepper

3½ tbsp vegetable oil

2 medium onions, finely sliced

100 g/4 oz button mushrooms

1 tsp sugar

50 g/2 oz roasted peanuts, coarsely ground

FOR THE GARNISH

sprigs of coriander

● Combine the beef, lemon grass, chilli, half the garlic, 2 tablespoons fish sauce, cornflour, black pepper and 2 tablespoons oil in a bowl. Set aside for 30 minutes.

● Pour 1 tablespoon oil in the wok over a medium heat and add the onions and the remaining garlic. Stir-fry for 1–2 minutes until they are golden brown. Remove the onions and set aside. Add ½ tablespoon more oil and, when hot, add the beef, the mushrooms, the rest of the fish sauce and the sugar. Sauté over a high heat for 1–2 minutes or until the beef is just cooked.

● Scoop the food from the wok and arrange it on a warmed serving platter. Arrange the sautéed onions around it and sprinkle the peanuts and black pepper over everything. Garnish with coriander sprigs.

Green Beef Curry

SERVES 4

Definitely green, but rarely sweet, this is one of the basic Thai curry styles, and can be used with pork, chicken or duck as a variation from beef.

1.2 litres/2 pt thin coconut milk

325 g/11 oz beef sirloin, cut into 2.5 x 2 x 0.5 cm/ 1 x ¾ x ¼ in slices

2 tbsp fish sauce

½ tbsp palm sugar

10 small white aubergines, quartered

3 fresh red chillies, quartered lengthways

3 kaffir lime leaves, torn into small pieces

10 g/¼ oz sweet basil leaves

FOR THE CHILLI PASTE

1 tbsp sliced shallot

1 tbsp chopped garlic

1 tbsp sliced galangal

½ stalk of lemon grass, sliced

½ tbsp coriander seeds

2 tsp salt

1 tsp shrimp paste

½ tsp chopped kaffir lime zest

½ tsp coriander root or stalk

6 white peppercorns, crushed

20 fresh small green chillies, roughly chopped

● Pound all the chilli paste ingredients, except the green chillies, together to form a fine paste, using a pestle and mortar or blender if you have one. Stir in the green chillies.

● Heat 250 ml/8 fl oz of the coconut milk in a pan, add the chilli paste and cook for 2 minutes. Add the beef and the rest of the coconut milk, and bring to the boil.

● Add the fish sauce and palm sugar, boil for 2 more minutes, then add the aubergine and chilli, and cook for 1 minute. Stir in the lime leaf, boil for 1 minute, add the basil and remove from the heat.

● Serve in bowls accompanied by rice, pickled vegetables, salted eggs and sun-dried beef.

Stir-fried Beef with Peppers and Bamboo Shoots

SERVES 4

1 tbsp vegetable oil

450 g/1 lb rump steak, thinly sliced

3 spring onions, cut in 1 cm/ ½ in lengths

2 cloves garlic, crushed

100 g/4 oz canned bamboo shoots, sliced

1 large green pepper, seeded and sliced

2 tbsp fish sauce or 2 tbsp light soy sauce and ½ tsp anchovy essence

150 ml/¼ pt beef stock

2 tbsp sugar

2 tsp cornflour mixed with a little water

● Heat the oil in a wok over a high heat, add the beef and stir-fry for 2–3 minutes, stirring all the while, to seal in the flavours of the meat. Scoop out the beef and place it in a warm oven.

● Add the spring onions and garlic to the wok and stir-fry over a moderate heat for 3 minutes. Increase the heat to high, stir in the bamboo shoots and pepper, and stir-fry for 1–2 minutes.

● Stir in the fish sauce, stock and sugar. Cover and cook for 3 minutes. Return the beef to the wok and stir for 1 minute. Add the cornflour to the beef mixture and stir constantly until the mixture thickens. Serve immediately.

Beef in Oyster Sauce

SERVES 4

If you include this dish as part of a Chinese menu, reduce the quantities by half, or serve it with plain cooked rice or chow mein.

450 g/1 lb frying steak, cut into small, thin slices

4 tbsp oyster sauce

3 tbsp soy sauce

1 clove garlic, crushed

5 tbsp dry sherry

4 large dried Chinese mushrooms

5 tbsp oil

1 green pepper, seeded and cut into chunks

1 red pepper, seeded and cut into chunks

1 onion, cut into chunks

● Place the meat in a dish. Mix the oyster sauce, soy sauce, garlic and sherry together, pour the mixture over the meat, and mix well. Cover and leave to marinate for 2–4 hours.

● Place the mushrooms in a small basin or mug and pour in just enough hot water to cover them. Place a saucer or the base of another mug on the mushrooms to keep them submerged, then leave to soak for 20 minutes. Drain, reserving the soaking liquid, discard tough stalks and slice the mushroom caps.

● Heat the oil, then stir-fry the peppers and onion for 3 minutes. Use a draining spoon to add the beef to the pan, then continue stir-frying until the meat is cooked and lightly browned. Add the mushrooms.

● Pour the soaking liquid into the oyster sauce marinade left from the meat and mix well, then pour the liquid into the pan. Bring to the boil and boil rapidly for a few minutes so that the meat is coated in a slightly thickened sauce. Serve at once.

Quick Beef

SERVES 2

The original concept of this recipe is that it is prepared and cooked quickly for people who are waiting to eat, but the beef can be marinated with the remaining ingredients for 1–3 hours to give it extra flavour.

225 g/8 oz good quality steak

2 cloves garlic, finely chopped

2 spring onions, finely chopped

2 tbsp sesame oil

1 tbsp beef stock

salt and freshly ground black pepper

● Preheat the grill. Cut the beef across the grain into slices about 1 cm/½ in thick. Score the slices on both sides. Put into a bowl.

● Mix the remaining ingredients together and pour over the beef. Stir to coat in the marinade, then grill for 5–7 minutes, turning halfway through, until cooked to your liking.

Beef in Oyster Sauce

Stir-fried Beef with Garlic and Chillies

SERVES 3–4

Garlic and chillies give the character to this simple, tasty stir-fry, but the number of each can be adjusted according to personal taste.

450 g/1 lb sirloin steak, cut into strips

2 tbsp soy sauce

1 spring onion, white and green part thinly sliced

1½ tsp sesame oil

2 tbsp rice wine or dry sherry

1½ tsp sugar

1½ tbsp vegetable oil

3 cloves garlic, cut into slivers

4 fresh red chillies, seeded and cut into strips

FOR THE GARNISH

½ egg, beaten, fried and cut into strips

toasted sesame seeds

● Put the beef in a bowl. Add the soy sauce, spring onion, sesame oil, rice wine or dry sherry and sugar. Stir, then cool for 1 hour.

● Heat the oil in a frying pan. Add the garlic and chillies, and stir-fry over a high heat until fragrant, about 1 minute. Remove with a slotted spoon and reserve.

● Lift the beef from the marinade and add to the pan. Stir-fry for 2–3 minutes. Return the chillies and garlic to the pan. Add the marinade and cook, stirring, over a medium heat for about 2 minutes.

● Serve the beef garnished with egg strips and toasted sesame seeds.

Grilled Beef

SERVES 4

*This dish, **pulgogi**, is one of the most popular Korean dishes. **Pulgogi** is also the name of the domed-shape metal hotplate that is put on a table-top burner for cooking the beef. A grill and grill rack or a barbecue can be used instead.*

4 spring onions, coarsely chopped

3 cloves garlic, finely chopped

1 tbsp crushed toasted sesame seeds

3 tbsp soy sauce

2 tsp rice wine or dry sherry

1 tbsp sesame oil

2 tbsp sugar

freshly ground black pepper

550 g/1¼ lb fillet steak or sirloin, frozen for 1 hour

vegetable oil for brushing

● Mix together the spring onions, garlic, sesame seeds, soy sauce, rice wine or sherry, sesame oil, sugar, 2 tablespoons water and plenty of black pepper.

● Cut the beef crossways into 5 mm/¼ in thick slices. Lay in a shallow dish. Pour over the spring onion mixture, cover and let marinate for 1 hour.

● Preheat the grill or barbecue. Lightly oil a grill rack or table-top grill plate. Cook the beef in batches in a single layer for about 1 minute on each side until browned on the outside but still pink inside.

Steak with Garlic and Soy Sauce

SERVES 2

A combination of a Western cut of meat with a Japanese sauce that works really well. Remember that the frying times given for the steak will vary depending on the thickness of the meat and personal preference. This flexible dish can be served with Japanese side dishes or vegetables.

2 x 150–200 g/5–7 oz sirloin
   or rump steaks

freshly ground black pepper

1 tbsp vegetable oil

5 cloves garlic, sliced

1 tbsp *sake*

15 g/½ oz butter

1 tbsp soy sauce

● Beat the meat on both sides using a steak hammer or a rolling pin, then season with the pepper.

● Heat the oil in a frying pan and fry the garlic briefly. Remove and set aside.

● Fry the steaks lightly on both sides, then add the *sake* and fry for a further minute before placing the steaks on warmed serving plates.

● Return the garlic to the pan, add the butter and soy sauce and when the mixture begins to bubble pour over the steaks and serve immediately.

Coconut Beef Curry

SERVES 8

This is one of the driest of Thai curries, and it is usually quite fiery.

FOR THE CURRY PASTE

6 dried red chillies, chopped roughly

7 white peppercorns

40 g/1½ oz garlic, roughly chopped

25 g/1 oz shallots, roughly chopped

2 coriander roots, roughly chopped

2 tsp salt

1 tsp roughly chopped galangal

1 tsp roughly chopped lemon grass

1 tsp roughly chopped kaffir lime rind

1 tsp shrimp paste

4 tbsp peanut or corn oil

325 g/11 oz beef sirloin, cut into 3 x 2 x 0.5 cm/ 1¼ x ¾ x ¼ in pieces

750 ml/1¼ pt thin coconut milk

1 tbsp fish sauce

2 tsp sugar

2 fresh red chillies, sliced

2 kaffir lime leaves, sliced finely

15 g/½ oz sweet basil leaves

● Pound all the curry paste ingredients together with a pestle and mortar or in a blender to form a paste.

● Heat the oil in a pan or wok and fry the curry paste for 3–4 minutes. Add the beef and fry for 2 minutes, then add the coconut milk and boil until the beef is tender, about 15 minutes.

● Add the fish sauce, sugar and chilli. Remove from the heat, transfer to a serving plate and sprinkle with the lime rind and basil. Serve accompanied by rice.

● Serve in bowls accompanied by rice, pickled vegetables, salted eggs and sun-dried beef.

Korean Meatballs

SERVES 2–3

These flavourful meatballs are served as one of the side dishes in a Korean meal. They are also good cold, so a useful item for a picnic.

450 g/1 lb lean minced beef

3 tbsp soy sauce

2 spring onions, finely chopped

2 cloves garlic, finely chopped

1 tbsp crushed toasted sesame seeds

1½ tsp sesame oil

freshly ground black pepper

seasoned plain flour for coating

2 eggs, lightly beaten

vegetable oil for frying

vinegar dipping sauce to serve

● Mix together the beef, soy sauce, spring onions, garlic, sesame seeds, sesame oil and plenty of pepper. Leave for 30 minutes.

● Form the meat mixture into flattened rounds, about 4cm/1½ in in diameter. Toss in seasoned flour to coat evenly, then dip in beaten egg, letting excess egg drain off.

● Heat a little oil in a frying pan, preferably nonstick, and fry the meatballs until brown and crisp on both sides and cooked through.

● Serve with vinegar dipping sauce.

Parties and Special Occasions

Whether you are planning a small buffet party or an elegant dinner, you will find recipes to suit any occasion here—from pretty marbled eggs to whole suckling pig. Many of these dishes are perfect for buffet or cocktail parties, and they are sure to win the praises of your guests for innovation, flavour and style.

Sizzling Butterfly Prawns

SERVES 4

Uncooked Mediterranean or jumbo prawns are available frozen from good fishmongers and oriental supermarkets. Since they tend to be rather expensive, the portions can be small but the end result need not look mean with the right accompaniments—for example, serve a chow mein with some sliced scallops.

24 uncooked large
  Mediterranean prawns,
  shelled with tails on

cornflour for coating

5 cm/2 in piece fresh ginger,
  peeled and grated, then
  chopped into small pieces

1 clove garlic, crushed

1 green chilli, seeded and finely
  chopped (optional)

2 tsp sugar

2 tsp white wine vinegar

½ tsp tomato purée

1 tbsp light soy sauce

1 tbsp dry sherry

pinch of five-spice powder

1 tsp sesame oil

120 ml/4 fl oz vegetable oil

**FOR THE VEGETABLE
GARNISH**

6 spring onions, cut into very
  fine strips

½ red pepper, seeded and cut
  into short, very fine strips

¼ cucumber, peeled and cut into
  short, fine strips

lemon wedges to serve

● To prepare the prawns, first remove the fine black cord that runs down the back (this may have been removed). Using a small sharp knife, take a prawn and cut it down the back, almost through in half, then press it open. Repeat with all the shellfish. Coat them generously with cornflour and shake off excess.

● In a bowl, mix the ginger, garlic, chilli, sugar, vinegar, tomato purée, soy sauce, sherry, five-spice powder and sesame oil. Add the prawns and mix well to coat them with the flavouring ingredients. They should be thoroughly tossed to ensure that they are all flavoured with the paste.

● Heat the vegetable oil until it is shimmering hot, then stir-fry the prawns over high heat until they are crisp and golden—this takes only a few minutes. Use a slotted spoon to transfer them to a serving plate.

● Add all the vegetables for garnish to the oil remaining in the pan and stir-fry for 2 minutes. Spoon them on the plate with the prawns and add the lemon wedges. Serve the dish immediately.

Seaweed-wrapped Avocado

SERVES 2

Avocado is not a traditional ingredient of Japanese cooking but it is certainly popular in many Japanese homes. This popularity is said to be due to the similarity between the taste of the avocado and the taste of raw tuna as used in **sushi** *and* **sashimi**. *You can mix in* **wasabi**, *the green Japanese mustard powder, to spice up the soy sauce, which can be used as a dressing, if you wish.*

1 avocado

nori (2 sheets of dried seaweed)

2 tsp soy sauce

1 tsp *wasabi* (optional)

● Slice the avocado in two, remove the stone and peel. Cut in half again, then slice into 1 cm/½ in widths.

● Cut the *nori* into strips and wrap the avocado slices in the *nori*.

● Pour soy sauce into a small dish. If you are using *wasabi*, mash in a small amount. Dip the avocado into the sauce before eating.

Oysters

SERVES 4

Instead of the traditional lemon juice, try spooning a little of this Korean sauce over oysters before sucking them, with their juices, from their shells.

12–24 oysters in the shell, opened

FOR THE SAUCE

2 tbsp rice vinegar

1 tbsp chilli bean paste

1 cm/½ in piece ginger, crushed and finely chopped

1½ tsp sugar

few drops of soy sauce to taste

- Mix together all the ingredients for the sauce, adjusting the levels of flavourings to taste. Pour into a small bowl. Cover and chill until ready to serve.

- Spoon the prepared sauce over the oysters.

Oyster Fritters

SERVES 4–6

Use Pacific oysters for these fritters—not only are they the authentic ones, but they are cheaper than European flat oysters, also known in Britain as 'native' oysters. Save the liquid that is in the oyster shells to strain into the batter; reduce the water by the amount of oyster liquid added and omit the salt from the recipe if you do this. Add some sesame seeds to the batter for an extra nutty, crunchy texture.

100 g/4 oz plain flour

2 tsp baking powder

very small pinch of Korean chilli powder, or cayenne pepper mixed with paprika

salt

1 egg, beaten

about 24 oysters, opened

vegetable oil for deep-frying

sesame or vinegar dipping sauce

- Sift the flour, baking powder, Korean chilli powder, or cayenne pepper, and paprika, and salt into a bowl. Slowly pour in 150 ml/¼ pt water, stirring, to make a smooth batter. Leave for 30 minutes.

- Half fill a deep-fat fryer with vegetable oil and heat to about 180°C/350°F. Dip the oysters in the batter, then fry for about 2 minutes until the batter is crisp and golden; take care not to overcook the oysters as they will become tough.

- Drain the oysters on absorbent kitchen paper and serve hot with sesame or vinegar dipping sauce.

Oysters

Spicy-fried Frogs' Legs

SERVES 4

5 tbsp peanut or corn oil

2 tbsp red chilli paste

8 sets frogs' legs

50 g/2 oz green peppercorns

5 small white aubergines, quartered

3 fresh red chillies, sliced lengthways

25 g/1 oz galangal or fresh ginger, cut into fine matchsticks

2 tsp fish sauce

½ tsp palm sugar

15 g/½ oz sweet basil leaves

● Heat the oil in a wok or pan, add the chilli paste and fry for 2 minutes, then mix in the frogs' legs and peppercorns.

● Add the aubergines, chilli, galangal or ginger, fish sauce and sugar, mix well and fry for 3 minutes.

● Stir in the basil and take off the heat. Serve accompanied by rice.

Tea Eggs

MAKES 12 EGGS

12 eggs

2 tsp salt

3 tbsp light soy sauce

2 tbsp dark soy sauce

1 tsp five-spice powder

1 tbsp red tea leaves

● Cook the eggs in water for 5–10 minutes. Remove and gently tap the shell of each egg with a spoon until it is cracked finely all over.

● Place the eggs back in the pan and cover with fresh water. Add the salt, soy sauces, five-spice powder and tea leaves (the better the quality of the tea, the better the result). Bring to the boil and simmer for 30–40 minutes. Leave the eggs to cool in the liquid.

● Peel off the shells—the eggs will have a beautiful marbled pattern. They can be served either on their own or as part of a mixed hors d'oeuvre, whole or cut into halves or quarters.

Salmon Roe Sushi

SERVES 2

Salmon roe is an expensive but popular ingredient in Japan. This dish makes a rather nice starter, although you can eat it combined with rolled **sushi** *or with fried bean curd* **sushi** *as a main dish.*

4 tbsp cooked *sushi* rice

1½ x 13 cm/5 in strips *nori*

2 slices cucumber, cut in half

4 tsp salmon roe

● Wet your palm with a little water. Take 1 tablespoon of rice and form it into a square-shaped ball. Make three other balls in the same way.

● Place each rice ball in the middle of a strip of *nori*. Roll the *nori* around it, then stand it on a plate.

● Place the sliced cucumber on top of each of the rice balls, and put 1 teaspoon of salmon roe on top of the cucumber. Serve with a dash of soy sauce.

Sukiyaki

SERVES 2

Sukiyaki *is one of the few examples of Japanese cuisine to have become popular throughout the West. In Japan, a special, heavy pan is used, however* sukiyaki *can be prepared with any large, deep frying pan. Like fondue,* **sukiyaki** *is always cooked at the table.*

1 tbsp vegetable oil

150 ml/¼ pt *dashi* stock

1½ tsp sugar

2 tbsp *mirin*

1 tbsp *sake*

2½ tbsp soy sauce

1 medium onion, halved and sliced

200 g/7 oz bean curd, cut in half lengthways and sliced

300 g/10 oz Chinese leaves, halved lengthways and sliced

6 shiitake mushrooms, halved

1 short leek, sliced on a slant

300 g/10 oz beef, sliced paper thin

2 eggs (optional)

● Heat the oil in a frying pan and add the *dashi* stock, sugar, *mirin, sake* and soy sauce. When this mixture begins to simmer, add half the amount of onions, bean curd, Chinese leaves and shiitake mushrooms, keeping each ingredient in its own separate group in the pan. Simmer for 7 minutes and then add half the beef, placing it in the centre of the pan. Continue to simmer for several minutes until cooked.

● Break the raw eggs into 2 serving bowls and mix the yolk and white with your chopsticks. Take the cooked meat, bean curd and vegetables a little at a time from the pan, dip them into the raw egg and eat with a bowl of rice. As the cooked ingredients are taken from the pan, replenish with the raw ingredients.

Steamed Crab with Light Wine Sauce

SERVES 4

Vietnamese people eat crabs a lot as they are plentiful and inexpensive; they are found in the lakes, rivers, mangrove swamps and coastal waters. The freshwater crab is highly prized for its sweet-flavoured meat.

675 g/1½ lb crab claws

2 stalks lemon grass, peeled and finely chopped, or grated rind of 1 lemon

1 slice fresh ginger, peeled and finely chopped

FOR THE SAUCE

4 tbsp rice wine, dry sherry or dry white wine

1 tbsp fish sauce or 1 tbsp light soy sauce

1 tbsp sesame seed oil

1 tbsp finely chopped lemon grass

½ tbsp spring onions, finely chopped

● Break open the crab claws by placing a newspaper on top and tapping with the back of a cleaver or a steak mallet. Carefully extract the flesh and discard any shell and cartilage. Place in a bowl and flake with a fork.

● Add the lemon grass and ginger. Mix well, cover and steam for about 15 minutes.

● Mix together the sauce ingredients and serve separately.

Sukiyaki

Ramen with Crab Omelette

SERVES 4

Typically, crab omelette is served on its own. The inspiration behind the dish is Chinese, but the Japanese have a preference for it served on a bowl of noodles. Ideally, individual omelettes should be made, but if time is against you, make one large one and cut it into four portions.

45 g/1 lb *ramen* noodles or 400 g/14 oz fresh or 350 g/ 12 oz dried thin egg noodles

1.5 litres/2½ pt soy sauce stock

FOR THE OMELETTE

6 eggs

175 g/6 oz crabmeat (canned)

4 shiitake mushrooms, sliced

2 spring onions, thinly sliced

4 tbsp canned bamboo shoots, thinly sliced

salt and white pepper

2—3 tbsp vegetable oil

1 spring onion, chopped

● To make the omelette, put the eggs, crabmeat, mushrooms, spring onion and bamboo shoots in a bowl. Season with salt and pepper, and mix.

● Heat the oil in a frying pan or wok until very hot. Pour in the egg mixture and heat for 30 seconds. Stir lightly with chopsticks or a spatula a few times. When it is nearly set, turn it over. The mixture should be soft like scrambled eggs, but be cooked just enough to be able to retain the shape of an omelette.

● Boil plenty of water in a large pan. Add the noodles and cook for 3 minutes, or according to the instructions on the packet. Drain, then divide into four bowls.

● Heat the soy sauce stock. Place the crab omelette on the noodles, and pour the stock over the top. Sprinkle with the chopped spring onion and serve.

Crab Stuffed with Minced Pork and Coriander

SERVES 4

2 cooked crabs

225 g/8 oz chopped lean pork

1 onion, chopped

1 tsp black pepper

1 tbsp sugar

1 tbsp fish sauce (optional)

1 tbsp chopped coriander root

2 eggs, separated

1 tbsp chopped spring onions

1 tbsp fresh coriander leaves, chopped

1 fresh red or green chilli, finely sliced

● Remove the claws from the crabs. Remove the flesh from the shells, taking care to keep them intact. Remove the flesh from the claws as well. Flake all the flesh and set aside.

● Combine the pork, onion, pepper, sugar, fish sauce, if used, and coriander root in a food processor or blender. Remove and place in a bowl. Add the crab meat and egg white. Add the spring onions and coriander leaves and mix by hand, using more egg white if necessary.

● Fill the crab shells with the mixture to form a generous mound. Carefully break the egg yolk and place ½ teaspoon yolk on the top of each mound. Sprinkle with chilli. Be very careful when moving the crab shells or else the yolk will run. (If you think this is too difficult, brush the filling with the beaten egg yolk and sprinkle with the sliced chilli and some coriander leaves.)

● Place each crab, stuffed side up, in a large steamer and steam for 20 minutes. Serve with a generous green salad.

Tempura

SERVES 2

One of the most famous dishes in the Japanese repertoire, **Tempura** needs no introduction. Ironically, strong evidence exists that **Tempura** is not originally Japanese, but was introduced into Japan by Portuguese traders in the seventeenth century. One of the great advantages of **Tempura** is its versatility. Virtually any seafood and vegetable can be prepared and served in this way. The ingredients suggested below are those most commonly served in Japan. Mix the dip first, so that the **Tempura** can be served and eaten immediately after being fried.

½ green pepper, seeded and cut into four pieces lengthways

4 shiitake mushrooms

225 g/8 oz sweet potatoes, unpeeled but sliced into 2 cm/¾ in circles

100 g/4 oz carrots, peeled and cut into 6 cm/2½ in lengths, then cut into matchsticks

4 large prawns, peeled but tails on

vegetable oil, for deep frying

small amount of plain flour

1 small white radish, peeled and grated

FOR THE BATTER

25 g/1 oz plain flour

25 g/1 oz cornflour

1 egg, beaten

175 ml/6 fl oz water

FOR THE DIP

2 tbsp *mirin*

2 tbsp soy sauce

175 ml/6 fl oz *dashi* stock

● To make the dip, put the *mirin*, soy sauce and *dashi* stock in a pan, bring to the boil and simmer for 1 minute. Leave to cool.

● To make the batter, place the flour, cornflour, egg and water into a bowl and mix lightly using chopsticks or a fork. The batter should be quite lumpy with some flour visible on top of the mixture.

● Heat the oil in a pan to 180˚C/350˚F. Check the temperature by dropping in some batter or a piece of bread; if it bubbles and floats to the surface, the oil is at the right temperature.

● Dip the vegetables into the batter and deep-fry until the batter has turned golden brown. Check the harder vegetables, such as sweet potatoes, are cooked by piercing with a skewer. If it runs through smoothly with no resistance, the vegetables are ready. The carrot matchsticks should be picked up in small bunches, dipped in the batter and then fried, held together by the batter.

● To deep-fry the prawns, coat them with a little flour before dipping into the batter as this will stop them from spitting while frying.

● When all the ingredients have been fried, serve immediately. Place the dip in small bowls and into the centre, add a spoonful of grated radish. Dip the pieces of *tempura* into the dip before eating.

Tempura

Steamed Crab

SERVES 6

The crab mixture can be steamed in a large crab shell. It is well worth using fresh crab meat for better flavour and texture.

50 g/2 oz bean sprouts

scant 40 g/1½ oz medium-firm bean curd

about 450 g/1 lb mixed white and brown crabmeat, finely chopped

1 cm/½ in fresh ginger, grated

2 spring onions, very finely chopped

1 tsp sesame oil

salt and freshly ground black pepper

1 tbsp plain flour

1 egg, beaten

diagonally sliced white and green parts of spring onions for garnish

● Add the bean sprouts to a saucepan of boiling water. Quickly return to the boil and boil for 1 minute. Tip into a colander and rinse under cold water. Drain well, then squeeze out as much water as possible. Chop finely.

● Wrap the bean curd in a clean cloth and squeeze firmly to express surplus liquid. Finely crumble the bean curd. Mix the crabmeat, bean sprouts, bean curd, ginger, spring onions, sesame oil and seasonings together. Divide among six individual heatproof dishes.

● Sift the flour over the tops of the dishes, then brush with beaten egg. Put in a steaming basket. Cover the dishes with baking parchment and cover the steaming basket. Put the steaming basket over a saucepan of boiling water and steam the crab for about 10 minutes. Garnish with spring onions.

Stuffed Crab Shells

SERVES 4

This dish is as well-known in Thailand for its name, **poo jag,** *as for anything else—it means, literally, dear crab, for reasons that no one has ever been able to explain convincingly.*

4 crab shells, well cleaned

3 eggs, beaten

1.2 litres/2 pt peanut or corn oil for deep-frying

10 g/¼ oz coriander leaves

2 fresh red chillies, cut into lengthways strips

FOR THE STUFFING

225 g/8 oz cooked minced pork

100 g/4 oz minced prawns

60 g/2½ oz crabmeat, fresh or drained very well if canned

2 tbsp finely chopped onion

1 tbsp finely sliced spring onion

1 tsp ground white pepper

1 tsp sugar

¼ tsp light soy sauce

¼ tsp salt

● Mix all the stuffing ingredients together and fill the crab shells. Heat the oil in a pan or wok to approximately 180°C/350°F.

● Dip the stuffed crabs in the beaten egg to coat them well all over, and then deep-fry until thoroughly cooked, about 10–15 minutes. Remove and drain well on absorbent kitchen paper. Sprinkle with the coriander and chilli before serving. Serve as an hors d'oeuvre or with rice and bottled Chinese plum sauce.

Korean Crab Cakes

SERVES 4

Although not quite authentic, these crab cakes go very well with a crisp green salad.

350 g/12 oz floury potatoes, unpeeled

1½ cloves garlic, crushed

1 fresh red chilli, seeded and finely chopped

2.5 cm/1 in fresh ginger, grated

3 spring onions, finely chopped

350 g/12 oz white and brown crabmeat

finely grated rind of ½ lime

2 tbsp chopped fresh coriander

salt and freshly ground black pepper

1½ tbsp sesame seeds

50 g/2 oz fresh bread crumbs, for coating

flour for coating

1 egg, beaten

vegetable oil for deep-frying

ginger dipping sauce to serve

● Boil the potatoes in their skins until tender. Drain and leave until cool enough to handle. Peel the potatoes and mash the flesh.

● Mix the mashed potato with the garlic, chilli, ginger, spring onions, crabmeat, lime rind, coriander and salt and pepper. Form into eight round cakes, about the size of golf balls. Chill for 30 minutes.

● Stir the sesame seeds into the breadcrumbs. Coat the crab cakes in the flour, then the egg and finally coat in the breadcrumbs.

● Half fill a deep-fat fryer with vegetable oil and heat to about 170˚C/325˚F. Fry the crab cakes in batches for about 8 minutes until golden. Transfer to absorbent kitchen paper to drain while frying the remaining crab cakes. Serve hot with ginger dipping sauce.

Marinated Thinly Sliced Chicken Breast

SERVES 3 – 4

Traditionally, vegetables, rice and pickles are served with the chicken, but this is also delicious with a crisp salad, or on firm white, crusty bread.

3 tbsp Japanese dark soy sauce

2 tbsp sesame oil

1 tbsp crushed toasted sesame seeds

2.5 cm/1 in fresh ginger root, grated

2 cloves garlic, crushed

2 spring onions, white and green parts thinly sliced into rings

2 tbsp rice wine

salt and freshly ground black pepper

350 g/12 oz skinned, boneless chicken breast, chilled

2 tbsp vegetable oil

2 fresh hot red chillies, thickly sliced crossways

4 large brown mushrooms, oyster or shiitake, each cut into 4 slices

● Mix together the soy sauce, sesame oil and seeds, ginger, garlic, spring onions, rice wine or sherry, salt and plenty of black pepper to taste.

● Holding the knife at a slight angle, cut across the chicken breasts to make 3 mm/⅛ in wide slices. Using a meat mallet or the flat side of a cleaver, pound each slice, at the same time dragging the mallet or cleaver across the slice. Lay the slices in a large, shallow dish, pouring some of the soy/sesame sauce over each layer. Cover and leave for 1 hour.

● Heat the vegetable oil in a large, preferably nonstick, frying pan. Lift some of the chicken slices from the marinade and add to the pan so they lie flat in a single layer. Cook for 1 minute on each side until lightly browned and cooked through. Transfer to a warm plate and keep warm while frying the remaining chicken.

● When all the chicken has been cooked through, add the chillies, mushrooms and remaining marinade to the pan. Stir continuously and cook for 1 more minute. Pour the sauce evenly over the chicken and serve immediately.

Japanese Chicken Shish Kebab

SERVES 2

The Japanese name for this dish, **yakitori,** *lends its name to the Japanese* **yakitori bar,** *a popular place to meet, eat, drink and socialize throughout Japan. Chicken and chicken livers are the two most commonly eaten* **yakitori.**

FOR THE STUFFING

4 tbsp soy sauce

4 tbsp *mirin*

1 tbsp caster sugar

1 tbsp honey

skin from the chicken

FOR THE *YAKITORI*

2 boneless chicken breasts (with skin), diced, making 24 pieces

1 leek, cut into 2.5 cm/1 in lengths, making 8 pieces

½ green pepper, seeded and diced, making 8 pieces

8 bamboo or steel skewers

● To make the sauce, put the soy sauce, *mirin*, sugar, honey and chicken skin into a saucepan, bring to the boil and simmer for about 10 minutes.

● Turn up the heat to medium and brush the *yakitori* with the sauce frequently, turning from time to time, for about 6–7 minutes or until the meat is cooked through. Serve with rice and a vegetable dish.

● To prepare the *yakitori*, thread onto a skewer pieces of chicken, leek, chicken, pepper and chicken again, in that order.

● Preheat the grill to low and cook the *yakitori* until the meat has turned white, about 3 minutes.

Duck with Plums and Port

SERVES 4

Serve this rich stir-fry with rice or noodles.

3 duck breasts, skinned and thinly sliced across (into medallions)

120 ml/4 fl oz port

grated rind and juice of 1 orange

1 bay leaf

1 sprig of parsley

1 sprig of thyme

1 sprig of rosemary

25 g/1 oz plain flour

salt and freshly ground black pepper

3 tbsp oil

knob of butter

225 g/8 oz plums, halved, stoned and quartered

FOR THE GARNISH

orange slices

fresh herbs

● Place the duck in a dish. Add the port, orange rind and juice, and all the herbs. Mix well, cover and leave to marinate overnight.

● Strain the duck well, reserving the marinade. Pick out the herbs, then pat the duck on absorbent kitchen paper. Toss the slices of duck in the flour, adding plenty of seasoning.

● Heat the oil and butter with the herbs. Add the duck and stir-fry the pieces until lightly browned. Sprinkle any leftover flour into the pan, then stir in the marinade and add the plums. Stir all the time until the juices boil and thicken. Reduce the heat and cook for 2 minutes, then taste for seasoning before serving. Halved orange slices and fresh herbs may be added for garnish.

Japanese Chicken Shish Kebab

Crispy Roast Duck with Pancakes and Fresh Herbs
SERVES 4

If you prefer not to make pancakes, buy 12 wheaten pancakes, which are available in good delicatessens.

450 g/1 lb of Ho Chi Minh duck (see Duck with Ginger Sauce, page 138)

FOR THE PANCAKES

225 g/8 oz plain flour

175 ml/6 fl oz boiled water

½ tbsp cold water

1 tsp sesame seed oil

FOR THE VEGETABLE PLATTER

1 bunch spring onions, cut into 5 cm/2 in lengths

50 g/2 oz fresh coriander

50 g/2 oz fresh mint

50 g/2 oz fresh basil

½ cucumber peeled in alternating strips, halved lengthways and sliced thinly crossways

300 g/10 oz fresh bean sprouts

sweet plum sauce to accompany (this can be obtained from supermarkets and delicatessens)

● To make the pancakes sift the flour into a mixing bowl. Pour in the boiled water, stirring quickly and then stir in the cold water. When cool enough, mould with your hands and form a dough. Cover with a cloth and leave for 30 minutes.

● When ready, knead lightly on a lightly floured board. Roll the dough into a sausage shape and cut into 2.5 cm/1 in portions. This will make about 12 rounds. With the heel of the hand flatten into circles of about 6 cm/2½ in across.

● Using a pastry brush paint half the pieces with the sesame oil. Place the remaining pieces onto the oiled surfaces making six pairs in total. With a lightly floured rolling pin roll out each pair to about 15 cm/ 6 in across. Turn them to make them round.

● Fry for 1–2 minutes in a heavy un-oiled pan until they begin to turn light brown. Turn them over and repeat. They will puff up.

● Remove and separate the two thin pancakes. Repeat until all the dough is used up. Put on a plate and cover with a cloth to prevent from drying. Steam all the pancakes in a steamer for 7 minutes just before serving with the duck.

● Arrange the duck on a plate. Arrange the vegetables on a plate. Put some plum sauce into a dish. Place the pancakes on a flat plate. Guests place a teaspoon of plum sauce and some duck and vegetables on a pancake.

Marinated Quail in Honey

SERVES 4

1 tsp coriander seeds, lightly crushed

2 tbsp clear honey

2 onions, sliced

300 ml/½ pt dry cider

300 ml/½ pt chilli vinegar

8 quails

25 g/1 oz butter

2 tbsp vegetable oil

salt and freshly ground black pepper

FOR THE GARNISH

fresh parsley, chopped

● Mix the coriander, honey, onion, cider19 and vinegar in a large bowl (not a metal one). Add the quails and marinate overnight.

● Preheat the oven to 180°C/350°F/Gas Mark 4. Drain and reserve the marinade. Dry the quails with absorbent kitchen paper. Heat the butter and oil in a large casserole. Add the quails, 4 at a time, seasoning them with salt and black pepper. Brown on both sides.

● Put all the birds in the casserole and pour the marinade over them. Cover and cook in the oven for 40–45 minutes, basting occasionally, or until tender. Garnish with chopped parsley to serve.

Vietnamese Pork au Caramel

SERVES 4

50 g/2 oz sugar

2 tbsp water

450 g/1 lb leg of pork, cut into large cubes

3 white radishes, peeled and thinly sliced

½ onion, chopped

5 tbsp fish sauce or light soy sauce

freshly ground black pepper

● Put the sugar in the wok and heat gently until it starts to smell as though it is burning. Stir in the water very carefully so that the mixture does not break up.

● Add the pork and radishes, and cover with water. Add the remaining ingredients and bring to the boil. Reduce the heat, cover and allow to simmer for about an hour or until the pork is cooked.

Pork Meatballs in Sweet Soy Sauce

MAKES 16 MEATBALLS

*The use of minced meat is widespread in Japan, and this form, **niku-dango**, is sold ready-made in delicatessens as well as being prepared at home. Take care, as the sweet-tasting sauce makes it all too easy to gorge oneself on these little balls of pork!*

FOR THE MEATBALLS

225 g/8 oz minced pork

25 g/1 oz leek, finely chopped

1 tbsp *sake*

large pinch of salt

½ egg, beaten

1 tbsp cornflour

vegetable oil, for deep frying

FOR THE SAUCE

4 tbsp water

1 tbsp *sake*

1 tbsp *mirin*

1 tbsp caster sugar

1 tbsp soy sauce

2 tsp cornflour

● To make the meatballs, mix the pork, leek, *sake*, salt, beaten egg and cornflour in a bowl. Knead the mixture until the beaten egg is well combined and gives a stickiness to the rest of the mixture. Then, take 1 tablespoon of the mixture in your hand and mould it into a ball.

● Fill a pan about one-third full with cooking oil. Heat to 180°C/350°F and then deep-fry the meatballs for 5 minutes or until browned. Remove and drain off any excess oil using absorbent kitchen paper.

● Put the water, *sake, mirin*, sugar, soy sauce and cornflour together in a pan. Mix together over a low heat, stirring until the sauce has thickened. Add the meatballs and continue to stir until they are all covered in the sauce. Serve with a bowl of hot, plain boiled rice and a vegetable dish.

Stuffed Roast Suckling Pig

SERVES 20

4.5 kg/10 lb prepared suckling pig (ask your butcher to leave enough flesh and skin on the belly for sewing)

juice of 1 lime

2 tbsp sea salt

4 cloves, ground

freshly ground black pepper

vegetable oil

FOR THE STUFFING

heart, liver and kidneys of the pig

75 g/3 oz butter

2 onions, finely chopped

4 cloves garlic, finely chopped

350 g/12 oz fresh breadcrumbs

1 red chilli, chopped

4 tbsp chopped spring onions

1 large sprig of parsley, finely chopped

1 tbsp fish sauce or light soy sauce

175 ml/6 fl oz rice wine

½ tsp finely chopped thyme

½ tsp allspice, crushed

juice of 1 lime

salt

FOR THE SAUCE

600 ml/1 pt chicken stock

600 ml/1 pt clear honey

120 ml/4 fl oz light soy sauce

4 tbsp tomato purée

4 tsp five-spice powder

120 ml/4 fl oz rice wine or sherry

salt

2 tbsp cornflour mixed with a little water

● Run cold water over the suckling pig and dry thoroughly inside and out. Rub the inside of the pig with lime juice. Mix the salt, cloves and black pepper and use half of it to rub the inside of the pig.

● Clean and wash the liver, heart and kidney. Dry and mince. Melt the butter in a pan on a low heat, add the onions and garlic, and sauté until softened. Add the minced liver, heart and kidney mixture and continue to sauté for a further 5 minutes. Remove from heat and allow to cool.

● Add the other ingredients, mixing well. (If the stuffing is too dry, add 1–2 tablespoons water or milk.) Fill the cavity with the stuffing and sew it up with kitchen string. Stuff a ball of foil in the pig's mouth. Tie each pair of legs together and fold under the animal. Place belly downwards in a shallow tin. Brush the back with oil and sprinkle the remainder of the ground cloves, sea salt and black pepper over the suckling pig. Cover the ears with foil for the first 90 minutes of cooking.

● Preheat the oven to 170°C/325°F/Gas Mark 3 and cook the pig for 2½ hours or until the juices run clear when pricked with a knife, basting regularly. Remove from the tin and allow to cool for 15 minutes. Replace the foil in the mouth with an orange and put the pig on a dish.

● Drain the juices from the roasting tin to a wok. Add all the sauce ingredients except the cornflour. Bring the juices to the boil and add the cornflour, stirring gently until it thickens.

Wild Boar Country Curry

SERVES 4

Well, wild boar is not strictly necessary (and in any case in Thailand these days is bred, not hunted). Substitute pork.

4 tbsp peanut or corn oil

225 g/8 oz boar or pork loin, cut into 3 x 2 x 0.5 cm/ 1¼ x ¾ x ¼ in slices

1.2 litres/2 pt water

200 g/7 oz bamboo shoots, diced

150 g/5 oz small white aubergines

115 g/4½ oz green beans

25 g/1 oz krachai, sliced lengthways

3 fresh red chillies, quartered

2 tbsp fish sauce

3 kaffir lime leaves, torn

10 g/¼ oz sweet basil leaves

FOR THE CHILLI PASTE

25 g/1 oz shallots, chopped

25 g/1 oz cloves garlic, chopped

15 g/½ oz dried red chillies, chopped

2 coriander roots, chopped

1 tbsp chopped lemon grass

1 tsp chopped galangal

1 tsp kaffir lime rind, chopped

1 tsp salt

½ tsp shrimp paste

● Pound all the chilli paste ingredients together with a pestle and mortar or in a blender to a fine paste.

● Heat the oil in a wok or pan and fry the chilli paste for 3 minutes. Add the meat and stir-fry for 2 minutes; then add the water and bamboo shoots and cook until the shoots are tender, about 3–5 minutes.

● Add the aubergines, green beans, krachai, chillies, fish sauce and lime leaf, boil for 3 minutes more and then remove from the heat. Stir in the basil and serve.

● Serve accompanied by pickled garlic, salted eggs and sticky rice.

One-Pan Dishes

Braised and steamed dishes, which often constitute the main courses in the serving sequence of a traditional Asian meal, take a little longer to cook than stir-fried dishes, but most can be prepared and cooked in advance. Some of these recipes can be served cold, making them ideal buffet dishes, and most blend well with Western food, so that they can be used in conjunction with non-Asian food as part of your family's regular menu.

Lion's Head Casserole

SERVES 4

'Lion's head' in Chinese cuisine means pork meatballs with cabbage. Here the 'meatballs' are entirely made from vegetables.

4 cakes of bean curd

100 g/4 oz gluten

50 g/2 oz cooked carrots

4–5 dried Chinese mushrooms, soaked

50 g/2 oz bamboo shoots

1 tbsp salt

1 tsp fresh ginger, finely chopped

2–3 tbsp ground rice or breadcrumbs

1 tbsp cornflour

2 tsp sesame seed oil

plain flour for dusting

6 cabbage or lettuce hearts

oil for deep-frying

1 tsp sugar

approx. 600 ml/1 pt water

5 large cabbage leaves

1 tsp ground white pepper

2 tbsp rice wine or dry sherry

● Squeeze as much liquid as possible from the bean curd using muslin, then mash.

● Finely chop the gluten, carrots, mushrooms and bamboo shoots. Place them with the mashed bean curd in a large mixing bowl. Add 1 teaspoon salt, the finely chopped ginger ground rice or breadcrumbs,

cornflour and sesame seed oil, and blend everything together until smooth. Make 10 'meatballs' from this mixture and place them on a plate, lightly dusted with flour.

● Trim off any hard or tough roots from the cabbage or lettuce hearts.

● Heat the oil in a wok or deep-fryer. When hot, deep-fry the 'meatballs' for about 3 minutes, stirring very gently to make sure that they are not stuck together. Scoop out with a slotted spoon or strainer, and drain.

● Pour off the excess oil leaving about 2 tablespoons in the wok. Stir-fry the cabbage hearts with a little salt and sugar. Add about 600 ml/1 pt water and bring to the boil. Reduce the heat and let the mixture simmer.

● Meanwhile, line the bottom of a casserole with the cabbage leaves and place the 'meatballs' on top. Pour the cabbage hearts with the soup into the casserole and add the remaining salt, ground pepper and rice wine. Cover, bring to the boil, reduce the heat and simmer for 10 minutes.

● To serve, take off the lid and rearrange the cabbage hearts so that they appear between the 'meatballs' in a star-shaped pattern.

Stewed Gluten in Sweet Bean Sauce

SERVES 4

325 g/11 oz gluten in small
    pieces

3 tbsp oil

1 tbsp dark soy sauce

1 tbsp sugar

1 tsp five-spice powder

2 tbsp rice wine or dry sherry

1 tbsp sweet bean paste or
    hoisin sauce

1 slice fresh ginger, peeled

2 tsp sesame seed oil

● Boil the gluten pieces in a pan of water for about 4–5 minutes or until they float to the surface. Remove and drain off as much water as possible.

● Heat the oil in a hot wok or pan. When hot, add the boiled gluten, stir for a few seconds and then add the soy sauce, sugar, five-spice powder, wine, sweet bean paste, crushed ginger and 120 ml/4 fl oz water.

● Bring to the boil and cook over high heat for 20–25 minutes or until there is very little juice left, stirring now and again to make sure that each piece of gluten is well covered by the gravy.

● Add the sesame seed oil, blend well and serve hot or cold.

Chinese Cabbage and Straw Mushrooms in Cream Sauce

SERVES 4

400 g/14 oz Chinese cabbage

350 g/12 oz canned straw
  mushrooms or 225 g/8 oz
  fresh straw mushrooms

4 tbsp oil

1½ tsp salt

1 tsp sugar

1 tbsp cornflour mixed with 3
  tbsp cold water

120 ml/4 fl oz milk

● Separate the cabbage leaves and cut each leaf in half lengthways.

● Drain the straw mushrooms. If using fresh ones, do not peel them, but just wash and trim off the roots.

● Heat 3 tablespoons of the oil in a hot wok and stir-fry the cabbage leaves for about 1 minute. Add the salt and sugar, and continue stirring for another minute or so. Remove the cabbage leaves and arrange them neatly on one side of a serving dish.

● Heat the remaining oil until hot, then reduce the heat and add the cornflour and water mixture and the milk, and stir until thickened. Pour about half of the sauce into a jug and keep warm.

● Add the mushrooms to the remaining sauce in the wok and heat them thoroughly over high heat. Remove the mushrooms and place them next to the cabbage leaves on the plate. Pour the sauce evenly over the cabbage and mushrooms and serve hot.

Cashew Casserole

SERVES 4

Soy sauce is excellent in casseroles, its piquancy adding a hint of Asia to this cashew nut and chicken dish.

2 tbsp sunflower oil

4 chicken pieces

8 shallots

225 g/8 oz chestnut mushrooms, quartered

100 g/4 oz baby turnips

2 celery sticks, sliced

1 carrot, diced

25 g/1 oz plain flour

600 ml/1 pt chicken stock

2 tbsp light soy sauce

150 ml/¼ pt dry white wine

50 g/2 oz unsalted cashew nuts

1 tbsp tomato purée

salt and ground black pepper

FOR THE DUMPLINGS

100 g/4 oz self-raising flour

40 g/1½ oz shredded beef suet

1 tbsp light soy sauce

1 tsp chopped fresh rosemary

● Heat the oil in a large frying pan. Add the chicken and cook until browned, about 10 minutes. Remove with a slotted draining spoon and place in an ovenproof casserole dish.

● Heat the oven to 180°C/350°F/Gas Mark 4. Add the shallots, mushrooms, turnips, celery and carrot to the frying pan and cook for 5 minutes, stirring. Add the flour and cook 1 minute.

● Gradually add the stock, soy sauce and wine, then bring to the boil, stirring. Add the cashew nuts and tomato purée and season well. Pour onto the chicken in the casserole dish. Cover and cook in the oven, about 45 minutes.

● Place the dumpling ingredients in a bowl. Stir in 120 ml/4 fl oz cold water and bring together to form a dough. Divide into eight and roll into balls.

● Uncover the casserole and place the dumplings on top of the chicken mixture. Return to the oven, uncovered, until cooked through, about 15 minutes.

Casserole of Vegetables

SERVES 4

2 tbsp dried wood ears

1 cake bean curd

100 g/4 oz green beans or
mange tout

100 g/4 oz cabbage or broccoli

100 g/4 oz baby corn or
bamboo shoots

100 g/4 oz carrots

3–4 tbsp oil

1 tsp salt

1 tsp sugar

1 tbsp light soy sauce

1 tsp cornflour mixed with
1 tbsp cold water

● Soak the wood ears in water for 20–25 minutes, rinse and discard the hard roots, if any.

● Cut the bean curd into about 12 small pieces and harden the pieces in a pan of lightly salted boiling water for 2–3 minutes. Remove and drain.

● Trim the beans or mange tout. Leave whole if small; cut in half if large.

● Cut the vegetables into thin slices or chunks.

● Heat about half of the oil in a flameproof casserole or saucepan. When hot, lightly brown the bean curd on both sides. Remove with a slotted spoon.

● Heat the remaining oil and stir-fry the rest of the vegetables for about 1½ minutes. Add the bean curd pieces, salt, sugar and soy sauce, and continue stirring to blend everything well. Cover, reduce the heat and simmer for 2–3 minutes.

● Mix the cornflour with water to make a smooth paste, pour it over the vegetables and stir. Increase the heat to high just long enough to thicken the gravy. Serve hot.

Chinese Cabbage Casserole

SERVES 4

450 g/1 lb Chinese cabbage

50 g/2 oz deep-fried bean curd
  or 2 cakes fresh bean curd

100 g/4 oz carrots

3 tbsp oil

1 tsp salt

1 tsp sugar

2 tbsp light soy sauce

2 tbsp rice wine or dry sherry

1 tsp sesame seed oil

● Separate the cabbage leaves, wash and cut them into small pieces. If using fresh bean curd, cut each cake into about 12 pieces and fry them in a little oil until golden.

● Peel the carrots and cut them into diamond-shaped chunks.

● Heat the oil in a hot wok and stir-fry the cabbage with the salt and sugar for a minute or so. Transfer it to a Chinese sand-pot or casserole and cover with the bean curd, carrots, soy sauce and sherry. Put a lid on the pot and when it comes to the boil, reduce the heat and simmer for 15 minutes.

● Stir in the sesame oil. Add a little water if necessary and cook for a few more minutes. Serve hot.

Steamed Eggs

SERVES 4

5 eggs

4 tbsp hot water

1 tsp salt

2 tsp rice wine

spinach leaves, chopped (optional)

1 tbsp soy sauce

● Beat the eggs in a bowl, and mix in the water, salt and rice wine.

● Place the bowl, uncovered, in a saucepan half-filled with boiling water. Cover the saucepan and steam gently for 20 minutes. If the heat is too high, the eggs will not congeal, or holes will form.

● A garnish of chopped spinach leaves may be added before steaming. Add the soy sauce before serving.

Braised Quails' Eggs with Bean Curd and Vegetables

SERVES 4

1 piece bean curd, cut into 6
pieces 1 cm/½ in thick

6 tbsp vegetable oil

10 straw mushrooms or firm
button mushrooms

8 quails' eggs, hard-boiled and
shelled

1 spring onion, cut into 2.5 cm/
1 in lengths

2 pieces canned bamboo shoots,
cut into 2.5 cm/1 in cubes

4 tsp bottled satay sauce

1 tsp cornflour

3 tsp fish sauce or light soy
sauce

2 tsp sugar

½ cup water

● Fry the bean curd in 4 tablespoons hot oil until
brown, taking care not to let it stick. Set aside and
discard the oil.

● Put the remaining oil into a small casserole dish
with a tight-fitting lid. Heat over a medium heat. Add
the straw mushrooms, quails' eggs, spring onion, bean
curd, bamboo shoots and satay sauce.

● Mix the cornflour, fish sauce and sugar to form a
smooth paste. Mix into the water. Stir this into the
casserole and cover. Cook for 4 minutes.

Cod and Chinese Cabbage Pot

SERVES 2

This popular winter dish is normally cooked on the table using a portable gas or electric ring. Everyone at the table takes food from the pan, transferring it to their own individual dishes while the host takes care to keep the pan stocked up with fresh raw ingredients. You will need an 20 cm/8 in casserole dish.

900 ml/1½ pt water

7.5 cm/3 in piece dried *konbu* (kelp)

1 small leek, sliced on a slant into 1 cm/½ in widths

1 medium onion, sliced

2 x 300 g/10 oz cod fillets or steaks, cut into large, bite-sized pieces

200 g/7 oz Chinese leaves, cut in half lengthways and then sliced into 1 cm/½ in strips

100 g/4 oz *momen* or cotton bean curd, cut into 1 cm/½ in cubes

100 g/4 oz carrots, peeled and thinly sliced

4 shiitake mushrooms, cut into halves

6 mange tout

FOR THE *PONZU* DRESSING

3 tbsp soy sauce

1 tbsp lemon juice

1 tbsp vinegar

1 tbsp *mirin*

½ tbsp Japanese instant stock granules

FOR THE GARNISH

450 g/1 lb white radish, peeled, grated and lightly squeezed

pinch of seven-spice powder or chilli pepper

● Put the water and *konbu* in a flameproof casserole and bring to the boil. Add half the leek, onion, cod, Chinese leaves, *tofu*, carrots, shiitake mushrooms and mange tout, keeping groups together in the pan. Cook for 5–8 minutes, or until the vegetables are cooked.

● Meanwhile, mix the soy sauce, lemon juice, vinegar, *mirin* and stock granules in a jar and stir well.

● When roughly half of the cooked food has been taken from the casserole, replenish with the raw ingredients.

● To serve, put 2 tablespoons of radish and 1 tablespoon *ponzu* dressing into each serving bowl.

● As you take food from the casserole with your chopsticks, dip it into the dressing and eat. Add some seven-spice if you wish to add a little more fire to the meal. As you eat, add more *ponzu* dressing and radish when you need to. Serve with rice.

Cod and Chinese Cabbage Pot

Fishballs with Noodles

SERVES 4

450 g/1 lb white fish, skinned and cut in chunks

25 g/1 oz cornflour

1 egg white

salt and freshly ground white pepper

175 g/6 oz Chinese egg noodles

4 tbsp oil

4 thin slices fresh ginger

1 piece lemon grass or strip of lemon rind

1 celery stick, cut diagonally into thin slices

1 bunch spring onions, sliced

100 g/4 oz mange tout, trimmed

4 tbsp soy sauce

4 tbsp dry sherry

● Pound the fish with the cornflour until it is reduced to a paste, then work in the egg white and seasoning. Wet your hands and shape the mixture into small balls, kneading it together so that the fish binds well.

● Place the noodles in the pan and pour in enough boiling water to cover them. Bring back to the boil and cook for 2 minutes, then drain and set aside.

● Heat the oil, then stir-fry the ginger and lemon grass or lemon rind for 1 minute before adding the fish balls. Stir-fry the fish balls until firm and golden.

● Add the celery, spring onions, and mange tout, and continue to stir-fry for 5–8 minutes, or until the vegetables are slightly tender but not soft.

● Add the noodles, soy sauce and sherry, and stir the mixture over high heat until the noodles are hot. Serve the dish at once.

Chicken with Mustard Sauce

SERVES 4

Wholegrain mustard is used here for a strong flavour with added texture. Any strong mustard could be used in the recipe if preferred.

1 tbsp vegetable oil

2 cloves garlic, finely chopped

450 g/1 lb chicken breast, boned and skinned

1 fennel bulb, trimmed and sliced

2 tbsp light soy sauce

50 g/2 oz butter

150 ml/¼ pt double cream

300 g/10 oz open cap mushrooms, peeled and sliced

2 tbsp wholegrain mustard

3 tbsp chopped fresh chives

salt and ground black pepper

● Heat the oil in a large frying pan and cook the garlic 1 minute. Cut the chicken into 2.5 cm/1 in cubes, add to the pan and cook for 2–3 minutes, stirring.

● Add the fennel, soy sauce and butter, and stir-fry for 5 minutes. Stir in the cream, mushrooms and mustard, and cook 5 minutes. Sprinkle with chopped chives. Season and serve.

Szechwan Noodles

SERVES 4

350 g/12 oz Chinese egg noodles

1 tbsp cornflour

3 tbsp dry sherry

5 tbsp chicken stock

5 tbsp light soy sauce

5 tbsp oil

2 green chillies, seeded and chopped

2 cloves garlic, crushed

5 cm/2 in piece fresh ginger, peeled and cut into fine strips

225 g/8 oz lean boneless pork, cut into fine strips

1 red pepper, seeded and cut into fine, short strips

1 bunch spring onions, cut diagonally into fine slices

200 g/7 oz can bamboo shoots, drained and cut in strips

2.5 cm/1 in slice Chinese cabbage, separated into pieces

● Place the noodles in the pan and pour in enough boiling water to cover them. Bring back to the boil and cook for 2 minutes, then drain the noodles. While the noodles are cooking, blend the cornflour with the sherry, stock, and soy sauce, then set aside.

● Wipe the pan and heat the oil. Add the noodles, spreading them out thinly, and fry over medium to high heat until they are crisp and golden underneath, patting them down slightly into a thin cake—they will set more or less in shape. Use a large slice to turn the noodles over and brown the second side. Don't worry if the noodles break up slightly—the aim is to end up with some that are crisp and others that remain soft. Transfer the noodles to a large serving dish and keep hot until needed.

● Add the chillies, garlic, ginger and pork to the oil remaining in the pan. Stir-fry the mixture over high heat until the pork is browned. Add the pepper and spring onions and stir fry for a further 2 minutes before adding the bamboo shoots. Stir fry for 1 minute to heat the bamboo shoots.

● Give the cornflour mixture a stir and pour it into the pan. Bring to the boil, stirring, and cook over high heat for 30 seconds. Mix in the Chinese cabbage, stir for less than a minute to heat the cabbage. Spoon the pork mixture over the noodles and serve at once.

Chicken Balls with Rice Sticks

SERVES 4

3 boneless chicken breasts, skinned and ground

40 g/1½ oz plain flour

4 tbsp *sake* or dry sherry

6 tbsp soy sauce (use Japanese sauce if possible)

1 small egg

1 bunch spring onions

salt and pepper

2 tsp sugar

225 g/8 oz ribbon rice sticks

4 tbsp peanut oil

2 small carrots, cut lengthways into very thin strips

225 g/8 oz mange tout, trimmed

½ cucumber, peeled, halved crossways, and thinly sliced lengthways

● A food processor is ideal for mincing the raw chicken, otherwise it may be done by hand using a chef's large knife and a chopping action: eventually the chicken will progress from being chopped in fine dice into a fine, almost minced, mixture.

● Mix the flour with the chicken, pounding the mixture well. Add 1 tablespoon each of the *sake* or dry sherry and soy sauce, then mix in the egg. Finely chop the white parts from 2 spring onions, then add them to the mixture with the seasoning. When all the ingredients are thoroughly combined the mixture may seem a little soft, but don't worry—if it is too firm at this stage the cooked balls will be slightly tough in texture. Cover the mixture and chill it on a low shelf in the refrigerator for 30 minutes, or put it in the freezer for about 15 minutes.

● Heat the remaining *sake* and soy sauce with the sugar, stirring, then bring the mixture to the boil and boil hard for 1 minute, set aside. It is best to do this in a saucepan but you can use your stir-fry pan, then pour the mixture into a large bowl, making sure you

scrape it all out of the pan by using a plastic spatula. In a wide pan 1 minute's cooking may be too long as the liquid evaporates more speedily.

● Slice the remaining spring onions diagonally. Place the rice sticks in the pan and pour in boiling water to cover them. Bring to the boil and cook for 1–2 minutes, until just soft. Drain and rinse under cold water.

● Wet your hands and shape the chicken mixture into balls, slightly smaller than walnuts—they do not have to be perfect in shape, but if you keep your hands well wetted with cold water the mixture is easier to shape.

● Heat the oil and stir-fry the chicken balls over medium to high heat, until they are golden brown all over. At first they should be coaxed and stirred around the pan gently until the mixture firms. If they are stirred smoothly and constantly they will form neat balls. Then they may be stir-fried with more vigor so that they brown evenly and cook through.

● Use a slotted spoon to remove the chicken balls from the pan, adding them to the boiled soy sauce mixture. Toss the balls in the sauce to coat them.

● Add the carrots, mange tout and spring onions to the oil remaining in the pan and stir-fry the vegetables for about 3 minutes before adding the cucumber. Continue stir-frying for about 2 minutes, until the vegetables are just cooked and piping hot.

● Toss in the rice sticks (you may have to rinse them quickly under cold water if they have set in a block—shake off excess water) and stir-fry them for a minute or so to heat them up. Replace the chicken balls in the pan and mix well, then serve.

Casserole of Duck with Dumplings

SERVES 4

1 duck, about 2.25 kg/5 lb

1 tsp peeled fresh ginger

salt and black pepper

2 tbsp dry sherry

4 x 2.5 cm/1 in slices fresh ginger, peeled

1 large whole spring onion

100 g/4 oz sliced cooked ham

225 g/8 oz can bamboo shoots, cut into 2.5 cm/1 in pieces

salt

FOR THE DUMPLINGS

225 g/8 oz plain flour

250 ml/8 fl oz boiling water

450 g/1 lb minced pork

100 g/4 oz prawns, peeled and deveined

175 g/6 oz white cabbage, finely chopped

salt

2 x 2.5 cm/1 in slices fresh ginger, peeled and ground

1 spring onion, finely chopped

2 tbsp light soy sauce

2 tbsp dry sherry

¼ tsp sugar

1 tbsp sesame oil

1 tbsp cornflour dissolved in 3 tbsp water

black pepper

plain flour

● Remove the fat from the cavity of the duck, discard the tail end and trim off any excess neck skin. Rinse and drain the duck. Mix the ginger, salt and black pepper, and rub well into the duck, inside and out. Leave to stand for 1 hour.

● Place the duck in a large casserole, add the sherry, ginger slices and spring onion, cover and bring to a slow boil over moderate heat. Turn down the heat, skim off any scum, adding enough liquid so that the duck does not burn and adjust the heat so that it simmers at its gentlest. Cover and leave for 3 hours.

● Make the dumplings by mixing the flour and boiling water in a large bowl, a little at a time, with a wooden spoon. Do not concern yourself with what it looks like at this stage.

● Chop the pork to loosen it and put it in a second bowl. Slice the prawns lengthways and then cut them into 5 mm/¼ in pieces. Mix with the pork.

● Cut the white cabbage leaves lengthways into narrow strips and then cross-cut to dice them. Mince and mix with salt and leave for 5 minutes. Squeeze dry and add to the meat mixture with the rest of the ingredients except the flour. Stir until smooth and pasty. Divide the mixture into 16 portions.

● Knead the dough for a few minutes until it is soft and smooth, dusting with flour if necessary. Roll it out into a 40 cm/16 in long sausage and cut with a sharp knife into 2.5 cm/1 in pieces. Dip the cut sides in flour, press into small round cakes with the palm of your hand and roll out into round wrappers 10 cm/4 in across.

● Lay a wrapper in the palm of one hand and put a portion of filling in it with the other. Spread with a table knife to within 1 cm/½ in of the edge. Gather the wrapper up and press the ends to make a little 'basket'. Press the back of a knife deep into the basket about 10 times to form indentations, which help to hold the filling in place. You should have 16 dumplings. Put them on a plate and steam over a medium-high heat for 20 minutes. Set aside.

● Skim off the fat from the casserole after it has been cooking for 3 hours and discard it. Scatter in the ham, bamboo shoots and the dumplings. Cover and simmer for another 5–10 minutes. Add salt to taste.

● Serve in the casserole. Guests help themselves by tearing the bird apart with chopsticks. If they are not sufficiently proficient, you could chop it in the kitchen, put the pieces back into the casserole and bring it back to the boil before serving at the table. Ladle into individual soup bowls.

Rice with Pork and Peppers

SERVES 4

4 tbsp oil

1 large onion, thinly sliced

350 g/12 oz lean boneless pork, cut in thin strips

1 red pepper, seeded and thinly sliced

1 green pepper, seeded and thinly sliced

salt and freshly ground black pepper

a little grated nutmeg

grated rind of 1 orange

100 g/4 oz long-grain rice, freshly cooked

100 g/4 oz wild rice, freshly cooked

● Heat the oil and stir-fry the onion for 2 minutes before adding the pork. Stir-fry the meat and onion together until the meat is cooked through and lightly browned, keeping the heat fairly high to seal the strips of meat.

● Add the peppers, seasoning, nutmeg and orange rind. Reduce the heat slightly and stir-fry for 3–5 minutes, or until the peppers are cooked.

● Stir in both types of rice and cook for a few minutes so that the ingredients are well combined. If the rice has been allowed to cool, it should be reheated thoroughly at this stage—the result is best if the rice is freshly cooked and piping hot when added to the pan.

Southern Chilli Curry

SERVES 4

As with most of the **nam phriks** *(spiced dishes), this thick, spicy southern curry is intended to be eaten with plain rice. Don't be fooled by the simplicity: it's both tasty and satisfying.*

600 ml/1 pt water

225 g/8 oz pork loin, cut into 3 x 2 x 0.5 cm/ 1¼ x ¾ x ¼ in pieces

3 tbsp fish sauce

1 tsp curry powder

3 kaffir lime leaves, torn into quarters

FOR THE CHILLI PASTE

8–10 dried small green and red chillies, chopped

6 white peppercorns

2 tbsp sliced shallot

1 tbsp sliced garlic

1 tsp sliced galangal

1 tsp shrimp paste

¼ stalk of lemon grass, sliced

● Pound all the ingredients for the chilli paste finely with a pestle and mortar or in a blender.

● Boil the water in a pan or wok, add the chilli paste and boil briefly before adding the pork, fish sauce, curry powder and lime leaf.

● Boil again for 10 minutes before transferring to bowls. Serve accompanied by rice.

Rice with Pork and Peppers

Northern Thai Pork Curry

SERVES 6

This dish originally came from across the Burmese border, as shown by the use of tamarind and turmeric. The palm sugar adds an intentional slight sweetness.

4 stalks lemon grass, chopped

1 tbsp chopped galangal

1 tbsp shrimp paste

4 dried red chillies, chopped

1 kg/2¼ lb belly of pork, cut into small 1 cm/½ in thick strips

750 ml/1¼ pt cold water

1 tbsp turmeric

1 tsp black soy sauce

10 shallots, sliced

50 g/2 oz palm sugar

25 g/1 oz ginger, chopped and pounded

4 tbsp tamarind juice

2 tbsp chopped garlic

½ tbsp marinated soya beans

fish sauce, to taste (optional)

● Pound the lemon grass, galangal, shrimp paste and chillies with a pestle and mortar or in a blender until fine, then mix with the pork.

● Put in a pan with the water, turmeric and soy sauce. Bring to the boil and cook until tender, about 15 minutes, then add the rest of the ingredients. Boil again for 5–8 minutes and remove from the heat.

● Taste and season with fish sauce if necessary.

Five-spice Pork with Noodles

SERVES 4

450 g/1 lb lean boneless pork, cut in thin slices

½ tsp five-spice powder

salt and freshly ground black pepper

2 spring onions, finely chopped

1 clove garlic, crushed

225 g/8 oz Chinese egg noodles

5 tbsp peanut oil

225 g/8 oz can bamboo shoots, sliced

225 g/8 oz mange tout, trimmed

4 tbsp soy sauce

3 tbsp roasted sesame seeds

● Mix the pork with the five-spice powder, seasoning, spring onions, and garlic. Cover and leave to marinate for at least an hour or as long as overnight.

● Cover the noodles with boiling water and bring back to the boil. Cook for 2 minutes, then drain and rinse under cold water.

● Heat the oil and stir-fry the pork until well browned. Add the bamboo shoots and mange tout, and continue to stir-fry for 3–4 minutes, or until the vegetables are cooked.

● Push the meat mixture to one side of the pan or make a space in the middle and add the noodles. Stir the noodles for 2 minutes to heat them through, then stir in the other ingredients, soy sauce and sesame seeds. Cook for 1 minute before serving.

Pigs' Trotters Stew

SERVES 4

1 kg/2 lb pigs' trotters, washed, blanched and chopped into 4–5 cm/1½–2 in pieces

1.2 litres/2 pt chicken or pork stock

1 large onion, sliced

3 boiled potatoes, quartered

3 tomatoes, diced

50 g/2 oz green beans or similar vegetable, sliced

3 tbsp bean sprouts

FOR THE VIETNAMESE BOUQUET GARNI

2 large celery sticks with leaves, roughly chopped

6 small coriander plants with roots, roughly chopped

2 large stalks lemon grass, chopped

6 large cloves garlic, finely chopped

1 cinnamon stick

2 star anise

1 tbsp black peppercorns

FOR THE GARNISH

3 tbsp chopped fresh coriander

3 tbsp chopped spring onions

● Put the pigs' trotters in a large saucepan and bring to the boil. Allow to boil for about 20–30 minutes until the meat pulls away from the bones. Drain.

● Put the trotters back into the washed saucepan and add the stock and, if necessary, a little extra water, to cover the meat. Bring to the boil. Wrap the bouquet garni in a piece of cloth and tie to form a little bundle. Drop this into the saucepan when it starts to boil. Simmer for 10 minutes or so until you get the right consistency, which should be slightly thickened.

● Add the onion, potatoes and tomatoes and simmer for a little while, just long enough for them to get warmed through but not long enough for them to disintegrate. Just before serving, add the beans and cook until they are just tender.

● Remove the bouquet garni and stir in the bean sprouts. Sprinkle the garnish over the stew.

Pork Knuckle and Peanut Stew

SERVES 4

3 fresh pork knuckles

1 smoked pork knuckle or ham hock

50 g/2 oz fresh peanuts, blanched

4 x 2.5 cm/1 in slices peeled fresh ginger, 1 cm/½ in thick

2 large spring onions

2.75 litres/5 pt water

salt

● Put the fresh and smoked knuckles, peanuts, ginger and spring onions into a large, heavy pan together with the water and bring to the boil over a high heat. Turn down the heat to a simmer and skim off any scum. Cover and simmer for 2½ hours, stirring once in a while.

● Skim off scum and season with salt to taste. Discard the ginger, spring onions and the knuckle bones, if so desired. The meat may be served in chunks or cut into small pieces. Serve hot with a dip of fish sauce with a sprinkling of ground Szechwan peppercorns.

Simmered Belly of Pork and White Radish

SERVES 2

Simmering is a widely used technique in Japanese cooking as it brings out the flavours of the ingredients. Its European equivalent, the white radish, contains more water than the Japanese giant radish or **daikon,** *making it easier to cook. From the point of view of taste, though, there is little different between the two.*

2 tsp vegetable oil

225 g/8 oz pork, cut into
    1 cm/½ in lengths

225 g/8 oz white radish,
    peeled and chopped into
    randomly-shaped, bite-sized
    pieces

1 tbsp *sake*

2 tbsp soy sauce

● Heat the oil in a saucepan and add the meat. Fry until browned.

● Add the white radish and stir well, then add the *sake* and simmer, covered, for 10 minutes.

● Add the soy sauce and continue to cook, covered for a further 5 minutes or until the white radish is cooked through. Serve hot with a bowl of boiled rice.

Braised Beef with Carrots and Onions

SERVES 4

The beef is marinated, then cooked slowly for a long time so that it can easily be removed from the bone with chopsticks.

1.5 kg/3 lb beef short ribs

1½ tbsp vegetable oil

2 carrots, cut into chunks

1 onion, cut into chunks

FOR THE MARINADE

2 tbsp sesame oil

6 tbsp soy sauce

4 spring onions, white and green parts thinly sliced

4 tbsp rice wine or dry sherry

2 tbsp crushed toasted sesame seeds

2.5 cm/1 in fresh ginger, finely chopped

3 cloves garlic, crushed and finely chopped

freshly ground black pepper

FOR THE GARNISH

pine nuts

sesame seeds

coriander

● Separate the beef into individual ribs and cut each one into 5-cm/2-in lengths. Make four deep slashes in a lattice pattern on the meaty sides of each piece of rib, going right through to the bone. Put into a bowl. Add the marinade ingredients and stir together well. Cover and leave in a cool place for 4 hours, stirring the beef occasionally.

● Remove the beef from the marinade; reserve the marinade for later.

● Heat the vegetable oil in a heavy flameproof casserole and fry the beef for 5 minutes. Add the onion and carrot chunks, and fry for 3 minutes more. Pour in the reserved marinade and add enough water just to cover the beef and vegetables. Bring to the boil, cover and simmer slowly for 1½–2 hours, turning the beef and vegetables occasionally, until the beef is very tender. Uncover the casserole about half to three-quarters of the way through the cooking so the sauce reduces.

● At the end of the cooking, boil the sauce hard to reduce it to a thickish syrup, turning the ribs to make sure they are evenly coated. Skim any fat from the surface and serve garnished with pine nuts, sesame seeds and coriander.

Spicy Beef Stew

SERVES 4

3 tbsp vegetable oil

2 medium onions, finely chopped

5 cloves garlic, finely chopped

10 spring onions, trimmed

1 stalk lemon grass, cut into 5 cm/2 in sections and crushed

1 kg/2 lb stewing beef, cut into 2.5 cm/1 in cubes

1.2 litres/2 pt water

6 tbsp yellow bean sauce, chopped and crushed

1 tsp chilli powder

4 star anise

2.5 cm/1 in cinnamon stick

½ tsp whole peppercorns

sugar

● Heat 1 tablespoon oil in a wok over a medium high heat. Put in the onions, garlic and whole spring onions, and stir-fry for 2 minutes. Add the lemon grass and continue to stir until the spring onions become lightly brown, remove the spring onions and set aside.

● Heat the remaining oil over a high heat. Stir-fry as many pieces of beef as are convenient until they are brown, turning them over from time to time. Continue until all the beef has been cooked.

● Add the water. Add the lemon grass mixture, yellow bean sauce, chilli powder, star anise, cinnamon, peppercorns and sugar, and bring to the boil. Cover and lower the heat to simmer gently for 1½ hours.

● Add the reserved spring onions; cover again and allow to simmer for a further 15 minutes or until the sauce has thickened a little and the meat is tender.

Spicy Beef Stew II

SERVES 4

1 kg/2 lb stewing beef, cut into 5 cm/2 in cubes

2 stalks lemon grass, sliced paper-thin and finely chopped

2 fresh red chillies, finely chopped

2 tsp sugar

2 tbsp grated fresh ginger

2 tsp ground cinnamon

2 tsp curry powder

3 tbsp fish sauce or 3 tbsp light soy sauce and ½ tsp anchovy essence

salt and freshly ground black pepper

4½ tbsp vegetable oil

1 large onion, finely chopped

6 cloves garlic, finely chopped

5 tbsp tomato purée

4 star anise

1.2 litres/2 pt water

2 medium carrots, cut into 2.5 cm/1 in chunks

2 medium potatoes, peeled and cut into 2.5 cm/1 in chunks

1 small white radish, peeled and cut into 2.5 cm/1 in chunks

● Mix the beef, lemon grass, chillies, sugar, ginger, cinnamon, curry powder, fish sauce, salt and black pepper, and leave to stand for 1 hour.

● Heat 4 tablespoons of oil in the wok over a high heat. Add the beef and marinade and stir quickly to sear. This should not take much more than 2 minutes. Remove the meat to a bowl and set aside.

● Add a little more oil and, when hot, add the onion and garlic and stir-fry until fragrant. Add the tomato purée and stir for 2 minutes. Add the beef, star anise, a little salt and the water. Bring the mixture to the boil, reduce the heat to low, cover the wok and simmer until the beef is tender, about 1½ hours.

● Add the carrots and simmer for 10 minutes. Add the potatoes and simmer for a further 10 minutes. Finally, add the white radish and cook for another 10 minutes.

Simmered Beef and Potatoes

SERVES 2

This dish is one of several described in Japan as 'mother's taste dishes', and it is very much a family-style creation.

3 tbsp water

1½ tbsp *sake*

2 tbsp caster sugar

2 tbsp soy sauce

225 g/8 oz thinly sliced beef, cut into 5 cm/2 in lengths

250 g/9 oz potatoes, peeled and cut into bite-sized pieces

75 g/3 oz frozen peas

● Put the water, *sake*, sugar and soy sauce in a pan and bring to the boil.

● Add the meat and simmer for a few minutes or until the meat browns. Remove from the pan and set aside. Put the potatoes in the pan and simmer, covered, for 10 minutes or until tender. Add the peas and simmer for a further 3 minutes.

● Return the meat back to the pan and simmer for about 3 minutes. Serve hot with a bowl of rice and one or two vegetable dishes.

Simmered Beef and Potatoes

Beef and Vegetable Hotpot

SERVES 4–6

This communal one-pot meal, known as **chongol**, *allows every person to dip into the pot to select their chosen morsels. Any number of a wide variety of ingredients can be added, according to what is available or to suit the occasion. Traditionally, it is prepared over a burner at the table.*

550 g/1¼ lb sirloin or fillet steak, partly frozen

750 ml/1¼ pt brown veal or chicken stock

6 celery sticks, cut into 5 cm/ 2 in pieces

2 young carrots, finely sliced diagonally

8 spring onions, cut diagonally into 5 cm/2 in pieces

6 Chinese leaves, cut into 5 cm/ 2 in pieces

8 chestnut mushrooms

1½ 100-g/4-oz cakes of bean curd, cut into 2.5 cm/1 in cubes

FOR THE MARINADE

2 tsp sesame seeds

3 tbsp sugar

1 fresh red chilli, seeded and finely chopped

6 tbsp soy sauce

1 plump clove garlic, crushed

● For the marinade, heat a dry heavy-bottomed saucepan, add the sesame seeds and toast until pale brown. Remove and crush finely. Mix with the remaining marinade ingredients.

● Slice the beef and cut into 2.5 x 5 cm/1 x 2 in strips. Put into a bowl. Pour over the marinade and stir to coat. Leave for 1 hour.

● Heat a dry heavy-bottomed pan. Remove the beef from the marinade and add to the pan. Cook briefly and quickly to sear the meat. Remove. Add the stock and any remaining marinade to the pan and bring to the boil. If using a fondue pot, boil the stock in a saucepan, then pour into the fondue pot.

● Add the celery and carrots to the pot. Boil for 5 minutes, then add the mushrooms, spring onions, Chinese leaves, bean curd and beef. Simmer together for 2–3 minutes, then lower the heat so the stock simmers slowly while the *chongol* is eaten.

Quick-Cook Beef, Bean Curd and Vegetable Stew

SERVES 3–4

Richness and depth is given to the flavour of this 'stew' by making the stock with **twoenjang,** *Korean fermented bean curd. The beef is then cooked for just two minutes.*

225 g/8 oz sirloin steak, cut into 2.5 x 5 cm/1 x 2 in slices

2 tsp sesame oil

1½ tsp sugar

freshly ground black pepper

8 dried Chinese black mushrooms, soaked in hot water for 30 minutes, drained, and stalks removed

1 onion, thinly sliced into rings

1 courgette, sliced

2 spring onions, white and green parts sliced

1–2 fresh red chillies, seeded and thickly sliced

2 x 100 g/4 oz cakes of medium-firm bean curd, cut into 4 cm/1½ in chunks

FOR THE STOCK

8 tbsp *twoenjang* (fermented bean curd) or *miso*

2 cloves garlic, lightly crushed

1 onion, cut into chunks

1 carrot, cut into chunks

3 spring onions cut into 7.5 cm/ 3 in lengths

● Put the *twoenjang* or *miso* in a strainer placed over a saucepan. Slowly pour through 1 litre/1¾ pt water, pushing the *twoenjang* or *miso* with the back of a wooden spoon so it is all pushed through. Add the remaining stock ingredients and bring to the boil. Cover and simmer slowly for 30 minutes.

● Meanwhile, mix the beef with the sesame oil, sugar and plenty of black pepper. Leave for 30 minutes.

● Drain the stock, squeezing out as much liquid as possible. Pour the stock back into the pan and add the mushroom caps, onion, courgette, spring onions and chillies. Bring to the boil, then simmer for 2 minutes. Add the beef slices to the stock with the bean curd. Return to the boil, then simmer for 2 minutes.

Rice and Noodles

Rice and noodles provide the bulk in many Asian dishes, and they are served, in one form or another, from the wastes of northern China to the heart of busy Tokyo. Most of the recipes in this section can be served as a light meal or snack—they are filling and nutritious on their own—but these dishes will more often be served with one or two other dishes from this section and a meat or seafood main dish to create a satisfying meal for four or more people.

Boiled Rice

SERVES 4–6

Boiled rice not only provides a foundation for other dishes but is enjoyed on its own.

400 g/4 oz short-grain rice

● Put the rice in a large bowl and add water to cover. Swish the rice around with your hand. When the water has become milky white, pour it away. Repeat the washing until the water is virtually clear.

● Put the rice into a heavy-bottomed saucepan. Add 600 ml/1 pt water and bring to the boil. Stir once, cover, and turn the heat right down. Cook the rice for 20 minutes, without removing the lid even once.

● Turn up the heat as high as it will go for 30 seconds, then turn it off, or remove the pan from the heat. Leave, without removing the lid at all, for 10–15 minutes before serving.

Vegetable Rice

SERVES 4

400 g/14 oz short-grain rice, washed and drained

2 tbsp vegetable oil

450 g/1 lb Chinese cabbage, cut crossways in 2.5 cm/1 in pieces

salt

600–750 ml/1–1¼ pt water

● Wash the rice several times until the water runs clear. Drain thoroughly.

● Heat a heavy saucepan over a high heat. Add the oil, swirl and heat for a further 30 seconds or so. Add the Chinese cabbage and stir rapidly. The leaves should now be shiny with oil. Sprinkle some salt and stir and the leaves will brighten.

● Put the rice and water in a saucepan and bring to the boil. Let it bubble for a couple of minutes, stirring occasionally. Turn the heat to medium and let it bubble for another 2 minutes, stirring occasionally.

● Turn to the lowest possible heat, cover and let the rice cook for 20 minutes. When it is cooked, leave it to rest for 10 minutes before serving.

● Lay the rice on a flat dish, placing the Chinese cabbage on top, and serve.

Rice with Millet

SERVES 2–4

Traditionally, this kind of rice was prepared for the same reasons as Rice with Barley (see page 238). A nuttier flavour can be obtained by toasting the millet, prior to boiling, in a dry saucepan over a moderate heat for 3 minutes.

300 g/10 oz short-grain rice, washed and soaked (see above)

100 g/4 oz millet

● Put the rice and millet into a saucepan. Add 750 ml/1¼ pt water and bring to the boil. Stir once, cover and turn the heat right down. Cook the rice for 20 minutes, without removing the lid even once.

● Turn up the heat as high as it will go for 30 seconds, then turn it off, or remove the pan from the heat. Leave, without removing the lid at all, for 10–15 minutes before serving.

Rice with Prawns

SERVES 4

2 tbsp vegetable oil

450 g/1 lb prawns, peeled

1 spring onion, chopped

50 g/2 oz button mushrooms

1 courgette, thinly sliced

½ carrot, thinly sliced

50 g/2 oz fine beans, cut into
2.5 cm/1 in lengths

1 tbsp rice wine or dry sherry

1 tsp light soy sauce

freshly ground black pepper

salt

450 g/1 lb plain boiled rice

FOR THE GARNISH

2 spring onions, neatly chopped
into rounds

● Heat ½ tablespoon oil in a wok and stir-fry the prawns for 1 minute. Remove and set aside.

● Add the remaining oil and lightly cook the spring onion. Add the mushrooms and the other vegetables and stir-fry for about 2 minutes over a high heat.

● Put the prawns back into the wok with the vegetables and add the rest of the ingredients, except the rice, continuing all the while to stir.

● Add the rice and stir-fry until the rice has changed colour. Place in a large serving bowl and garnish with the chopped spring onions.

Sticky Rice

SERVES 4

400 g/14 oz glutinous rice
(specified on packet)

1 tsp salt

METHOD 1

● Rinse and drain the rice after soaking overnight. Spread the soaked rice mixed with the salt over a dampened muslin in the top of a steamer and steam for about 40 minutes, sprinkling water over it occasionally. Taste while cooking for consistency. It should not be crunchy; Vietnamese prefer it well boiled.

METHOD 2

● Boil about 750 ml/1¼ pt water in a thick saucepan. Add the rice and salt and bring it back to the boil. Let it boil for 1 minute or so and then cover it with a well-fitting lid. Take it off the heat and hold the lid tightly on the saucepan. Turn it over and drain it fairly dry.

● Return to a very low heat and allow the rice to cook for about 20 minutes. After cooking, set it aside for 10 minutes to complete the cooking. When ready to serve, fluff it up with a ladle or chopsticks, whichever you prefer.

Rice with Prawns

Mixed Rice

SERVES 2

Japanese-style mixed rice is easy to make and can be served either as a main course with a soup and salad or instead of plain boiled rice.

150 g/5 oz Japanese short-grain rice

50 g/2 oz carrot, peeled and cut into short matchsticks

3 shiitake mushrooms, cut into short matchsticks

½ sheet *abura-age*, rinsed in hot water and cut into short matchsticks

5 mm/¼ in piece bean curd, soaked in water for 5 minutes, then cut into matchsticks

8½ tbsp *dashi* stock

1 tbsp sugar

1½ tbsp soy sauce

3 mange tout

pinch of salt

1 egg

½ tbsp water

vegetable oil, for frying

FOR THE GARNISH

2 red radishes, thinly sliced

nori strips

● First make *sushi* rice according to the instructions on page 242.

● Put the carrots, shiitake, *abura-age*, bean curd, *dashi* stock, sugar and soy sauce in a pan. Bring to the boil and simmer for 15 minutes.

● Meanwhile, boil the mange tout in salted water for 3 minutes, then remove and cut finely on the slant.

● Mix the egg, water and a pinch of salt together in a bowl. Heat the vegetable oil in an omelette pan and make two thin omelettes. Let the omelettes cool, then cut each one in half then slice it into thin strips.

● When the vegetables are cooked, mix the ingredients with the rice. Place the rice mixture onto a large plate. Spread the egg, then the mange tout over the top and decorate with the radish and strips of *nori*.

Egg Fried Rice

SERVES 4

2 eggs

2 tbsp water

2 tbsp vegetable oil

2 spring onions, finely chopped

450 g/1 lb plain boiled rice

2 tbsp soy sauce

salt

½ tsp sugar

● Beat the eggs with the water in a bowl. Heat ½ teaspoon oil in a wok and add the egg mixture. Swirl it around to make an omelette. Transfer to a plate and allow to cool. When cool, cut into strips.

● Heat the remaining oil, add the spring onions, and stir-fry for 2 minutes. Add the plain boiled rice and cooled omelette strips.

● Stir in the soy sauce, salt and sugar and cook for a further 2–3 minutes, until all ingredients have been coated. Serve in a large bowl.

Perfumed Rice

SERVES 4

400 g/14 oz Thai perfumed
rice

600 ml/1 pt water

1 tsp salt

● Wash the rice several times and drain; when the washing water is clear, the rice is as clean as it can possibly be. In large families rice needs washing with both hands but cooking for a small family does not require more than the rubbing between the fingers.

● Put the rice and water in a saucepan, add the salt and bring quickly to the boil. Reduce the heat immediately and cover. Allow to simmer for as long as necessary—30 minutes is about right.

● The rice should be taken off the heat and allowed to rest for about 10 minutes before serving. The result should be a rather moist, slightly sticky boiled rice that people east of the Ganges prefer.

Prawn-fried Rice

SERVES 6

120 ml/4 fl oz peanut or corn
oil

1 tbsp chopped garlic

200 g/7 oz raw peeled prawns

3 eggs, beaten

50 g/2 oz onion, sliced

1 tomato, cut into 6 pieces

550 g/1¼ lb cooked rice

15 g/½ oz spring onions,
chopped

½ tbsp light soy sauce

1 tsp sugar

1 tsp salt

1 tsp ground white pepper

50 g/2 oz cucumber, peeled
and sliced into circles

● Heat the oil in a wok or pan and add the garlic.

● Stir-fry and then add the prawns and fry for 1 minute. Add the eggs and cook for another minute, stirring well, then add the onion and tomato.

● Stir-fry for 1 minute then add the rice, soy sauce, sugar, salt and pepper. Stir well over a high heat for a further 3 minutes.

● Scoop onto serving plates and arrange the cucumber pieces around.

● Serve accompanied by fish sauce with chillies, and eat with whole spring onions and sliced cucumber.

Japanese Rice Balls

SERVES 2

The Japanese name for this dish is **onigiri**, and it is a simply prepared and handy 'eat anytime' meal, which can be packed up in a picnic or served as an accompaniment at dinner. The use of the word 'ball' is slightly misleading as the shape of the finished product more closely resembles a triangle. The use of Japanese rice for making rice balls is strongly recommended as other varieties tend to lack the characteristic stickiness of the Japanese grains.

165 g/5½ oz Japanese short-grain rice, rinsed well

pinch of flaked *bonito*

½ tbsp soy sauce

1 Japanese pickled plum (*ume-boshi*), seeded and halved

4 strips 5 x 15 cm/2 x 6 in *nori*

● Rinse the rice until the water runs off almost clear.

● Cook the rice the same way as making *sushi* rice (see page 242) but do not add the *sushi-zu*.

● Let the rice cool down before use. Mix the *bonito* flakes with the soy sauce in a small saucer or plate to make a paste.

● Wet and then sprinkle your palms with a little salt. (You will need to repeat this process with every ball you make.) Scoop up 3 heaped tablespoons of rice and mould it lightly into a round shape.

● Once the rough ball shape is formed, make a small hole in the middle and put either half of the *bonito* paste or one half of the Japanese plum inside.

● Cover the hole while at the same time trying to form the rice into a triangular shape.

● When the four rice balls have been formed, wrap each with a strip of *nori*.

Fried Rice with Spicy Sauce

SERVES 4–6

2 tbsp peanut or corn oil

550 g/1¼ lb cooked rice

3 tbsp fish sauce with chillies

● Heat the oil in a wok or pan, add the rice and mix well, stir-frying for 1 minute.

● Add the sauce, mix well and cook for 1 more minute. Remove from the heat.

● Serve accompanied by preserved salted eggs, cucumber slices, fried eggs and raw vegetables.

Pineapple Rice

SERVES 4–6

A 'show-off' dish that is quite easy to make but always impressive to present. Although the pineapple also adds flavour to the rice, there is scarcely any point attempting it just with pineapple pieces—appearance is everything.

1 pineapple	2 tbsp chicken stock
4 tbsp peanut or corn oil	2 tsp curry powder
550 g/1¼ lb cooked rice	1 tsp sugar
100 g/4 oz ham, finely diced	1 tsp salt
½ tbsp chopped garlic	¼ tsp ground white pepper
40 g/1½ oz raisins	

● Cut one side off the pineapple lengthways to expose the inside. Carefully remove the inside fruit and cut into small dice. Reserve the outside of the pineapple.

● Heat the oil in a pan or wok, add the ham and garlic, stir-fry, then add 75 g/3 oz of the diced pineapple and all the rest of the ingredients. Mix well.

● Spoon into the empty pineapple, cover with the pineapple lid and bake in a preheated 140°C/275°F/ Gas Mark 1 oven for 30 minutes.

Rice with Spinach, Bean Sprouts and Laver

SERVES 4–6

This dish is generally eaten with a dipping sauce.

225 g/8 oz young fresh
   spinach, cut across into 2 cm/
   ¾ in strips

225 g/8 oz mung bean sprouts

1 clove garlic, chopped

1 carrot, cut into fine strips

2 spring onions, white and
   green parts, sliced diagonally

1½ sheets *kim* (*nori* or laver),
   cut into thin strips

2 tsp sesame oil

3 tbsp soy sauce

2 tsp crushed toasted sesame
   seeds

½ tsp sugar

freshly ground black pepper

scant 400 g/14 oz short-grain
   rice, washed and soaked

● Add the spinach and bean sprouts to a large saucepan of water. Cover and quickly return to the boil. Boil for 1 minute, then tip into a colander. Drain well, then squeeze out as much water as possible. Mix with the remaining ingredients except the rice and leave for 30 minutes.

● Drain the rice and put into a saucepan with the vegetable mixture and 600 ml/1 pt water. Stir, then cover and bring to the boil. Stir once, cover again and turn the heat to very low. Cook for 20–30 minutes, without removing the lid even once. Turn the heat up as high as it will go for 30 seconds, then turn it off, or remove the pan from the heat. Leave, without removing the lid at all, for 10–15 minutes before serving.

Rice with Soya Bean Sprouts

SERVES 4–6

The bean sprouts provide a crisp contrast to the softness of the rice.

225 g/8 oz soya bean sprouts

400 g/14 oz short-grain rice, washed and soaked

● Add the bean sprouts to a saucepan of boiling water, cover and quickly return to the boil. Boil for 2 minutes, then drain.

● Drain the rice and put it into a saucepan. Put the bean sprouts on top and pour in 600 ml/1 pt water. Cover and bring to the boil. Stir once and cover again. Turn the heat to very low and cook for 20–30 minutes, without removing the lid. Turn the heat up high for 20 seconds, then turn it off. Leave for 10–15 minutes before serving.

Rice and Mushrooms

SERVES 3–4

Using mushrooms (of which Koreans are very fond) with a small amount of beef to flavour rice is a good way of boosting the meaty flavour and giving the illusion that there is more meat than there actually is.

150 g/5 oz lean minced beef

225 g/8 oz open-cap mushrooms, preferably brown cap, chopped

2 cloves garlic, crushed and finely chopped

2 spring onions, white and some green parts, chopped

2 tbsp soy sauce

1½ tsp sesame oil

1 tbsp crushed toasted sesame seeds

freshly ground black pepper

2 tsp vegetable oil

200 g/7 oz short-grain white rice, washed and soaked

FOR THE GARNISH

very fine slices of red chilli

● Mix together the beef, mushrooms, garlic, spring onions, soy sauce, sesame oil, sesame seeds and plenty of pepper. Leave for at least 30 minutes.

● Heat the vegetable oil in a saucepan. Add the mushroom and beef mixture, and stir until the beef just changes colour. Stir in the rice and 300 ml/½ pt water. Cover and bring to the boil. Stir once and cover again. Turn the heat to very low and cook for 20–30 minutes, without removing the lid even once. Turn up the heat as high as it will go for 30 seconds, then turn it off, or remove the pan from the heat. Leave, without removing the lid at all, for 10–15 minutes. Stir before serving garnished with very fine slices of red chilli.

Rice with Beef and Bean Sprouts

SERVES 3–4

This dish is traditionally eaten by poorer people as adding plain rice and bean sprouts to beef makes the meat go further.

2 tbsp soy sauce

2 cloves garlic, crushed

2 spring onions, white and a
   little green part finely
   chopped

1½ tbsp crushed toasted sesame
   seeds

1 tbsp sesame oil

freshly ground black pepper

150 g/5 oz lean beef, chilled

1 tbsp vegetable oil

200 g/7 oz short-grain rice,
   washed, soaked and drained

225 g/8 oz bean sprouts

FOR THE GARNISH

very thin strips of red chilli

● Mix the soy sauce, garlic, spring onions, sesame seeds, sesame oil and pepper in a bowl.

● Slice the beef very thinly and cut into strips. Stir into the bowl with the soy mixture to coat evenly and leave for 1 hour, stirring two or three times.

● Heat the vegetable oil in a large saucepan. Add the beef and stir-fry for 2–3 minutes until darker brown. Stir in the rice and bean sprouts, then add 350 ml/ 12 fl oz water. Bring to the boil. Stir once, cover and turn the heat to very low. Cook the rice for 20 minutes, without removing the lid even once. Turn up the heat as high as it will go for 30 seconds, then turn it off, or remove the pan from the heat. Leave, without removing the lid at all, for 10–15 minutes. Serve garnished with very thin strips of red chilli.

Rice with Barley

SERVES 4

Barley used to be added to rice toward the end of summer when rice stocks were getting low, to eke it out until the next crop was harvested.

300 g/10 oz short-grain rice,
   washed and soaked

100 g/4 oz pearl barley

● Put the rice and pearl barley into a saucepan. Add 750 ml/1¼ pt water and bring to the boil. Stir once, cover and turn the heat right down.

● Cook the rice for about 20 minutes, without removing the lid even once. Continue as in the recipe for Rice with Millet (see page 227).

Rice with Beef and Bean Sprouts

Chicken Rice

SERVES 4

325 g/11 oz boneless skinned capon or chicken breasts

1.2 litres/2 pt water

3 coriander roots

2 tsp salt

200 g/7 oz rice, rinsed

10 cloves garlic, chopped

15 g/½ oz fresh ginger, sliced and crushed

3 tbsp peanut or corn oil

13 cm/5 in piece of cucumber, cut into 5 mm/¼ in slices

10 g/¼ oz coriander leaves

FOR THE *KHAO MAN* SAUCE

5 fresh small green chillies, chopped

2 tbsp pickled soya beans

½ tbsp chopped fresh ginger

½ tbsp white vinegar

1 tsp sugar

1 tsp soy sauce

¼ tsp chopped garlic

● Boil the water in a pan, add the chicken with the coriander root and salt, and cook until the chicken is soft, about 15 minutes. Remove the meat with a slotted spoon and put to one side. Strain the cooking liquid, put 1 litre/1¾ pt back in the pan and add the rice, garlic, ginger and oil. Bring back to the boil and cook, covered, until the rice is tender but not soft, about 15–18 minutes.

● Place the rice on serving plates. Slice the chicken across into 1 cm/½ in pieces and place on top of the hot rice. Arrange the cucumber slices around the sides and sprinkle with the coriander leaves.

● Mix all the ingredients for the sauce together in a bowl and serve with the chicken and rice, and with the remaining chicken stock if desired.

Vegetarian Special Fried Rice

SERVES 4

Vegetarian special fried rice is one stage richer and more elaborate than egg-fried rice and almost a meal in itself.

4–6 dried Chinese mushrooms

1 green pepper, cored and seeded

1 red pepper, cored and seeded

100 g/4 oz bamboo shoots

2 eggs

2 spring onions, finely chopped

2 tsp salt

4–5 tbsp oil

800 g/1¾ lb cooked rice

1 tbsp light soy sauce (optional)

● Soak the dried mushrooms in warm water for 25–30 minutes, squeeze dry and discard the hard stalks. Cut the mushrooms into small cubes.

● Cut the green and red peppers and the bamboo shoots into small cubes.

● Lightly beat the egg with about half of the spring onions and a pinch of the salt.

● Heat about 2 tablespoons of oil in a hot wok, add the beaten eggs and scramble until set. Remove.

● Heat the remaining oil. When hot, add the rest of the spring onions followed by all the vegetables and stir-fry until each piece is covered with oil. Add the cooked rice and salt, and stir to separate each grain of rice. Finally add the soy sauce, blend everything together, and serve.

Rice Crackers with Pork and Coconut Sauce

SERVES 4–6

450 g/1 lb cooked rice

750 ml/1¼ pt peanut or corn oil for deep-frying

1 tsp coriander root, chopped

1 tsp chopped garlic

450 ml/¾ pt thin coconut milk

175 g/6 oz cooked pork, chopped

130 g/5 oz raw shelled prawns, chopped

1 tsp coriander leaf and stalk, lightly chopped

1 fresh red chilli, cut into lengthways strips

100 g/4 oz unsalted peanuts, chopped small

2 tbsp sliced shallots

¼ tsp ground white pepper

½ tbsp palm sugar

1 tsp salt

● Knead the rice slightly until it is sticky, then press it onto a slightly soiled nonstick baking tin in a layer 3 mm/⅛ in thick. Place in the sun for 1–2 days or in a warm 170°C/325°F/Gas Mark 3 oven until very dry, 3–5 hours. Remove the rice from the pan and break it into 5 cm/2 in pieces.

● Heat the oil in a wok or pan to a temperature of 180°C/350°F. Fry the rice crackers until a light tan colour, 3–5 minutes. Remove them with a slotted spoon and drain well on absorbent kitchen paper.

● To make the sauce, pound the coriander root and garlic together in a pestle and mortar. Heat the coconut milk in a pan and add the coriander and garlic mixture. Bring to the boil, add the pork, prawns, and remaining ingredients, and continue to boil until the meat is cooked, about 7–10 minutes. Remove the pan from the heat, pour into a bowl and sprinkle with the coriander leaf and chilli.

● Serve the sauce with the rice crackers.

Basic Sushi Rice

SERVES 2

This is the basic technique for producing the glutinous, vinegar-flavoured rice that forms the basis of all the variants of **sushi.** *Japanese short-grain rice is essential for making* **sushi** *rice. The ratio of Japanese rice to water should be 1:1¼ parts water.*

165 g/5½ oz Japanese short-grain rice

2.5 cm/1 in strip dried kelp

250 ml/8 fl oz water

FOR THE SUSHI-ZU

1½ tbsp rice vinegar

1 tbsp caster sugar

½ tsp salt

● Put the rice in a pan and rinse several times with cold water until the water is almost clear. Leave the rice in a sieve for approximately 30 minutes so that individual grains can begin to absorb the water remaining in the sieve.

● Add the water, rice and kelp to a pan. Bring to the boil, taking the kelp out just before boiling point. Simmer, covered, for about 10 minutes. (Simmering time depends on the amount of rice you cook.)

● Test the rice to see if it has softened. Turn off the heat and leave for 10 minutes.

● Mix the vinegar, sugar and salt in a bowl. Put the rice in a large bowl. Wet the wooden spoon and add the *sushi-zu* a little at a time, 'cutting' it into the rice with the wooden spoon (not stirring or mashing), until you have used all the liquid. The rice will now be giving off the sharp aroma of the *sushi-zu*. Leave to cool before using.

"Roll Your Own" Sushi

SERVES 2

A modern and very popular variant on the sushi *theme. This makes a great change for dinner parties.*

1 quantity basic *shushi* rice (see page 244)

5 sheets of *nori*, each cut into 4 pieces

5 diagonal slices of cucumber, cut into long matchsticks

¼ avocado, sliced

1 rollmop herring, sliced

1 bunch cress

soy sauce

FOR THE FILLING

90 g/3½ oz tuna in brine

1 tbsp mayonnaise

FOR THE OMELETTE

1 egg

1 tsp caster sugar

pinch of salt

2 tsp vegetable oil for frying

● To prepare the filling, drain the tuna and mix with the mayonnaise. Make a Japanese-style omelette (see page 320), which should be cut into strips after cooling down. Now lay all the ingredients out on a large serving platter. The rice is laid out on a separate plate as are the strips of *nori*.

● Each diner takes a piece of *nori* in one hand and scoops about a tablespoon of rice onto it, spreading it quite thinly.

● Next, a portion of one or a combination of the fillings are taken with *hashi* and laid in the centre of the sheet. Last, the diner rolls the *nori* into a cornet shape, dipping it into his or her small bowl of soy sauce before eating.

Large Sushi Rolls

SERVES 2

You might think it takes real skill and experience to produce good sushi rolls or **futo-maki,** *but after a couple of practice runs, you should get the hang of it. Nevertheless well-made* **futo-maki** *will undoubtedly impress your dinner guests.*

1 quantity basic *sushi* rice (see page 242)

3 dried shiitake mushrooms, rinsed and soaked in 4 tbsp water

1 tsp caster sugar

1 tsp soy sauce

2 sheets *nori* seaweed sheets

6 seafood sticks

1 bunch cress

FOR THE OMELETTE

1 egg, beaten

1 tsp caster sugar

pinch of salt

vegetable oil, for frying

● To prepare the filling, slice the mushrooms and put in a pan with the water they were soaked in, the sugar and the soy sauce. Bring this mixture to the boil and simmer for 5 minutes. Put the sugar and salt into a bowl with the beaten egg and mix together well. Heat the oil in an omelette pan and make a Japanese-style omelette (see page 320). Let the omelette cool and then cut lengthways into three strips.

● Place the *nori* squarely on a *sushi* mat or a chopping board covered with cling film. Spread the rice onto the *nori*, leaving a 2.5 cm/1 in strip free of rice at the far edge.

● Next, lay, in order, half the omelette, shiitake, seafood sticks and cress in lines across the bed of rice, leaving a small strip of bare rice between each ingredient.

● Now, holding the egg in place, pull the near edge of the *nori* sheet up and over in one motion until the *nori* has enfolded all the ingredients laid on the rice. Next, use your fingers to tuck the near edge of the *nori* inside the roll. Then, rotate the mat until the join is turned to the bottom of the roll.

● Grip the far end of the *sushi* mat with your right hand and hold the roll with your left. Now, pull the roll firmly towards you to ensure that the roll becomes well packed. Finally, line up the sides of the mat by gently patting with the palms of your hands to clean up the ends of the roll. Gently unroll the mat to reveal the finished roll inside.

● Repeat with the remaining half of the ingredients. When finished, slice the rolls into pieces the thickness of your thumb. Use a knife dipped in water mixed with vinegar so that the rice will not cling to the blade. Serve displayed on a large plate. The slices should be taken from the plate and then dipped into individual dishes of soy sauce before being eaten by your guests.

Large Sushi Rolls

Thin Rolls of Cucumber and Pickled Radish

SERVES 2

1 quantity *sushi* rice (see page 242)

2.5 sheets *nori*, cut into half

1 cucumber

2 *takuwan* sticks of 5 mm x 19 cm/¼ x 7½ in

2½ tsp toasted sesame seeds

little *wasabi* (optional)

● Cut the cucumber into three 19 cm x 5 mm/ 7½ x ¾ in pieces.

● Place the *nori* on a *sushi* mat or a chopping board, covered with cling film or polythene. Spread the rice evenly on the *nori*, except for a 2 cm/¾ in strip clear along the far edge. Using the tip of your finger, smooth a small amount of *wasabi* paste over the rice.

● Place the cucumber sticks on the rice and sprinkle over ½ teaspoon of toasted sesame seeds.

● Roll over the *sushi* mat and form to shape. The *nori* is sealed by the moisture from the rice. In the same way, make two more rolls with the cucumbers and make two with pickled radish. Cut each roll into five pieces using a knife wetted with a mixture of water and vinegar to give a clean cut.

Fresh Bean Curd

SERVES 4

Fresh bean curd, which is as white and soft as the white of poached eggs, is not difficult to make.

350 g/12 oz yellow soya   juice of 2 lemons
    beans, soaked overnight

● Drain the beans and put half of them in a blender or food processor with 600 ml/1 pt warm water. Mix to a smooth purée. Pour the contents of the blender or food processor into a fine strainer lined with a large piece of muslin and placed over a large bowl.

● Repeat with the remaining beans and another 600 ml/1 pt warm water, adding the purée to the strainer. Fold the muslin over the pulp in the strainer and press firmly to extract as much liquid as possible.

● Return the residue in the strainer to the blender or food processor and add another 600 ml/1 pt warm water. Mix again for a couple of minutes, then pour into the strainer to drain. Discard the residue in the strainer. The thickish white liquid is soya milk.

● Bring the soya milk to the boil in a large saucepan. As soon as it begins to rise in the pan, lower the heat and simmer the milk, uncovered, for 15–20 minutes, stirring occasionally.

● Remove from the heat and stir in the lemon juice, which should make the milk curdle. Pour the curds and liquid into a fine strainer lined with a large clean piece of muslin, and leave to drain.

● To make medium-firm bean curd, fold the muslin over the curds, cover the surface of the curd with a weight (a heavy saucepan will do) and let drain for 15 minutes. To make firm bean curd, let drain for 2 hours. It will keep for up to two days.

Braised Bean Curd with Sesame Seeds

SERVES 2–4

Braised bean curd is a typical dish of Korean home cooking. Serve braised bean curd as a side dish, accompanied by rice and vegetables, and meat or fish as liked.

2 tbsp Japanese soy sauce

1 tsp sesame oil

1½ cloves garlic, crushed

2 tsp sugar

¼ tsp chilli powder

2 tsp crushed toasted sesame
    seeds

2 spring onions, white and
    green parts thinly sliced

200 g/7 oz medium-firm bean
    curd, cut into 5 mm/ ¼-in
    thick rectangular slices

1½ tbsp vegetable oil

freshly ground black pepper

● Mix together the soy sauce, sesame oil, garlic, sugar, chilli powder, sesame seeds and spring onions.

● Put the bean curd in a single layer between two layers of absorbent kitchen paper. Cover with a plate and put a weight on the plate. Leave for 30 minutes or so.

● Heat the vegetable oil in a large frying pan. Add the bean curd in a single layer and fry for about 1½ minutes on each side until browned. Using a slotted spatula, transfer to a large plate. Pour or wipe the oil from the pan.

● Return the bean curd to the pan in a single layer. Pour over the soy sauce mixture, partially cover the pan, and simmer for 6–7 minutes, turning the bean curd halfway through. Most of the sauce should be absorbed into the bean curd during this time.

● Transfer the bean curd to a warm plate and pour over the remaining sauce.

Braised Bean Curd with Pork

SERVES 4

This is a family way of braising bean curd.

2 tbsp soy sauce

1 tsp sesame seeds

2 tbsp sugar

1½ tbsp chilli bean paste

2 cloves garlic, crushed

2.5 cm/1 in fresh ginger, grated

1½ tsp crushed toasted sesame seeds

350 g/12 oz lean pork loin, very thinly sliced on the diagonal

3 tbsp vegetable oil

2 100-g/4-oz cakes of medium-firm bean curd

FOR THE GARNISH

spring onions, shredded diagonally

● Mix together the soy sauce, sesame seeds, sugar, chilli bean paste, garlic and ginger.

● Lay the pork slices in a shallow dish and pour over the soy sauce mixture. Coat the pork with the mixture and leave for 30 minutes.

● Heat half the vegetable oil in a frying pan. Add the pork mixture and cook for 12–15 minutes, turning the pork halfway through, until cooked through. Add a little water, as necessary, to keep the mixture fairly liquid.

● Meanwhile, cut each bean curd cake horizontally in half, then cut across each half into three pieces. Fry in the remaining oil in another frying pan for about 3 minutes on each side, until golden. Transfer to absorbent kitchen paper to absorb excess oil.

● Pour the oil from the second frying pan, then make a layer of bean curd in the pan. Cover with some of the pork mixture. Repeat, then cover and heat through gently for 5 minutes. Serve garnished with spring onions.

Fried Bean Curd

SERVES 6

A little sesame oil adds a subtle yet distinctive flavour that 'lifts' simple fried bean curd.

4 x 100-g/4-oz cakes of
medium-firm bean curd

vegetable and sesame oil for
frying

vinegar dipping sauce to serve

● Cut the bean curd into rectangles approximately 4 x 2 x 2 cm/1½ x ¾ x ¾ in. Dry on kitchen paper.

● Heat a thin film of vegetable oil mixed with a little sesame oil in a nonstick frying pan over a medium heat. Add half the bean curd and cook for 3 minutes on each side until golden. Using a slotted spoon, transfer to absorbent kitchen paper to drain while frying the remaining bean curd in the same way.

● Serve the bean curd on a warm plate with vinegar dipping sauce.

Fried Bean Curd Sushi

SERVES 2

These sweet-tasting sacks of **sushi** *rice can be eaten along with other* **sushi** *dishes or alone as a tasty and filling snack.* **Inari-zushi** *also forms a part of many a Japanese picnic as well as being a firm favourite as a lunch box filler. Refer to the instructions for making basic* **sushi** *rice while cooking the rice.*

½ quantity of basic *sushi* rice (see page 242)

2 sheets *abura-age* (thin bean curd)

120 ml/4 fl oz *dashi* stock

1½ tbsp caster sugar

1 tbsp *mirin*

2 tsp soy sauce

1 tsp toasted sesame seeds

● Gently roll the *abura-age*, using a chopstick as a rolling pin, to make it easier to handle. Place in a colander and rinse with hot water. Cut in half and gently open the 'sack'.

● Put the *dashi* stock, *mirin*, soy sauce and *abura-age* in a pan, bring to the boil and simmer for 20 minutes or until the *dashi* mixture has almost evaporated. Make a small lid with some foil and place on top of the *abura-age*. Continue to cook until the remaining liquid has been completely absorbed.

● Remove the *abura-age* and leave on a plate or chopping board until dry.

● Mix the *sushi* rice with the sesame and divide into four equal portions. Fill each *abura-age* with rice and fold to create a small sack.

Poached Bean Curd

SERVES 4

This plainly cooked bean curd can be eaten as it comes, or served with a dipping sauce. The role of cooking liquid in the serving dish is to keep the bean curd hot; it is not drunk. The bean curd can also be served in individual dishes with seaweed and bonito flakes.

15 g/½ oz *wakame*

3 cakes of medium-firm bean curd, each about 100 g/4 oz

vinegar dipping sauce to serve (optional)

● Bring 2.5 litres/4½ pt water to the boil in a wide saucepan. Add the *wakame* and bean curd, and simmer gently for 5 minutes.

● Using a slotted spoon, transfer the bean curd to a warm serving dish deep enough to let the cakes be almost covered by the cooking liquid. Pour in simmering cooking liquid to come three-quarters of the way up the sides of the bean curd cakes. Serve straightaway, accompanied by vinegar dipping sauce, if liked.

Spicy Fried Noodles

SERVES 4

You can make your own chilli powder by roasting 100 g/4 oz red chillies in the oven at 200°C/400°F/Gas Mark 6 until brown. Blend briefly if you want flakes. Process more for powder. Store in an airtight container.

2 tbsp vegetable oil

2 cloves garlic, finely chopped

100 g/4 oz pork, sliced

4 large uncooked prawns, peeled, deveined, tails intact

1 tbsp dried shrimp

2 tbsp pickled white radish, finely chopped

50 g/2 oz diced bean curd

3 tbsp lemon juice

3 tbsp fish sauce or light soy sauce and ½ tsp anchovy essence

3 tbsp sugar

175 g/6 oz rice stick noodles (preferably the thicker ones), soaked in warm water for 15 minutes and drained well

2 eggs, beaten

50 g/2 oz bean sprouts

3 tbsp peanuts, crushed

2 tbsp chopped spring onions

2 tbsp chopped fresh coriander

FOR THE GARNISH

½ tsp roasted chilli powder or flakes

lemon wedges

● Heat the oil in a wok and gently stir-fry the garlic for 3–4 minutes until golden-brown. Increase the heat, add the pork and fry for 6 minutes until cooked. Add the prawns, dried shrimp and pickled radish, and continue stir-frying for 1 minute. Add the bean curd, stir, reduce the heat and add the lemon juice, fish sauce and sugar, stirring all the while for 3 minutes.

● Add the noodles and stir the mixture thoroughly for 1–2 minutes. Push to one side and quickly add the beaten eggs. Once they begin to set, stir them, effectively scrambling them. Push to one side.

● Place most of the bean sprouts and a handful of crushed peanuts, spring onions and coriander over the noodles. Stir these in with the scrambled eggs and noodles. Serve on a large plate with little mounds of bean sprouts, peanuts, spring onions, coriander, chilli flakes and lemon wedges.

White Noodles with Spicy Meat Sauce

SERVES 4–6

4 tbsp peanut or corn oil

325 g/11 oz minced pork

325 g/11 oz pork spare ribs, cut into 2.5 cm/1 in pieces

100 g/4 oz chicken blood pudding, cut into 2.5 cm/1 in pieces

1.5 litres/2½ pt chicken stock

1 tbsp marinated black soya beans, finely pounded

1 tbsp salt

150 g/5 oz cherry tomatoes

425 g/15 oz fresh rice vermicelli (if dried, soak for 5 minutes and boil for 2 minutes) or cooked spaghetti

FOR THE CHILLI PASTE

7 dried red chillies, chopped

25 g/1 oz garlic, chopped

15 g/½ oz shallot, chopped

2 tbsp chopped lemon grass

1 tbsp chopped galangal

1 tsp coriander root or stalk, chopped

1 tsp shrimp paste

1 tsp salt

● Pound all the chilli paste ingredients together with a pestle and mortar or in a blender.

● Heat the oil in a wok or pan, fry the chilli paste and then add the minced pork and spare ribs. Cook for 10 minutes, mixing well, then add the blood pudding, stock, soya beans and salt. Bring to the boil, add the tomatoes and simmer for 20 minutes or until the spare ribs are tender.

● Boil the rice noodles in water until just done, 5–8 minutes, drain and place in serving bowls. Spoon the meat mixture over the noodles.

● Serve the dish accompanied by sliced fried garlic, deep-fried dried red chillies, spring onions, fresh coriander and lime wedges.

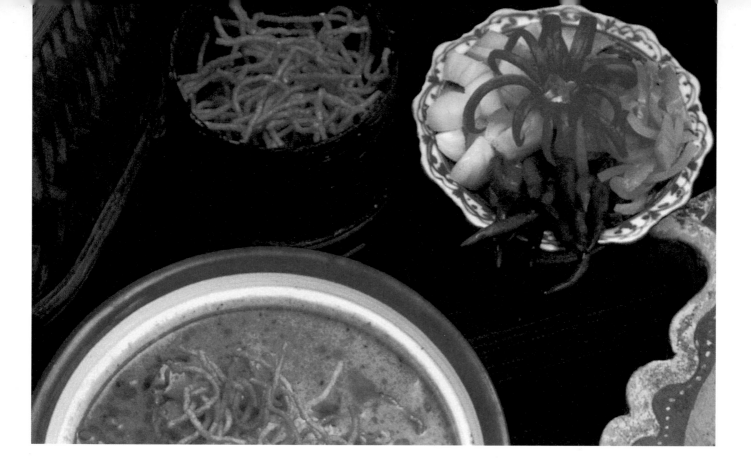

Curried Noodles

SERVES 4–6

A favourite lunch in Chiangmai and other towns in northern Thailand. The curry ingredients give away its Indian antecedents, but **khao soi,** *as it is known, has arrived via Burma, in particular from the Shan States. Diners add the crispy noodles at the last minute so that they do not go soggy, and the condiments allow individual choice of flavour.*

1.5 litres/2½ pt thin coconut milk

325 g/11 oz boneless skinned chicken breasts, cut lengthways into 1 cm/½ in thick slices

1 tbsp light soy sauce

1 tbsp dark soy sauce

2 tsp salt

425 g/15 oz dried or 200 g/ 7 oz fresh egg noodles

peanut or corn oil for frying

FOR THE CHILLI PASTE

4 dried red chillies, chopped roughly

1 tbsp chopped shallot

2 tsp fresh ginger, sliced

1 tsp coriander seeds

1 tsp turmeric

● Dry-roast the chilli paste ingredients in a 180°C/ 350°F/Gas Mark 4 oven until fragrant, about 8–10 minutes, then pound until fine with a pestle and mortar or in a blender.

● Heat 250 ml/8 fl oz of the coconut milk in a pan or wok, add the chilli paste and fry for 2 minutes, then add the chicken and soy sauces. Stir-fry for 3 minutes, then add the rest of the coconut milk and bring to the boil for 3 minutes. Add the salt and remove from the heat.

● Fry 100 g/4 oz of the noodles in a hot oil until crisp. Remove and drain well. Boil the rest of the noodles in water until firm but tender and drain.

● Place the boiled noodles in individual serving bowls, and pour the chicken mixture on top. Garnish with the fried noodles.

● Serve accompanied by bowls of diced shallots, pickled cabbage and chilli powder.

Stir-fried Egg Noodles with Barbecued Pork

SERVES 4

Literally translated as 'stir-fried noodles', **chow mein** *is an archetypical noodle fast-food, and one of the very first noodle dishes to become popularized in the West.*

450 g/1 lb fresh or 300 g/ 10 oz dried thin egg noodles

2 tbsp vegetable oil

2.5 cm/1 in fresh ginger, peeled and finely chopped

2 cloves garlic, finely chopped

1 medium onion, sliced

3 medium carrots, sliced into bite-sized pieces

12 mange tout, blanched

175 g/6 oz bean sprouts, rinsed

225 g/8 oz Chinese barbecued (*chasin*) pork, sliced and cut into bite-sized squares

1 tbsp sesame oil

4 tbsp light soy sauce

1 tbsp dark soy sauce

1 tbsp sugar

salt and black pepper

● Boil plenty of water in a pan and cook the noodles for 3 minutes. Rinse under running water, and drain.

● Heat the vegetable oil in a wok or frying pan until very hot. Stir-fry the ginger and garlic for 30 seconds. Add the onion, carrots and mange tout, and stir-fry for 2 minutes. Add the bean sprouts and *cha siu* pork, and stir-fry for another 2 minutes.

● Add the sesame oil, noodles, soy sauce and sugar, and stir-fry for 1 minute until the noodles are coated with sauce. Season if necessary, and stir once more. Serve immediately.

White Noodles with Sauce

SERVES 4–6

200 g/7 oz sea bass, perch or white fish fillets, skinned

325 g/11 oz thin rice noodles soaked for 3 minutes if dried

1.5 litres/2½ pt thin coconut milk

20 fish balls, frozen or bottled

3 tbsp fish sauce

100 g/4 oz bean sprouts, blanched

100 g/4 oz beans, cut into 1 cm/½ in lengths

100 g/4 oz morning glory, blanched

50 g/2 oz lemon basil leaves

FOR THE CHILLI PASTE

100 g/4 oz shallots, finely chopped

50 g/2 oz cloves garlic, chopped

50 g/2 oz dried salted mackerel or other fish, chopped lightly

250 ml/8 fl oz water

175 g/6 oz krachai, sliced

2 tbsp sliced lemon grass

4 dried red chillies, seeded

2 tsp sliced galangal

1 tsp shrimp paste

1 tsp salt

● Mix all the chilli paste ingredients together, put in a pan or wok and cook over medium heat for 1 minute. Cool and then chop in a blender or food processor. Put to one side.

● Boil fish in a small amount of water for 10 minutes. Remove, cool slightly and chop finely (or process quickly in a food processor). Boil the noodles quickly for 5 minutes, drain, cool and place in serving bowls.

● Heat the coconut milk in a pan, add the chilli paste mixture, the fish and the fish balls if using, the fish sauce, and boil for 3 minutes. Remove from the heat.

● Top the noodles with the fish mixture. Arrange the bean sprouts, beans, morning glory and lemon basil around the side.

Soft Noodles with Vegetable and Peanut Sauce

SERVES 4

This is a famous Indonesian dish comprising vegetables in a peanut sauce. Normally it is served as a salad, but it also makes a great noodle topping!

100 g/4 oz green cabbage, sliced

150 g/5 oz bean sprouts

100 g/4 oz green beans

4–5 small carrots, cut into matchsticks

400 g/14 oz fresh or 300 g/ 10 oz dried thin egg noodles

1 tbsp sesame oil

FOR THE PEANUT SAUCE

1 tbsp vegetable oil

1 clove garlic, finely chopped

1 shallot, finely chopped

½ tsp chilli powder

500 ml/8 fl oz water

1 tbsp light brown sugar

8 tbsp crunchy peanut butter

a pinch of salt

juice of ½ a lemon

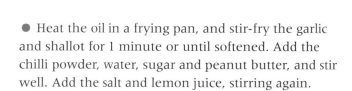

● Heat the oil in a frying pan, and stir-fry the garlic and shallot for 1 minute or until softened. Add the chilli powder, water, sugar and peanut butter, and stir well. Add the salt and lemon juice, stirring again.

● Boil water in a saucepan and blanch the cabbage, bean sprouts, green beans and carrots for 2–3 minutes. Drain well.

● Boil more water in the pan, then cook the egg noodles for 3 minutes. Rinse, drain and toss with the sesame oil. Divide them onto four plates.

● Pile the vegetables on the noodles, and pour the peanut sauce over the top. Serve at once.

Spicy Rice-stick Noodles with Chicken

SERVES 4

Authentic Thai spicy noodles are very, very hot. I have altered the amount of green chilli used in this recipe to cool them down and save your taste buds! However, if you feel like increasing the spices, you can add more green chilli if you dare.

900 g/2 lb fresh flat rice noodles or 300 g/10 oz dried rice-stick noodles

5 tbsp vegetable oil

2 cloves garlic, finely chopped

4–6 small green chillies, chopped

225 g/8 oz boneless chicken breasts, sliced into bite-sized pieces

175 g/6 oz frozen green beans, halved

100 g/4 oz spring greens or fresh spinach

16 canned or fresh baby corn, each cut diagonally into 3 pieces

4 tbsp fish sauce

2 tbsp dark soy sauce

2 tbsp light soy sauce

1 tbsp palm or brown sugar

2 small tomatoes, halved

● If you use fresh noodles, just rinse with warm water. Soak dried rice noodles in warm water for 2–5 minutes, or according to the instructions on the packet. Rinse, and drain.

● Heat 3 tablespoons of the oils in a wok or frying pan until very hot. Stir-fry the garlic and green chilli for 30 seconds, then add the chicken and fry for about 3 minutes more.

● Add the green beans, greens or spinach, and baby corn, stirring for 1–2 minutes. Add the remaining oil and the rice noodles, and stir. Then add the fish sauce, soy sauce and sugar, and stir well.

● Garnish with the tomatoes, and serve at once.

Fried Flat Rice Noodles with Beef and Black Bean Sauce

SERVES 4

Black bean sauce is just one of a number of end products that result from the fermentation of soya beans. Prepared with salt and spices, the black bean forms the basis of a very distinctive sauce to complement most meats. Here it is used with beef, but you will find it is equally good with pork.

900 g/2 lb fresh flat rice noodles or 300 g/10 oz dried rice-stick noodles

450 g/1 lb rump steak, sliced at a slant into bite-sized pieces

1 egg white

3 tbsp Chinese rice wine or dry sherry

4 tbsp light soy sauce

2 tsp cornflour

7 tbsp vegetable oil

2.5 cm/1 in fresh ginger, peeled and finely chopped

3 cloves garlic, finely chopped

2 spring onions, chopped

2 medium-sized onions, cut into bite-sized squares

1 large green pepper, cut into bite-sized squares

6 tbsp black bean sauce

2 tsp sugar

● Rinse fresh flat rice noodles with hot water, or soak dried noodles in warm water for 2–5 minutes. Rinse, and drain.

● Marinate the beef with 1 tablespoon of the rice wine, 1 tablespoon of the soy sauce and the cornflour for 30 minutes.

● Heat 3 tablespoons of the oil in a wok or frying pan. Fry the beef for 2–3 minutes, and set aside. Clean the wok before the next step.

● Heat 2 tablespoons of the oil in a wok and stir-fry the ginger and garlic for 30 seconds. Add the spring onions, onion and green pepper, and stir until the onion becomes transparent.

● Return the beef and noodles to the wok. Add 2 tablespoons of the oil, plus the black bean sauce, soy sauce, rice wine and sugar. Stir well until all the ingredients are thoroughly mixed. Divide the noodles onto four plates, and serve.

Fried Rice-stick Noodles with Bean Curd and Black Bean Sauce

SERVES 4

Bean curd is prepared by cutting it into small cubes. Be careful when you do this as it is delicate stuff and prone to disintegrate if handled too roughly. Nutritious and healthy as it undoubtedly is, bean curd will never win any awards for flavour, which is why its combination with the spicy, aromatic black bean sauce makes such a good pairing.

300 g/10 oz dried rice-stick noodles

4 tbsp vegetable oil

350 g/12 oz bean curd, diced

2.5 cm/1 in fresh ginger, peeled and finely chopped

2 cloves garlic, finely chopped

½ green pepper, diced

½ red pepper, diced

½ yellow pepper, diced

5 spring onions, chopped

6 tbsp black bean sauce

3 tbsp light soy sauce

2 tbsp Chinese rice wine or dry sherry

2 tsp sugar

● Soak the rice-stick noodles in warm water for 2–5 minutes, depending on the instructions on the packet. Rinse and drain.

● Heat 3 tablespoons of the oil in a wok or frying pan. Fry the bean curd until golden brown. Add the ginger and garlic, and stir. Add the peppers and spring onions, and stir-fry for 1–2 minutes.

● Add the remaining oil, noodles, black bean sauce, soy sauce, rice wine and sugar, then stir until the noodles are well coated with the sauce. Divide the noodles onto four plates, and serve at once.

Thai Fried Rice-stick Noodles

SERVES 4

The most widely eaten and best known of all the noodle dishes of Thailand. Like all the best noodle dishes, it is simply prepared and ready in minutes. The key lies in the use of salty dried shrimps and roasted peanuts. You can adjust the amount of chilli used depending on your liking for spiciness.

300 g/10 oz dried rice-stick noodles

12 large prawns with tails, peeled and deveined

5 tbsp vegetable oil

3 cloves garlic, finely chopped

4 shallots, sliced

2 eggs, beaten

2 tbsp roast peanuts, crushed

3–4 small green chillies, chopped

2 tbsp dried shrimps, chopped

2 spring onions, chopped

150 g/5 oz bean sprouts

2½ tbsp palm or brown sugar

6 tbsp fish sauce

120 ml/4 fl oz freshly squeezed lemon juice

coriander leaves

4 lime wedges

FOR THE PRAWN MARINADE

1 tsp freshly squeezed lemon juice

1 tsp fish sauce

½ tsp palm or brown sugar

● Soak the rice-stick noodles in warm water for 2–5 minutes, or according to the instructions on the packet. Rinse, and drain.

● Marinate the prawns in the lemon juice, fish sauce and sugar for at least 15 minutes.

● Heat 2 tablespoons of the oil in a wok or frying pan and stir-fry the garlic and shallots for 30 seconds. Make a well in the centre and add the eggs, then lightly scramble.

● Add the peanuts, chillies, dried shrimps, spring onions and bean sprouts, and stir.

● Add another 2 tablespoons of oil and the noodles, and stir. Add the sugar, fish sauce and lemon juice, then stir until the noodles are well coated.

● Quickly beat the remaining tablespoon of oil in the wok, and fry the prawns thoroughly. Put the noodles onto four plates. Lay the prawns on top, and garnish with coriander and lime wedges. Serve at once.

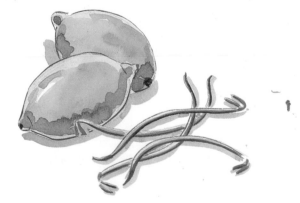

Thai Fried Rice–stick Noodles

Malaysian Flat Rice Noodles

SERVES 4

If you are ever lucky enough to visit Malaysia, you will find this dish being sold in restaurants and from roadside stalls wherever you go. The fish balls in this recipe are not available at supermarkets, but you should be able to pick them up at oriental food shops.

900 g/2 lb fresh flat rice
    noodles or 300 g/10 oz dried
    rice-stick noodles

5 tbsp vegetable oil

2 cloves garlic, finely chopped

1-cm/½-in fresh ginger, peeled
    and finely chopped

175 g/6 oz boneless belly of
    pork or chicken breasts,
    skinned and thinly sliced

2 small red chillies, chopped

16 large prawns with tails,
    peeled and deveined

8 fish balls or portions of
    imitation crabmeat, sliced

175 g/6 oz bean sprouts

100 g/4 oz fresh spinach

2 eggs, beaten

1 tsp sugar

3 tbsp light soy sauce

3 tbsp dark soy sauce

salt and black pepper

● Rinse the fresh flat rice noodles with warm water, or soak the dried rice-stick noodles in warm water for 2–5 minutes. Rinse and drain.

● Heat 3 tablespoons of the oil in a wok or frying pan until very hot. Stir-fry the garlic and ginger for 30 seconds. Add the pork and fry for about 3 minutes. Add the chilli and prawns, then stir for about 1 minute. Add the sliced fish balls or crabmeat, the bean sprouts and spinach, and stir again for about 1 minute.

● Make a well in the centre, then add the egg. Scramble quickly. Add the remaining oil, and the rice noodles, sugar and soy sauce, then stir well. Taste, and add salt and black pepper as required. Put onto four plates, and serve immediately.

Fried Rice Noodles with Coconut Sauce

SERVES 4

The coconut and its parent palm have a hallowed place in the Thai psyche. The coconut itself has a wide variety of culinary uses, while the palm is employed to make furniture, toys and musical instruments. Canned coconut milk varies in its consistency depending on the brand. A thicker product produces the richest, smoothest flavour. Remember to shake the can well before opening.

300 g/10 oz dried rice-stick noodles

3 tbsp vegetable oil

2 cloves garlic, finely chopped

3 shallots, chopped

400 g/14 oz rump steak, thinly sliced

16 canned or fresh baby corn, cut diagonally

4 spring onions, chopped

150 g/5 oz bean sprouts

400 ml/14 fl oz canned coconut milk

2 tsp palm or brown sugar

4 tbsp fish sauce

3 tbsp freshly squeezed lemon juice

1 tbsp Thai red curry paste

coriander leaves

● Soak the rice-stick noodles in warm water for 2–5 minutes, or follow the instructions on the packet. Rinse and drain.

● Heat the oil in a wok or frying pan, then stir-fry the garlic and shallots for 30 seconds. Add the beef and stir-fry for about 3 minutes, before adding the baby corn, spring onions, celery and bean sprouts.

● Add the coconut milk, sugar, fish sauce, lemon juice and curry paste, and stir well until the sauce is absorbed into the noodles.

● Put the noodles onto four plates, sprinkle with coriander leaves, and serve at once.

Fried Bean-thread Noodles with Bean Curd

SERVES 4

Bean curd is a favourite constituent of Thai cooking. This dish features fried bean curd. Like all other types of bean curd, it is best to use what you buy in one go as it quickly deteriorates, even if refrigerated.

225 g/8 oz bean-thread noodles

4 tbsp vegetable oil

300 g/10 oz bean curd, diced

3 cloves garlic, finely chopped

4 shallots, finely chopped

150 g/5 oz bean sprouts

150 g/5 oz frozen green beans, halved

2 spring onions, chopped

2 tbsp roast peanuts, crushed

2 tbsp dried shrimps, chopped

3–5 small green chillies, chopped

2½ tbsp palm or brown sugar

6 tbsp fish sauce

120 ml/4 fl oz freshly squeezed lemon juice

FOR THE GARNISH

2 tbsp crispy onion

coriander leaves

1 medium red chilli, sliced

4 slices lime

● Soak the bean-thread noodles in boiling water for 5 minutes. Rinse under cold water, and drain. Heat half the oil in a wok or frying pan, and fry the bean curd until golden brown. Drain on absorbent kitchen paper.

● Add the remaining oil to the wok, then fry the garlic and shallots for about 30 seconds. Add the bean sprouts, green beans and spring onions, and stir well.

● Add the bean-thread noodles, bean curd, crushed peanuts, dried shrimps and green chilli, then stir. Season with the sugar, fish sauce and lemon juice, stirring again.

● Divide the noodles onto four plates. Sprinkle with the crispy onions, coriander leaves and red chilli, and garnish with lime slices. Serve at once.

Fried Bean-thread Noodles
with Bean Curd

Wheatflour Noodles with Egg

SERVES 2

Udon is the name given by the Japanese to those noodles made from wheatflour. A great favourite in the winter months because of its warming properties, udon comes in various shapes, some flat, some round in section, some as thick as a little finger, others as thin as spaghetti.

300 g/10 oz fresh *udon*

FOR THE SOUP

600 ml/1 pt *dashi* stock (see page 62)

1 tsp salt

2 tsp caster sugar

2 tbsp *mirin*

2 tbsp soy sauce

1 egg, beaten

2 tsp cornflour

2 tsp water

2 spring onions, chopped

● Bring a large pan of water to the boil. Add the *udon* and boil for 2 minutes. Drain and then place in equal portions into two bowls.

● Put the *dashi* stock, salt, sugar, *mirin* and soy sauce in a pan and bring to the boil. Pour ⅔ of the liquid into the two bowls. Bring the remainder back to the boil and gradually add the beaten egg, mixing lightly so that when the egg rises to the surface, it is cooked in fronds.

● Mix the cornflour and water into a paste and then add this to the soup to thicken. Pour the egg mixture into the bowls. Sprinkle with the spring onion and serve immediately while still hot.

Rice-stick Noodles with Pork and Prawns

SERVES 4

This dish contains the three foundations of Thai flavouring: garlic, shallots and chillies. Thai garlic tends to be small compared to its western counterpart, so if the cloves you have are on the large side, use just one.

300 g/10 oz dried rice-stick noodles

5 tbsp vegetable oil

2 cloves garlic, finely chopped

3 shallots, chopped

225 g/8 oz lean pork, sliced into small pieces

100 g/4 oz peeled prawns

4–6 small green chillies, chopped

150 g/5 oz bean sprouts

8 canned or fresh baby corn, cut diagonally into bite-sized pieces

3 celery sticks, cut diagonally into bite-sized pieces

2 eggs, beaten

2½ tbsp palm or brown sugar

3½ tbsp tomato ketchup

6 tbsp fish sauce

120 ml/4 fl oz freshly squeezed lemon juice

coriander leaves

4 lime wedges

● Soak the noodles in warm water for 2–5 minutes, or according to the instructions. Rinse, then drain.

● Heat 3 tablespoons of the oil in a wok or frying pan, and stir-fry the garlic and shallots for 30 seconds. Add the pork and fry for about 3 minutes. Add the prawns and green chillies, stirring for another minute, then add the bean sprouts, baby corn and celery, and fry for another 2 minutes.

● Make a well in the centre, then pour in the egg and scramble quickly. Add the remaining oil and the rice-stick noodles, then stir. Add the sugar, tomato ketchup, fish sauce and lemon juice, and stir well.

● Divide the noodles onto four plates, and garnish with coriander and lime wedges.

Buckwheat Noodles Topped with Deep-fried Large Prawns

SERVES 2

Soba noodles are made from buckwheat and are distinguished by their brown colour. Like ramen noodles, they can be bought fresh or dried. Soba is considered to be a very healthy food by the Japanese, and topping a dish of the noodles with a large prawn turns a nourishing meal into a gourmet experience.

2 large prawns

plain flour

4 shiitake mushrooms

150 g/5 oz dried *soba*

FOR THE BATTER

2 tbsp plain flour

½ egg, beaten

4 tbsp water

FOR THE SOUP

600 ml/1 pt *dashi* stock

1 tsp salt

2 tsp caster sugar

2 tbsp *mirin*

2 tbsp soy sauce

2 spring onions, chopped

● To make the batter mix the flour, egg and water lightly in a bowl. Coat the prawns with flour and dip in the batter. Dip the mushrooms into the batter. Heat the oil to 180°C/350°F and deep-fry until light golden brown.

● Bring a large pan of water to the boil. Add the *soba* and cook for about 3 minutes. Briefly rinse with cold water and then drain. Divide the *soba* equally between two bowls.

● Put the *dashi* stock, salt, sugar, *mirin* and soy sauce in a pan and bring to the boil. Add the bowls of *soba*.

● Place one prawn and two mushrooms on the top of each bowl and sprinkle with chopped spring onion. Serve immediately.

Stir-fried Noodles and Bean Sprouts

SERVES 4

1 tbsp vegetable oil

2 small onions, thinly sliced

4 cloves garlic, chopped

50 g/2 oz bean sprouts

175 g/6 oz (dried weight) cellophane (glass) noodles, soaked in warm water for 30 minutes, drained and cut into 7.5 cm/3 in lengths

120 ml/4 fl oz chicken stock

1 tbsp fish sauce or light soy sauce

2 spring onions, thinly sliced

1 tbsp fresh coriander, chopped

freshly ground black pepper

● Heat the oil in a wok over high heat. Add the onions and garlic, and sauté for 2 minutes or so until the edges begin to brown.

● Add the bean sprouts and stir-fry for 30 seconds. Add the noodles and stir-fry for 1 minute. Stir in the chicken stock and fish sauce, and toss to combine. Add the spring onions and remove from heat. Serve on a serving dish with coriander and black pepper sprinkled all over.

Malaysian Egg Noodles with Chicken and Prawns

SERVES 4

A typical feature of Malaysian and Singaporean cuisine is the frequent use of egg, as in this dish, in which strands of beaten egg are stirred into the sauce.

400 g/14 oz fresh or 300 g/
  10 oz dried thin egg noodles

2 tbsp sesame oil

4 tbsp vegetable oil

2 cloves garlic, finely chopped

100 g/4 oz boneless chicken
  breasts, sliced into bite-sized
  pieces

100 g/4 oz peeled prawns

100 g/4 oz fish balls or
  imitation crabmeat, sliced

175 g/6 oz bean sprouts

100 g/4 oz spring greens or
  fresh spinach

1 tsp light soy sauce

1 tsp salt

white pepper

½ tsp sugar

600 ml/1 pt chicken stock

3 tbsp cornflour

4 tbsp water

2 eggs, beaten

● Boil plenty of water in a pan and add the egg noodles. Cook for 3 minutes, then rinse under cold water and drain. Heat the sesame oil in a wok or frying pan, and fry the noodles. Then divide onto four individual plates.

● Heat the vegetable oil in a wok or frying pan until very hot. Fry the garlic for 30 seconds. Add the chicken and fry for 2–3 minutes. Add the prawns and stir, then add the fish balls, bean sprouts and spinach or greens, stirring for 2–3 minutes.

● Add the soy sauce, salt, pepper, sugar and chicken stock; bring to the boil. Dissolve the cornflour in water, then add to thicken the sauce. When the sauce returns to the boil, stir in the beaten egg and wait for the egg strands to float up to the surface. Pour the sauce over the noodles, and serve.

Stir-fried Egg Noodles with Prawns and Black Bean Sauce

SERVES 4

These stir-fried noodles require cooking for only a short time. Large prawns add both flavour and a certain luxury to this dish, so if you are feeling extravagant, use them in place of their smaller cousins.

450 g/1 lb fresh or 300 g/
  10 oz dried medium egg
  noodles

3 tbsp vegetable oil

2.5 cm/1 in fresh ginger,
  peeled and finely chopped

3 cloves garlic, finely chopped

100 g/4 oz peeled prawns

12 large prawns, peeled and
  deveined

1 small red pepper, sliced

4 spring onions, chopped into
  2.5 cm/1 in lengths

black pepper

1 tbsp sesame oil

4 tsp light soy sauce

4 tsp dark soy sauce

2 tbsp Chinese rice wine

3 tbsp black bean sauce

● Cook the noodles in a pan of boiling water for 4 minutes. Rinse, and drain well.

● Heat the vegetable oil in a wok or frying pan. Stir-fry the ginger and garlic for 30 seconds. Add the prawns, pepper, spring onions, and black pepper, and stir for 1–2 minutes or until the prawns are heated.

● Add the sesame oil and noodles, and stir. Add the soy sauce, rice wine and black bean sauce, then stir again until the noodles are coated well with the sauce.

● Put the noodles onto four plates, and serve at once.

Malaysian Egg Noodles
with Chicken and Prawns

Sweet and Sour Fish on Pan-fried Egg Noodles

SERVES 4

Sweet and sour fish has never quite gained the same kind of popularity as sweet and sour pork, though it is every bit as good to eat and makes an especially good noodle topping.

vegetable oil for deep-frying

2 tbsp cornflour

1 egg, beaten

1 tsp water

450 g/1 lb cod or haddock steaks, cut into bite-sized pieces

300 g/10 oz dried or 400 g/ 14 oz fresh thin egg noodles

4 tbsp vegetable oil

FOR THE SAUCE

1 tbsp sesame oil

2 tbsp vegetable oil

1 medium-sized onion, cut into bite-sized squares

1 red pepper, cut into bite-sized squares

75 g/3 oz frozen green peas

100 g/4 oz can bamboo shoots, cut into halves

10 shiitake mushrooms, quartered

½ tsp chilli powder

600 ml/1 pt chicken stock

2½ tbsp sugar

100 g/4 oz tomato ketchup

4 tsp light soy sauce

4 tbsp Chinese rice wine or dry sherry

4 tbsp vinegar

salt and black pepper

3 tbsp cornflour

4 tbsp water

● Heat the oil in a pan until very hot. Meanwhile, mix the cornflour, egg and water together, then dip the fish in the mixture. Deep-fry for about 2 minutes or until golden brown.

● Cook the egg noodles in plenty of boiling water for 3 minutes. Rinse under running water, drain well and divide into four. Heat 1 tablespoon of oil in a wok or frying pan. Add a portion of noodles and press down lightly. Fry until lightly browned, then turn the noodles over, press down lightly, and fry until the other side turns golden brown.

● Put the pan-fried noodles on a chopping board, make a crisscross pattern of cuts, and place on an individual plate. Repeat the process for the other three portions.

● Heat 1 tablespoon sesame oil and 2 tablespoons vegetable oil in the wok or frying pan until very hot. Stir-fry the onion, red pepper and peas for 2 minutes. Add the bamboo shoots and shiitake mushrooms, and sprinkle with the chilli powder. Stir-fry for another 2 minutes.

● Add the chicken stock, sugar, tomato ketchup, soy sauce and rice wine, and bring to the boil. Add the vinegar, and season to taste with salt and black pepper.

● Dissolve the cornflour in the water, and add to thicken the sauce. Add the fish and stir gently. Pour the sweet and sour fish over the noodles. Serve immediately.

Indonesian Fried Egg Noodles with Chicken and Bean Curd

SERVES 4

Indonesian cooking has become increasingly popular over the last few years and this, one of the most commonly eaten dishes in Indonesia, has been at the forefront of this trend.

300 g/10 oz dried medium egg noodles

4 tbsp + 2 tsp vegetable oil

300 g/10 oz bean curd, diced

2 eggs, beaten

2.5 cm/1 in fresh ginger, peeled and finely chopped

4 shallots, finely chopped

1 tsp ground coriander seeds

1 red chilli, chopped

225 g/8 oz boneless chicken breasts, diced

4–5 small carrots, sliced

3 celery sticks, sliced

4 spring onions, chopped into 2.5 cm/1 in lengths

3 tbsp light soy sauce

salt and pepper

4 tomato wedges

sliced cucumber

● Cook the egg noodles in a pan of boiling water for 4 minutes. Rinse and drain well.

● Heat 1 tablespoon of the oil in a wok or frying pan, and fry the bean curd until lightly browned. Set aside, and clean the wok.

● To make the egg sheets, heat 1 teaspoon of the oil in an omelette pan. Add half the beaten egg and fry both sides, like a thin pancake. Repeat to make a second egg sheet. When the egg sheets are cooled, slice them thinly.

● Heat another 2 tablespoons of the oil in the wok, stir-fry the ginger, shallots, ground coriander and red chilli for 30 seconds. Add the chicken and stir for 2–3 minutes. Add the carrots, celery, bean curd and spring onions, stirring each time you add the ingredients.

● Add 1 tablespoon of the oil, the egg noodles and soy sauce to the wok, and stir well. Divide the noodles onto four plates, sprinkle the sliced egg sheets on top, and garnish with tomato wedges and cucumber slices. Serve at once.

Malaysian Spicy Egg Noodles

SERVES 4

This dish uses **belacan**, *the pungent shrimp-based paste commonly used in Malaysia and Thai cooking. Don't let the odor put you off when you use shrimp paste, but the aroma does tend to stick around unless you ensure your kitchen is well-ventilated!*

300 g/10 oz dried medium egg noodles

5 tbsp vegetable oil

4–6 small dried red chillies, soaked in hot water, then ground

2 cloves garlic, finely chopped

1 tsp dried shrimp paste (optional)

300 g/10 oz rump steak, sliced

1 medium-sized onion, sliced

2 green chillies, chopped

150 g/5 oz bean sprouts

100 g/4 oz spring greens or fresh spinach

salt and black pepper

3 tbsp light soy sauce

FOR THE GARNISH

coriander leaves

4 lime wedges

● Boil plenty of water in a pan and cook the noodles for 4 minutes. Rinse under water and drain. Set aside.

● Heat 3 tablespoons of the oil in a wok or frying pan. Add the chillies, garlic and shrimp paste, and stir. Add the beef and fry for 2–3 minutes.

● Add the onion, green chillies, bean sprouts and spring greens, stirring each time you add the ingredients. Season with salt and pepper.

● Add the remaining oil and the egg noodles, sprinkle soy sauce over the mixture, and mix all the ingredients well. Put the noodles onto four plates, and garnish with coriander leaves and lime wedges.

Stir-fried Egg Noodles with Yakisoba Sauce

SERVES 4

Maybe the most popular noodle dish eaten in Japan, this is found in noodle shops and is made and served in the street, at festivals, or cooked over a campfire during a trip out into the countryside.

350 g/12 oz dried egg noodles or 550 g/1¼ lb Japanese steamed noodles

1 tbsp sesame oil

2 tbsp sunflower oil

225 g/8 oz boneless belly of pork or chicken breasts, thinly sliced

1 medium-sized onion, sliced

4–5 small carrots, cut in half lengthways and thinly sliced

5 cabbage leaves, cut roughly

salt and black pepper

7 Tbsp *yakisoba* or Japanese brown sauce

nori seaweed flakes (optional)

red pickled ginger (optional)

● If you are using dried noodles, boil plenty of water in a pan, add the noodles and cook for 3 minutes. Rinse with water and drain. Toss the noodles in the sesame oil. If you use Japanese steamed noodles, just rinse with very hot water.

● Heat the sunflower oil in a wok or frying pan, then fry the pork or chicken for 3–4 minutes. Add the onions, carrots and cabbage, and stir-fry for 3–4 minutes. Sprinkle with the salt and pepper, add the noodles and *yakisoba* or brown sauce, and stir well.

● Put the noodles onto four plates, and sprinkle with the *nori* flakes and pickled ginger. Serve at once.

Malaysian Spicy Egg Noodles

Thai-fried Noodles

SERVES 6

The country's basic fried noodle dish. Quick and easy to prepare, it is usually eaten as a secondary rather than as a main dish.

120 ml/4 fl oz peanut oil

200 g/7 oz raw large prawns, shelled

100 g/4 oz firm bean curd, diced

3 tbsp preserved sweet white radish, chopped

3 tbsp sliced shallots

4 eggs

325 g/11 oz rice or cellophane (glass) noodles

4 tbsp chicken stock

3 tbsp dried shrimps, chopped

40 g/1½ oz unsalted peanuts, chopped

4 spring onions, sliced

425 g/15 oz bean sprouts

FOR THE SAUCE

250 ml/8 fl oz water

120 ml/4 fl oz tamarind juice

40 g/1½ oz palm sugar

1 tbsp light soy sauce

● Mix all the sauce ingredients together in a pan and boil until reduced to about 150 ml/¼ pt. Set aside to cool.

● Heat the oil in a wok or pan until very hot, then add the prawns and bean curd and stir-fry lightly for 1 minute. Add the preserved radish and shallot, fry for 1 minute, and break in the eggs. Stir-fry for a minute, then add the noodles and chicken stock. When the noodles are soft (about 2 minutes), add the dried shrimps, peanuts, spring onions and bean sprouts. Add the sauce, fry for a couple of minutes and serve.

● Serve accompanied by chopped peanuts, chopped dry chillies, sugar, lime wedges, spring onions and fresh bean sprouts, all in small saucers.

Crispy Egg Noodles with Chicken and Bean Sprout Sauce

SERVES 4

Take care when preparing the noodles for this dish, as the oil may boil over if an excessive amount is used. The best and safest method is to use a wok rather than a frying pan.

225 g/8 oz dried medium egg noodles

vegetable oil for deep-frying

1 egg white

2 tsp cornflour

6 tbsp vegetable oil

300 g/10 oz boneless chicken breasts, shredded

FOR THE SAUCE

1 tbsp sesame oil

2 cloves garlic, finely chopped

2.5-cm/1-in fresh ginger, peeled and finely chopped

400 g/14 oz bean sprouts

15 canned straw mushrooms, halved

4 spring onions, chopped

600 ml/1 pt chicken stock

2 tsp light soy sauce

2 tbsp Chinese rice wine or dry sherry

salt and black pepper

3 tbsp cornflour

4 tbsp water

● Boil plenty of water in a pan and cook the noodles for 4 minutes. Rinse and drain. Separate, and then spread the noodles on a tray to dry.

● Fill a saucepan or wok quarter full of oil and heat to 180°C/350°F. Deep-fry the noodles in small batches until golden and crispy. Drain on absorbent kitchen paper. Crush the noodles lightly to make them easier to handle, and divide onto three plates.

● Mix the egg white and 2 teaspoons of cornflour. Heat 5 tablespoons of the vegetable oil in the wok or frying pan. Coat the chicken with the cornflour mixture, then shallow-fry until golden brown. Discard the oil and clean the wok or frying pan.

● Heat the remaining tablespoon of vegetable oil and the sesame oil in the wok until very hot. Stir-fry the garlic and ginger for 30 seconds. Add the bean sprouts, mushrooms and spring onions, then stir-fry for 2 minutes.

● Return the chicken to the wok, then add the stock, soy sauce and rice wine. Season with salt and black pepper. Bring to the boil and simmer for 1–2 minutes.

● Dissolve the cornflour in the water, then add to thicken the sauce. Pour the sauce over the noodles just prior to eating.

Crispy Egg Noodles with Pork Sauce

SERVES 4

Deep-fried noodles might seem like a strange idea, but, in fact, they are very popular throughout Asia, and make a crunchy and refreshing alternative to the more traditional boiled noodles.

225 g/8 oz dried thin egg noodles

vegetable oil for deep-frying

FOR THE SAUCE

225 g/8 oz lean pork, sliced on a slant into bite-sized pieces

1 tbsp light soy sauce

4 tbsp cornflour

8 large dried shiitake mushrooms, rinsed

4 tbsp vegetable oil

2.5 cm/1 in fresh ginger, peeled and finely chopped

2 cloves garlic, finely chopped

1 medium-sized onion, cut into bite-sized squares

4–5 small carrots, thinly sliced

225 g/8 oz Chinese cabbage, cut into bite-sized squares

salt and black pepper

600 ml/1 pt chicken stock

2 tbsp Chinese rice wine or dry sherry

2 tsp sugar

4 tbsp water

● Boil plenty of water in a saucepan and cook the noodles for 3 minutes. Rinse and drain. Separate and spread the noodles on a tray to dry.

● Heat a wok or saucepan a quarter full of oil and heat until very hot. Deep-fry the egg noodles in small batches until golden and crispy. Drain on absorbent kitchen paper. Set aside.

● Put the pork, soy sauce and 1 tablespoon of the cornflour in a bowl, mix and leave for 15 minutes. Soak the shiitake mushrooms in a cup of hot water for 15 minutes, then remove and quarter. Retain the water. Heat 2 tablespoons of the oil in a wok or frying pan and fry the pork for about 3 minutes. Set aside and clean the pan.

● Heat 2 tablespoons oil in the wok or pan until very hot. Fry the ginger and garlic for 30 seconds, before adding the onion, carrots, mushrooms and cabbage. Stir-fry for 2–3 minutes. Add in the meat, season with salt and pepper, and stir.

● Add the water used to soak the mushrooms, plus the chicken stock, rice wine and sugar; bring to the boil, checking the saltiness.

● Dissolve the remaining 3 tablespoons cornflour with the water, and add to thicken the sauce. Crush the crispy noodles lightly and divide onto four plates. Pour the sauce over the noodles and serve at once.

Crispy Egg Noodles
with Pork Sauce

Soft Egg Noodles with Minced Pork Sauce

SERVES 4

Toban djan *is a fiery Chinese chilli bean sauce available from most Chinese or oriental food departments in supermarkets. Here, the power of the chilli sauce is tempered by the addition of yellow bean sauce, leaving the dish pleasantly spicy rather than breathtakingly hot.*

300 g/10 oz dried or 400 g/ 14 oz fresh thin egg noodles

2 tsp sesame oil

FOR THE SAUCE

2 tbsp vegetable oil

1 large clove garlic, finely chopped

1-cm/½-in fresh ginger, peeled and finely chopped

2 spring onions, chopped

450 g/1 lb minced pork

3 tbsp yellow bean sauce

1 tbsp chilli bean sauce

2 tbsp Chinese rice wine or dry sherry

2 tbsp dark soy sauce

scant 250 ml/8 fl oz chicken stock, mixed to a paste with 2 tbsp cornflour

salt and black pepper

● Cook the egg noodles in plenty of boiling water for 3 minutes. Rinse and drain. Toss in the sesame oil and divide into four servings.

● Heat the vegetable oil in a pan and stir-fry the garlic, ginger and spring onions for 30 seconds. Add the minced pork and fry for 3–4 minutes.

● Add the yellow bean sauce, chilli sauce, rice wine and soy sauce, and stir for 1 minute.

● Add the mixture of stock and cornflour, and stir until the sauce thickens. Season with salt and black pepper to taste.

● Pour the sauce over the noodles, and serve.

Fried Noodles with Chicken, Vegetables and Gravy

SERVES 4

325 g/11 oz large flat rice noodles

120 ml/4 fl oz peanut or corn oil

1 tsp dark soy sauce

2 tbsp finely chopped garlic

200 g/7 oz boneless skinned chicken breasts cut lengthways into 1 cm/½ in thick slices

2 tbsp light soy sauce

2 tbsp sugar

1 tsp ground white pepper

1.5 litres/2½ pt chicken stock

425 g/15 oz kale or broccoli, cut into 1 cm/½ in pieces

1 tbsp cornflour, mixed with a little water

● Boil the noodles for 1 minute and drain well. Heat half the oil in a wok or pan, add the noodles and fry lightly for 1 minute. Add the black soy sauce, fry lightly for another minute. Drain off the oil and transfer the noodles to a plate.

● Heat the rest of the oil in the wok. Add the garlic and chicken, and fry lightly for 2 minutes. Stir in the white soy sauce, sugar, white pepper and then the chicken stock. Boil well for 3–5 minutes, add the kale, boil again for 1 minute and then add the cornflour. Boil for 1 minute and pour over the noodles.

● Serve accompanied by sliced fresh red chilli in vinegar, fish sauce, sugar and chilli powder, in separate bowls.

Chicken and Red Pepper in Egg Noodle Basket

SERVES 6

Noodle baskets are a Chinese innovation that appeal as much to the eyes as to the taste buds. You will need two small sieves about 13 cm/5 in across. This recipe works best with thinner noodles, and the oil needs to be hot to get nice, crisp, golden baskets. This recipe makes six baskets, which can be presented as a main dish or as a starter with less filling.

225 g/8 oz dried thin egg
   noodles

vegetable oil for deep-frying

FOR THE FILLING

6 tbsp vegetable oil

450 g/1 lb boneless chicken
   breasts, sliced diagonally into
   bite-sized pieces

salt and black pepper

3 tbsp cornflour

4 cloves garlic, finely chopped

1 cm/½ in fresh ginger, peeled
   and finely chopped

100 g/4 oz can bamboo shoots,
   sliced into matchsticks

⅔ red pepper, diced

4 spring onions, chopped

FOR THE SAUCE

150 ml/¼ pt chicken stock

1 tbsp Chinese rice wine or dry
   sherry

1 tbsp light soy sauce

2 tsp dark soy sauce

4 tsp tomato ketchup

½ tsp sugar

salt and black pepper

½ tbsp cornflour

2 tsp water

● Boil the egg noodles for 3 minutes. Rinse with water, drain, separate and dry on a tray lined with absorbent kitchen paper.

● Heat the oil in a deep pan to 180°C/350°F. Oil the sieves, one on the inside, the other on the outside. Line one sieve with egg noodles and press the other sieve down lightly to sandwich them. Carefully deep-fry the noodles with the two sieves holding them together until crispy and golden, about 3–4 minutes. Remove the noodle basket, taking care not to break it. Create five more baskets in the same way.

● Heat 4 tablespoons of oil in a wok or frying pan. Sprinkle the chicken with the salt and pepper, then

coat with the cornflour. Shallow-fry the chicken for 3–4 minutes, or until golden brown. Drain on absorbent kitchen paper until needed.

● Heat the remaining 2 tablespoons of oil in the wok, stir-fry the garlic and ginger, then add the bamboo, pepper and onion. Stir well. Add the chicken stock, rice wine, soy sauce, ketchup and sugar; bring to the boil, and season if required.

● Combine the cornflour and water, then add to thicken the sauce. Return the chicken to the pan and stir. Place the noodle baskets on six plates and fill with the chicken mixture. Serve at once.

Sweet Crisp-fried Noodles

SERVES 4–6

This is a Thai embellishment of a Chinese dish, and for complete success depends on the noodles being fried just right—so that they are both crisp and puffy when served to guests.

1.5 litres/2½ pt peanut or corn oil for frying

200 g/7 oz raw prawns, shelled and cut into 3 pieces

150 g/5 oz pork loin, cut into cubes the same size as prawn pieces

50 g/2 oz firm bean curd, cut into small rectangles

150 g/5 oz thin rice vermicelli noodles, soaked in cool water for 1 minute if dried and drained well

½ tbsp chopped garlic

½ tbsp chopped onion

50 g/2 oz palm sugar

2 tbsp white vinegar

1 tbsp marinated soya beans

1 tbsp fish sauce

175 g/6 oz bean sprouts

3 spring onions, cut into 4 cm/ 1½ in pieces

2 tbsp pickled garlic, sliced

2 fresh red chillies, cut into very thin strips

● Heat the oil in a pan or wok and fry the prawns and pork until brown and well cooked, about 10 minutes.

● Remove with a slotted spoon and drain on absorbent kitchen paper. Set aside.

● Add the bean curd to the hot oil and fry until brown, about 2 minutes. Remove with a slotted spoon and drain on absorbent kitchen paper. Add the noodles to the hot oil and brown lightly, about 4–5 minutes. Remove and drain well.

● Remove all the oil from the pan except for 2 tablespoons. Add the garlic and onion and fry gently for a minute; then add the cooked pork, prawns and bean curd, the sugar, vinegar, marinated soya beans and fish sauce. Fry until thick and sticky, about 7–10 minutes.

● Reduce the heat and add the noodles. Mix well for 1 minute, then transfer onto a large plate in a mound. Arrange the bean sprouts, spring onions, pickled garlic and chilli on top.

Crabmeat Sauce on Pan-fried Egg Noodles

SERVES 4

300 g/10 oz dried or 400 g/ 14 oz fresh medium egg noodles

4 tbsp vegetable oil

FOR THE CRABMEAT SAUCE

2 tbsp vegetable oil

1 clove garlic, finely chopped

1-cm/½-in fresh ginger, peeled and finely chopped

10 shiitake mushrooms, sliced

175 g/6 oz canned bamboo shoots, sliced into matchsticks

4 spring onions, chopped

350 g/12 oz canned crabmeat

600 ml/1 pt water

4 tsp light soy sauce

salt and black pepper

3 tbsp cornflour

4 tbsp water

● Cook the egg noodles in plenty of water for 4 minutes. Rinse, drain well and divide into four. Heat 1 tablespoon of oil in a wok or frying pan until very hot. Press one portion of the egg noodles down lightly into the pan and fry until lightly browned on both sides. Place on a chopping board and cut a crisscross pattern. Remove to a plate. Repeat.

● Heat 2 tablespoons of oil in the cleaned wok. Fry the garlic and ginger for 30 seconds. Add the shiitake mushrooms, bamboo shoots and spring onions, and stir-fry for 1–2 minutes. Add the crabmeat, water and soy sauce, and season. Bring to the boil, and simmer for 1 minute more.

● Dissolve the cornflour in the water and add to thicken the sauce. Stir. Pour over the noodles and serve immediately.

Fried Egg Noodles with Seafood Sauce

SERVES 4

If you have a taste for slightly richer flavours in this hearty dish, try adding eight fresh abalone to the ingredients.

300 g/10 oz dried egg noodles

4 tbsp vegetable oil

1 tbsp sesame oil

2.5 cm/1 in fresh ginger, peeled and finely chopped

2 cloves garlic, finely chopped

300 g/10 oz squid, cleaned

175 g/6 oz peeled large prawns

4 fish balls or chunks of imitation crabmeat, sliced

250 g/9 oz Chinese cabbage, cut into bite-sized squares

salt and white pepper

600 ml/1 pt chicken or vegetable stock

1 tbsp Chinese rice wine or dry sherry

3 tbsp cornflour

4 tbsp water

● Cook the egg noodles in boiling water for 3 minutes. Rinse and drain. Heat 1 tablespoon of the vegetable oil and sesame oil in a wok or frying pan. Stir-fry the noodles and put on four plates.

● Heat the remaining vegetable oil in the wok, and stir-fry the ginger and garlic for 30 seconds. Add the squid and prawns, stirring for 1–2 minutes or until the squid is cooked thoroughly.

● Add the slices of fish ball and Chinese cabbage, sprinkle with salt and white pepper, and stir. Add the stock and rice wine, and bring to the boil. Simmer for 1–2 minutes.

● Combine the cornflour and water, and add to thicken the sauce. Pour over the noodles, and serve.

Crabmeat Sauce on Pan-fried
Egg Noodles

Shredded Beef and Yellow Bean Sauce on Pan-fried Egg Noodles

SERVES 4

Yellow bean sauce is available in two varieties, one using whole beans, the other puréed. The texture differs, but the taste is identical. You can use either in this dish.

450 g/1 lb rump steak, shredded

1 tbsp light soy sauce

1 tbsp Chinese rice wine or dry sherry

1 tbsp cornflour

400 g/14 oz fresh or 300 g/ 10 oz dried thin egg noodles

4 tbsp vegetable oil

FOR THE SAUCE

2 tbsp vegetable oil

1 cm/½ in fresh ginger, peeled and finely chopped

10 cm/4 in piece leek, cut in half and shredded

175 g/6 oz bean sprouts

1 small green pepper, sliced

salt and black pepper

400 ml/14 fl oz chicken stock

6 tbsp whole or puréed yellow bean sauce

1 tbsp light soy sauce

2 tbsp cornflour

3 tbsp water

● Marinate the beef in the soy sauce, rice wine and cornflour for 30 minutes.

● Meanwhile, cook the egg noodles in a pan of boiling water for 3 minutes. Rinse, drain and divide into four. Heat 1 tablespoon of oil in a wok or frying pan. Take one quarter of the noodles and fry them like a pancake. Press the noodles to form a round and, when they have started to turn golden in colour, turn to fry on the other side. Remove to a chopping board, and cut twice in a crisscross pattern to make the noodles easier to eat. Put the noodles on a plate. Repeat the process with the other three portions.

● Heat remaining 2 tablespoons of oil in the wok or frying pan; stir-fry the ginger for 30 seconds. Add the leek, bean sprouts and green pepper, stirring each ingredient as you add it. Season.

● Add the chicken stock, yellow bean sauce and soy sauce; bring to the boil. Combine the cornflour and water, then add to the sauce, stirring until it thickens. Pour the sauce over the noodles before serving.

Fried Egg Noodles with Pork and Aubergine Sauce

SERVES 4

Oyster sauce is a frequently used Chinese flavouring. The surprising thing about oyster sauce is that you would find it difficult to find any trace of fishiness in its flavour. It will last for long periods if kept refrigerated, and is widely available from supermarkets.

400 g/14 oz fresh or 300 g/ 10 oz dried medium egg noodles

2 tbsp sesame oil

FOR THE SAUCE

300 g/10 oz boneless belly of pork, skinned and thinly sliced

2½ tbsp light soy sauce

2½ tbsp Chinese rice wine or dry sherry

4 tbsp cornflour

4 tbsp vegetable oil

2.5 cm/1 in fresh ginger, peeled and finely chopped

2 cloves garlic, finely chopped

350 g/12 oz aubergine, sliced into bite-sized pieces and soaked in salted water

4–5 small carrots, sliced

16 canned straw mushrooms, halved

2 spring onions, chopped into 2.5 cm/1 in lengths

black pepper

600 ml/1 pt chicken stock

2 tbsp oyster sauce

1 tsp sugar

4 tbsp water

● Marinate the pork in 1 tablespoon each of soy sauce, rice wine and cornflour. Set aside for 30 minutes, then heat 1 tablespoon of the vegetable oil in a wok or frying pan, and fry the pork for about 3 minutes until lightly browned. Clean the wok.

● Heat the rest of the vegetable oil in the wok until very hot and stir-fry the ginger and garlic for 30 seconds. Add the drained aubergine and carrots, and stir-fry for a further 1–2 minutes. Add the pork, mushrooms and spring onions, sprinkle black pepper and stir thoroughly.

● Add the chicken stock, rice wine, oyster sauce, soy sauce and sugar, and bring to the boil, simmering for 1 minute. Dissolve the cornflour in the water and add to thicken the sauce.

● Boil the egg noodles in plenty of water for 4 minutes. Rinse under running water, and drain. Heat the sesame oil in a wok, add the noodles and quickly stir-fry for a few minutes.

● Divide the egg noodles into four plates, pour the pork and aubergine sauce over them, then serve.

Chow Mein

SERVES 4

After chop suey, chow mein (which means 'fried noodles' in Chinese) must be the next most popular dish in Chinese restaurants. Try to get freshly made noodles from an Oriental food shop or department or Italian delicatessen, as they taste much better than dried ones. As a rough guide, allow at least 50 g/2 oz dried noodles per person, and double the weight if using fresh ones.

25 g/1 oz dried bean curd skin sticks

25 g/1 oz dried tiger lily buds

50 g/2 oz bamboo shoots

100 g/4 oz spinach or any other greens

225 g/8 oz dried egg noodles

2 spring onions, thinly shredded

3—4 tbsp oil

1 tsp salt

2 tbsp light soy sauce

2 tsp sesame seed oil

● Soak the dried vegetables overnight in cold water or in hot water for at least an hour. When soft, thinly shred both the bean curd skins and tiger lily buds.

● Shred the bamboo shoots and spinach leaves into thin strips.

● Cook the noodles in a pan of boiling water according to the instructions on the packet. Freshly made noodles will take only about half that time.

● Heat about half the oil in a hot wok or frying pan. While waiting for it to smoke, drain the noodles in a sieve. Add them with about half the spring onions and the soy sauce to the wok and stir-fry. Do not overcook or the noodles will become soggy. Remove and place them on a serving dish.

● Add the rest of the oil to the wok. When hot, add the other spring onions and stir a few times. Then add all the vegetables and continue stirring. After 30 seconds or so, add the salt and the remaining soy sauce together with a little water if necessary. As soon as the gravy starts to boil, add the sesame seed oil and blend everything well. Place the mixture on top of the fried noodles as a dressing.

Stir-fried Udon with Yakisoba Sauce

SERVES 4

675 g/1½ lb parboiled fresh or 400 g/14 oz dried *udon*

3 tbsp sunflower oil

225 g/8 oz minced pork

1 medium-sized onion, sliced

225 g/8 oz Chinese cabbage, sliced

½ red pepper, sliced

175 g/6 oz mange tout, cut in half

salt and black pepper

8 tbsp *yakisoba* or Japanese brown sauce

nori seaweed flakes (optional)

red pickled ginger (optional)

● Rinse the parboiled *udon* with very hot water or, if using dried *udon*, cook according to the instructions on the packet.

● Heat the oil in a wok or frying pan until very hot. Add the pork and fry for 3 minutes. Add the onion, Chinese cabbage, red pepper and mange tout, and stir-fry for about 3 minutes. Season with salt and pepper.

● Add the *udon* and *yakisoba* or Japanese brown sauce, and stir well. Divide the *udon* onto four plates. Sprinkle *nori* flakes and pickled ginger over the top, and serve.

Cellophane Noodles with Vegetables

SERVES 4

Chapchae is a colourful vegetable-packed noodle dish with a multitude of different textures. After the vegetables have been prepared, it is very quick to assemble and cook.

6 dried Chinese black mushrooms, soaked in hot water for 30 minutes

150 g/5 oz young fresh spinach leaves

2 Chinese cabbage leaves

3 shiitake or oyster mushrooms, thinly sliced

4 spring onions, white and green parts thickly sliced diagonally

1 small courgette, cut into fine strips

1 carrot, cut into fine strips

4 tbsp vegetable oil

1 tbsp sesame oil

3 cloves garlic, crushed

2 small fresh red chillies, seeded and cut into fine strips

50 g/2 oz cellophane (glass) noodles, soaked for 30 minutes and drained

1 tbsp soy sauce

1 tsp sugar

salt

● Drain the dried mushrooms, and cut out and discard the stalks and any hard parts. Thinly slice the mushroom caps.

● Add the spinach to a large saucepan of boiling water. Cover and quickly return to the boil. Boil for 2 minutes, then drain and rinse under running cold water. Drain well and squeeze out as much water as possible. Separate the leaves.

● Cut away and discard the curly outer part of the Chinese cabbage leaves, saving only the V-shaped core of the leaves. Cut this into fine strips, then mix with the spinach, dried and fresh mushrooms, spring onions, courgette and carrot until well mixed.

● Heat the vegetable oil and sesame oil in a deep frying pan. Add the garlic and chilli, and stir-fry for 10 seconds. Add the mixed vegetables and stir-fry for 3–4 minutes until the vegetables are tender but still crisp. Turn the heat to low and stir in the noodles, soy sauce, sugar and salt. Cook for 2 minutes, then serve.

Cellophane Noodles
with Vegetables

Stir-fried Egg Noodles with Vegetables

SERVES 4

450 g/1 lb fresh or 300 g/ 10 oz dried medium egg noodles

2 tbsp vegetable oil

2.5 cm/1 in fresh ginger, peeled and finely chopped

2 cloves garlic, finely chopped

300 g/10 oz Chinese cabbage, chopped into bite-sized squares

150 g/5 oz bean sprouts

1 small red pepper, cut into bite-sized squares

1 small green pepper, cut into bite-sized squares

16 straw mushrooms (canned), halved

1 tbsp sesame oil

2 spring onions, chopped

4 tbsp light soy sauce

1 tbsp dark soy sauce

1 tbsp sugar

salt and black pepper

● Boil plenty of water in a pan and cook the noodles for 3–4 minutes. Rinse under cold water, and drain.

● Heat the vegetable oil in a wok or frying pan, then stir-fry the ginger and garlic for 30 seconds. Add the Chinese cabbage, bean sprouts, red and green peppers and straw mushrooms. Stir each ingredient as you add it. Fry together for about 2 minutes.

● Add the sesame oil, noodles, spring onions, soy sauce and sugar, and stir well. Check the taste, adding salt and pepper if necessary. Put the noodles onto four plates and serve immediately.

Rice Vermicelli and Egg

SERVES 4

50 g/2 oz rice vermicelli

1 tsp black jack (see method)

2 cloves garlic, crushed

2 spring onions, chopped

salt and freshly ground black pepper

6 eggs, beaten

1 crisp lettuce, shredded

½ cucumber, sliced

2 tbsp pickled carrots or gherkins

1 tbsp chopped fresh mint

1 tbsp chopped fresh coriander

1 tbsp vegetable oil

FOR THE NUOC MAM GIAM SAUCE

1 clove garlic, roughly chopped

1 fresh red chilli, roughly chopped

1 tbsp fish sauce

1 tsp lemon juice or vinegar

1 tbsp sugar

● To prepare the rice vermicelli, bring a large saucepan of salted water to the boil. Add the rice vermicelli and boil, stirring constantly to separate the vermicelli, for about 3 minutes. It should be tender but firm to the bite. Drain in a colander and rinse under cold running water to stop the cooking.

● Make the *nuoc mam giam* sauce by grinding the garlic and chilli together in a blender or, better still, pound in a mortar with a pestle. Transfer to a small bowl. Stir in the other ingredients and mix thoroughly, making sure that the sugar dissolves.

● Make some black jack if you cannot find any in a supermarket. Heat 1 tablespoon sugar in a wok until it darkens. Remove from the heat and carefully stir in 2 tablespoons cold water. Do this extremely carefully or you will finish up with burns on your hand. Save whatever is left over in refrigerator.

● Combine the garlic, spring onions and black jack in a shallow dish and add salt and black pepper, and the eggs. Mix well and set aside to marinate.

● Set out the lettuce, cucumber, pickled vegetables, mint and coriander into four individual bowls. Top each portion of vegetables with cooked vermicelli.

● Heat the oil in a wok and pour in the egg mixture. Flip it over once and let it cool for 1–2 minutes in a dish. Cut into eight pieces. Put two pieces in each bowl and top each with 2 tablespoons *nuoc mam giam* sauce. The guests mix the contents of their bowls.

Crispy Rice Vermicelli with Shredded Chicken

SERVES 4

You will be surprised at the rapid expansion of the vermicelli the first time you try this dish. The key is to deep-fry it in small amounts to prevent it from overflowing from your wok or pan. The noodles are ready when they have lost their transparency and have turned white.

100 g/4 oz rice vermicelli

vegetable oil for deep-frying

FOR THE SAUCE

450 g/1 lb boneless chicken breasts, shredded

2 tbsp light soy sauce

2 tbsp Chinese rice wine or dry sherry

3 tbsp cornflour

4 tbsp vegetable oil

2.5 cm/1 in fresh ginger, peeled and finely chopped

8 shiitake mushrooms, shredded

12 water chestnuts, sliced

4 spring onions, chopped into 2.5 cm/1 in lengths

salt and black pepper

400 ml/14 fl oz chicken stock

1 tsp sesame oil

1 tbsp tomato ketchup

½ tsp sugar

3 tbsp water

6 lettuce leaves, rinsed and quartered

● Fill a wok or saucepan a quarter full of vegetable oil and heat to 180°C/350°F. Deep-fry the rice vermicelli in small batches at a time. It will puff up in seconds. Drain on absorbent kitchen paper.

● Marinate the chicken in 1 tablespoon each of the soy sauce, rice wine and cornflour for 30 minutes. Heat 2 tablespoons of oil in a wok or frying pan, and fry the chicken for 3–4 minutes. Set aside.

● Heat the remaining 2 tablespoons of the vegetable oil in the wok. Add the ginger and stir-fry for 30 seconds. Add the *shiitake* mushrooms, water chestnuts, spring onions and chicken, sprinkle with salt and pepper, then stir-fry for 1–2 minutes.

● Add the chicken stock, sesame oil, tomato ketchup, sugar and remaining soy sauce and rice wine, and bring to the boil. Combine the remaining cornflour and water, then add to thicken the sauce. Stir well.

● To serve, pile the lettuce leaves onto a small plate. Put the crispy vermicelli onto four individual plates, and pour the chicken sauce over the top. When you eat, take one lettuce leaf and wrap some noodles and chicken sauce together in a bundle, then pop it into your mouth.

Thai Sweet Crispy Rice Vermicelli

SERVES 4

Although it requires a little more time than most noodle dishes, this dish is well worth the extra effort. It is essential that it is served as soon as it is ready as the vermicelli will become mushy if left for very long.

50 g/2 oz rice vermicelli, slightly crushed

vegetable oil for deep-frying

1 tbsp vegetable oil

2 cloves garlic, finely chopped

2 shallots, finely chopped

12 large prawns with tails, peeled and deveined

4 tbsp raw cashew nuts

FOR THE SAUCE

3 tbsp palm or brown sugar

2 tbsp freshly squeezed lemon juice

1 tsp vinegar

1 tsp light soy sauce

2 tbsp tomato ketchup

½ tsp chilli powder

FOR THE GARNISH

2 lettuce leaves, halved

coriander leaves

2 small tomato wedges

● Heat the oil in a wok or saucepan until very hot. Deep-fry the vermicelli for a few seconds until they puff up and become white. Drain on absorbent kitchen paper.

● Heat the oil in the wok or frying pan. Add the garlic and shallots, and stir. Add the prawns and cashew nuts, and stir-fry for about 2 minutes.

● Add the sugar, lemon juice, vinegar, soy sauce, ketchup and chilli powder, and simmer until the sauce thickens. Take out the prawns, and set aside.

● Add the crispy vermicelli and coat with the sauce. Put the vermicelli on a bed of lettuce on four plates. Garnish each serving with three prawns, coriander and tomato wedges. Serve.

Crispy Vermicelli with Chicken and Mango

SERVES 4

A modern Chinese dish that looks set to become a great favourite. Fried vermicelli must be eaten as quickly as possible once it is ready.

150 g/5 oz rice vermicelli

vegetable oil for deep frying

1 egg white

3⅔ tbsp cornflour

450 g/1 lb boneless chicken
  breasts, sliced into bite-sized
  pieces

salt and black pepper

4 tbsp vegetable oil

2 cloves garlic, finely chopped

2.5 cm/1 in fresh ginger,
  peeled and finely chopped

3 celery sticks, sliced diagonally

1 medium-sized onion, cubed

1 mango, cut into bite-sized
  pieces

600 ml/1 pt chicken stock

2 tbsp Chinese rice wine or dry
  sherry

3 tbsp light soy sauce

2½ tbsp sugar

4 tbsp water

● Fill a wok or saucepan a quarter full of oil, and heat to 180°C/350°F. Deep-fry the vermicelli in small batches only a few seconds until they turn white. Drain on absorbent kitchen paper.

● Mix the egg white and 2 teaspoons of the cornflour in a bowl. Sprinkle the chicken with salt and black pepper, and coat thoroughly with the cornflour mixture.

● Heat 2 tablespoons of the oil in a wok or frying pan until very hot. Fry the chicken for about 2 minutes. When finished, discard the oil and clean the pan.

● Heat the remaining 2 tablespoons of oil in the wok. Stir-fry the garlic and ginger for 30 seconds before adding the celery, onion and chicken. Stir-fry for a further 2–3 minutes.

● Add the chicken stock, rice wine, soy sauce and sugar, then bring to the boil. Add the mango, season with salt and black pepper, and simmer for 1–2 minutes. Combine the remaining cornflour with the water, and add to thicken the sauce.

● Divide the crispy vermicelli onto four individual plates and lightly crush. Pour the sauce over the top just before serving.

Stir-fried Vermicelli with Vegetables

SERVES 4

1 tbsp vegetable oil

1 clove garlic, finely chopped

1 carrot, thinly sliced

4 tbsp water

50 g/2 oz Chinese cabbage, shredded

½ celery stick, shredded

3 tbsp chicken stock

1 tbsp oyster sauce

1 tbsp fish sauce or 1 tbsp light soy sauce and ½ tsp anchovy essence

1 level tsp sugar

freshly ground black pepper

100 g/4 oz rice vermicelli, soaked in warm water for 5 minutes and drained well

● Heat the oil in a wok over high heat and fry the garlic until golden brown. Add the carrot and stir-fry for 1 minute.

● Add all the remaining ingredients, except the vermicelli, stirring gently. Cook for 2 minutes.

● Add the vermicelli and toss to combine all the ingredients. Stir for 1 minute. Serve in a large serving dish.

Sweet and Sour Pork on Crispy Vermicelli

SERVES 4

Perhaps the most popular Chinese dish in the West. It is equally at home with noodles as with rice.

150 g/5 oz rice vermicelli

vegetable oil for deep-frying

450 g/1 lb boneless belly of pork, skinned and cut into bite-sized pieces

1 tbsp Chinese rice wine or dry sherry

1 tbsp light soy sauce

3 tbsp cornflour

1 egg white

4–5 carrots, cut at random into bite-sized pieces

2 tbsp vegetable oil

1 tbsp sesame oil

1 medium-sized onion, cut into bite-sized pieces

1 green pepper, cut into bite-sized squares

FOR THE SAUCE

400 ml/14 fl oz chicken stock

2⅔ tbsp sugar

100 g/4 oz tomato ketchup

1½ tbsp light soy sauce

4 tbsp Chinese rice wine or dry sherry

4 tbsp vinegar

salt and black pepper

2 tbsp cornflour

3 tbsp water

● Fill a wok or saucepan a quarter full of oil, and heat to 180°C/350°F. Separate the vermicelli into small portions. Deep-fry the vermicelli in several batches in the wok. They puff up in a few seconds, so be ready to take them out promptly. Drain on absorbent kitchen paper. Put the crispy vermicelli onto four individual plates, and lightly crush.

● Marinate the pork in the rice wine and soy sauce for 20–30 minutes. Mix 2 tablespoons of the cornflour, the egg white and 1 teaspoon of water together in a bowl, and coat the pork with the cornflour mixture. Deep-fry the meat for about 4–5 minutes, or until golden brown. Drain on absorbent kitchen paper, then crush lightly and arrange on four plates.

● Cook the carrots in a pan of boiling water for about 15 minutes, then set aside. Heat 1 tablespoon

vegetable oil and 1 tablespoon sesame oil in the wok or frying pan until very hot. Stir-fry the onion and green pepper for 1–2 minutes, add the carrots and stir for a further minute.

● Add the chicken stock, sugar, tomato ketchup, soy sauce and rice wine, and bring to the boil. Add the vinegar and season.

● Combine the cornflour with the water, and stir well into the sauce. Add the pork. Scoop the sweet and sour pork onto the noodles, and serve immediately.

Thai Fried Vermicelli with Red Curry Paste

SERVES 4

Thai red curry paste is a result of the influence of Indian and Chinese cooking. The result is a novel and interesting combination of heat and sourness.

225 g/8 oz rice vermicelli

3 tbsp vegetable oil

225 g/8 oz bean curd, diced

3 cloves garlic, chopped

100 g/4 oz canned bamboo
   shoots

175 g/6 oz bean sprouts

100 g/4 oz spring greens or
   fresh spinach

2 tbsp Thai red curry paste

6 tbsp fish sauce

3 tbsp light soy sauce

1 tbsp palm or brown sugar

FOR THE GARNISH

coriander leaves

4 lime wedges

● Soak the rice vermicelli in warm water for 3–5 minutes. Rinse and drain.

● Heat the oil in a wok or frying pan, and fry the bean curd until golden brown. Add the garlic, bamboo shoots, bean sprouts and greens or spinach, stirring each time you add the ingredients.

● Add the red curry paste, fish sauce, soy sauce and brown sugar; then stir well. Add the vermicelli and stir until the noodles are well coated with sauce.

● Put the vermicelli onto four plates and garnish with coriander leaves and lime wedges. Serve at once.

Singapore Spicy Noodles

SERVES 4

The return home of itinerant Chinese over the years has resulted in a gradual increase in the popularity of curried dishes in China, especially in the south-western provinces. Although the origins of this dish lie in India, Singapore has been the cultural melting pot where most Chinese migrants have come into contact with Indian cuisine.

225 g/8 oz rice vermicelli

4 tbsp vegetable oil

2 cloves garlic, finely chopped

1 cm/½ in fresh ginger, peeled and finely chopped

1 red chilli, chopped

100 g/4 oz peeled prawns

6 small squid, cleaned and sliced

175 g/6 oz bean sprouts

100 g/4 oz spinach

225 g/8 oz Chinese barbecued pork, thinly sliced

2 eggs, beaten

3 spring onions, roughly chopped

⅔ tsp salt

a pinch of chilli powder

black pepper

2–3 tsp hot curry powder

1 tbsp light soy sauce

2 tsp sugar

150 ml/¼ pt chicken stock

- Soak the rice vermicelli in warm water for 3 minutes, or according to the instructions on the packet. Rinse with cold water, and drain.

- Heat 3 tablespoons of the oil in a wok or frying pan until very hot. Add the garlic, ginger and red chilli, and stir-fry for 30 seconds.

- Add the prawns and squid, and stir for another minute. Then add the bean sprouts, spinach and pork, and stir-fry for 1–2 minutes.

- Make a well in the centre, add the beaten egg and scramble lightly. Quickly add the remaining tablespoon of oil and the rice vermicelli, and mix all the ingredients well.

- Add the spring onions, salt, chilli powder, black pepper, curry powder, soy sauce, sugar and chicken stock. Stir until the sauce is absorbed. Put the noodles onto four plates, and serve at once.

Pork and Pineapple in Honey Sauce on Crispy Vermicelli

SERVES 4

Another dish with a sweet and sour theme. The honey and pineapple complement the pork very well.

150 g/5 oz rice vermicelli

vegetable oil for deep-frying

450 g/1 lb boneless belly of pork, skinned and cut into bite-sized pieces

salt and black pepper

1 tbsp Chinese rice wine or dry sherry

2½ tbsp cornflour

2 tbsp water

FOR THE SAUCE

2 tbsp vegetable oil

2.5 cm/1 in fresh ginger, peeled and finely chopped

1 clove garlic, finely chopped

2 medium-sized onions, cubed

4–5 carrots, sliced

4 pineapple rings (canned), chopped

salt and black pepper

400 g/14 oz chicken stock

2 tbsp honey

2 tsp brown sugar

1 tsp light soy sauce

4 tbsp pineapple juice (from the can)

2 tbsp cornflour mixed with 3 tbsp water

- Fill a wok or saucepan a quarter full of vegetable oil and heat to 180°C/350°F. Deep-fry the rice vermicelli in small batches. They will puff up in a few seconds. Drain on absorbent kitchen paper.

- Sprinkle the pork with salt and black pepper, then marinate in the rice wine for 15 minutes. Combine the cornflour and water, and coat the pork with the paste. Deep-fry the pork until lightly browned. Drain on absorbent kitchen paper.

- Heat the oil in the cleaned wok or frying pan. Stir-fry the ginger and garlic for 30 seconds. Add the onions and carrots, and stir-fry for about 2 minutes. Add the pineapple, lightly sprinkle with salt and pepper, and stir.

- Add chicken stock, honey, sugar, soy sauce and pineapple juice. When the sauce is boiling, add the combined cornflour and water to thicken the sauce. Add the pork and mix.

- Put the crispy vermicelli onto four plates, then lightly crush. Pour on sauce, and serve immediately.

Indonesian Fried Vermicelli with Squid

SERVES 4

Squid is a great favourite throughout Asia, and nowhere more so than in Indonesia. The flavourings used here are distinct, but without being so powerful as to cloak the taste of the seafood.

225 g/8 oz rice vermicelli

3 tbsp vegetable oil

2.5 cm/1 in fresh ginger, peeled and finely chopped

4 shallots, chopped finely

8 small squid, cleaned and sliced

4–5 small carrots, cut into matchsticks

150 g/5 oz bean sprouts

100 g/4 oz fresh spinach, chopped

1 small red chilli, chopped

1 tsp ground paprika

3 tbsp light soy sauce

salt and black pepper

4 tomato wedges

sliced cucumber

● Soak the rice vermicelli in warm water for 3 minutes, or according to the instructions on the packet. Rinse and drain. Heat 2 tablespoons of the oil in a wok or frying pan, and stir-fry the ginger and shallots for 30 seconds. Add the squid and stir until the squid turns white.

● Add the carrots, bean sprouts, spinach and chilli, and stir for 1–2 minutes. Add the remaining tablespoon of oil, the vermicelli, paprika and soy sauce, and stir well.

● Taste, and add the salt and black pepper if required. Put the vermicelli onto four plates, and garnish with the tomato wedges and sliced cucumber. Serve at once while still hot.

Stir-fried Udon with Seafood

SERVES 4

*Stir-frying coaxes maximum flavour out of the seafood ingredients, and gives the **udon** noodles a smooth, slippery texture in this filling dish.*

400 g/14 oz dried or 550 g/ 1¼ lb parboiled fresh *udon*

3 tbsp sunflower oil

175 g/6 oz squid, cleaned and sliced

175 g/6 oz peeled prawns

4 spring onions, chopped roughly

175 g/6 oz bean sprouts

300 g/10 oz *shimeji* mushrooms, roots cut off and separated, or 15 *shiitake* mushrooms, sliced

4 tsp dried *wakame* seaweed, soaked in hot water

4 tbsp bonito flakes

4 tbsp Japanese soy sauce

salt and black pepper

● Boil plenty of water in a large pan and add the *udon*. Cook for 7–15 minutes for dried, or 3 minutes for parboiled fresh *udon*. Rinse with cold water and drain well.

● Heat the oil in a wok or frying pan until very hot. Stir-fry the squid and prawns for 2 minutes. Add the spring onions, bean sprouts, mushrooms and *wakame*, and stir-fry for about 2 minutes.

● Add the *udon, bonito* flakes and soy sauce, and stir. Season with salt and pepper. Stir for another minute, and serve at once.

Chilled Udon with Fermented Soya Beans

SERVES 4

Fermented soya beans, or **natto,** *are not to everyone's taste. Even in Japan, where it originated,* **natto is very much a 'love it or hate it' food, despite it being a nutritious source of protein.**

400 g/14 oz dried or 550 g/ 1¼ lb parboiled fresh *udon*

500 ml/18 fl oz dipping stock, chilled

FOR THE TOPPING

6 okra

salt

225 g/8 oz Japanese fermented soya beans (*natto*)

10 g/¼ oz *bonito* flakes

1 spring onion, chopped

1 tsp hot prepared mustard

4 tsp Japanese soy sauce

½ sheet *nori* seaweed, shredded

● Remove the tiny hairs on the okra; the easiest way to do this is to first sprinkle the salt over the okra, then roll them over on a chopping board. Blanch in the boiling water for 1 minute, then drain and chop.

● Mix the okra, *natto, bonito* flakes, spring onion, mustard and soy sauce together in a bowl.

● Bring plenty of water to the boil in a large pan and add the *udon*. Cook according to the instructions on the packet. Rinse and drain. Divide the *udon* into four bowls.

● Pile the *natto* mixture on top of the *udon*. Gently pour the dipping stock into each bowl, sprinkle with *nori*, then serve immediately.

Stir-fried Udon with Miso Sauce

SERVES 4

This is another nouveau *stir-fried* udon *dish. The* **udon** *are coated in a salty sauce, making a very appetizing fast meal.*

400 g/14 oz dried or 550 g/
1¼ lb parboiled fresh *udon*

225 g/8 oz green cabbage

225 g/8 oz fresh green beans

3 tbsp sunflower oil

225 g/8 oz rump steak, sliced
on a slant into bite-sized
pieces

1 small red pepper, chopped
into bite-sized pieces

10 shiitake mushrooms,
quartered

a pinch of salt and chilli powder

2 tbsp red *miso* paste

2 tbsp Japanese soy sauce

2 tbsp *mirin*

1 spring onion, chopped

● Boil plenty of water in a large pan and cook dried *udon* for 7–15 minutes or parboiled fresh *udon* for 3 minutes. Rinse and drain.

● Blanch the cabbage leaves and green beans for 2 minutes. Rinse under cold water. Cut the cabbage leaves into bite-sized pieces, and halve the fresh green beans.

● Heat the oil in a wok or frying pan until very hot. Add the beef and fry for 2–3 minutes. Add the cabbage, green beans and shiitake mushrooms, and sprinkle on salt and chilli powder. Stir-fry for another 2–3 minutes.

● Mix the *miso*, soy sauce and *mirin* together in a bowl. Add the *udon* and *miso* mixture to the pan, and stir-fry for about 1 minute. Put the *udon* onto four plates. Sprinkle with chopped spring onions, and serve.

Chilled Soba with Deep-fried Mackerel

SERVES 4

Mackerel is one of the great mainstays of the Japanese diet. It is not only eaten raw as **sushi** *and* **sashimi**, *but is incorporated in many Japanese cooked dishes, as here.*

400 g/14 oz dried *soba*

500 ml/18 fl oz dipping stock

FOR THE TOPPING

vegetable oil for deep frying

8 tbsp flour

120 ml/4 fl oz water

450 g/1 lb mackerel, gutted,
filleted and cut into 4 pieces
per person

350 g/12 oz white radish,
peeled and grated

2 spring onions, chopped

alfalfa sprouts to garnish

● Heat the vegetable oil in a saucepan to 180°C/350°F. Mix the flour and water lightly in a bowl to a lumpy consistency to make a batter, then dip the mackerel pieces in. Deep fry for about 3 minutes, or until golden brown.

● Bring plenty of water to the boil in a large saucepan. Add the *soba* and cook for 5–6 minutes. Drain and rinse well under cold running water. Drain again, and then divide into four portions.

● Place four pieces of deep-fried mackerel in each bowl. Place the grated white radish in the centre and garnish with the spring onions and sprouts. Pour the dipping stock over the top, and serve immediately.

Stir-fried Udon with Miso Sauce

Cold Noodles with Vegetables

SERVES 4

This is a vegetarian version of kuksu, *a popular noodle dish, which is served surrounded by small bowls of condiments, relishes and side dishes, the most important of which are soy sauce, Korean chilli powder and spicy pickles. If you are unable to buy son* myon *noodles, use vermicelli and cook according to the directions on the packet.*

3 tbsp soy sauce

1 tbsp sugar

1 tbsp sesame oil

5 dried Chinese black mushrooms, soaked for 30 minutes in hot water

100 g/4 oz bean sprouts

450 g/1 lb young fresh spinach leaves, stalks removed

450 ml/¾ pt vegetable stock

225 g/8 oz *son myon* noodles or vermicelli

green part of 1 spring onion, diagonally sliced

1 tbsp crushed toasted sesame seeds

very small pinch of Korean chilli powder or cayenne pepper mixed with paprika

● Mix together 2 tablespoons of the soy sauce, 2 teaspoons of the sugar and the sesame oil.

● Drain the mushrooms and cut out and discard the stalks and any woody parts. Thinly slice the caps.

● Bring 750 ml/1¼ pt water to the boil in a saucepan and add the remaining sugar. Put the bean sprouts into a strainer and lower the strainer into the water. Return the water to the boil and cook the bean sprouts for 20 seconds. Remove the strainer of bean sprouts from the water and rinse them under running cold water. Leave to drain completely.

● Add the spinach to the saucepan and boil for 2 minutes or until wilted. Drain, rinse under running cold water and drain again.

● Pour the stock into a saucepan. Add the remaining soy sauce and bring to the boil. Add the noodles and boil for about 3 minutes until just tender. Quickly remove the noodles from the water using a slotted spoon and put into a warm serving dish. Add the spinach and mushrooms to the liquid and heat through, then quickly remove. Season with the soy sauce mixture and pile onto the noodles. Keep warm.

● Heat the bean sprouts in the stock, then remove and quickly season with the remaining soy sauce mixture. Place on top of the spinach and mushrooms. Pour the remaining stock around the noodles and sprinkle with the spring onion, sesame seeds and a little chilli powder or cayenne mixed with paprika. Serve immediately while still hot.

Chilled Udon with Five Toppings

SERVES 4

Dried, medium-sized udon is preferable for this dish if you can obtain them. A nonstick omelette pan will help you to prepare the egg sheets, which should resemble thin pancakes.

400 g/14 oz dried or 550 g/ 1¼ lb parboiled fresh *udon*

500 ml/18 fl oz dipping stock, chilled

FOR THE TOPPINGS

2 eggs

2 tsp sugar

1 tbsp vegetable oil

8 okra

salt

4 tsp dried *wakame* seaweed, soaked in warm water and drained

8 chunks imitation crabmeat, torn into shreds

handful alfalfa sprouts

● Boil plenty of water in a pan. Add the *udon* and cook 8–15 minutes for dried or 3 minutes for fresh noodles. Rinse and put the *udon* into four shallow bowls. Set aside.

● Mix the eggs and sugar together in a bowl. Heat the oil in a frying pan, and pour in a third of the egg mixture. When the egg starts bubbling, turn it over. (The method is the same as for making thin pancakes.) Repeat this and make two more egg sheets. Let them cool, then cut in half and then into shreds.

● Sprinkle the salt over the okra on a chopping board, then roll the okra with salt to remove the fine down. Boil some water in a pan, and blanch the okra for just a minute before chopping finely.

● Arrange the shredded egg, okra, *wakame*, crabmeat shreds and sprouts in separate groups on top of the *udon* portions.

● Just before eating, pour the chilled dipping stock over the noodles.

Chilled Udon with Aubergine and Miso Sauce

SERVES 4

Miso *sauce is a versatile ingredient, which can be paired with almost any vegetable you care to mention. Here it is combined with aubergine, which should be soaked in salted water to remove any bitterness.*

500 ml/18 fl oz *dashi* stock

4 tbsp vinegar

400 g/14 oz dried or 550 g/ 1¼ lb parboiled fresh *udon*

FOR THE TOPPING

1 tbsp sunflower oil

2 cloves garlic, finely chopped

1 cm/½ in fresh ginger, peeled and finely chopped

8 spring onions, chopped

225 g/8 oz aubergine, cut into matchstick-sized pieces and soaked in salted water

1 small green pepper, cut into matchstick-sized pieces

a pinch of salt

4 tbsp *miso* paste

1 tbsp Japanese soy sauce

2 tsp sugar

3 tbsp Japanese rice wine

● Mix the *dashi* stock and vinegar, then refrigerate. Heat the oil in a frying pan. Add the garlic, ginger and spring onion, and fry for 1 minute.

● Add the aubergine, green pepper and salt, and stir-fry for 4–5 minutes, or until the aubergine is softened. Add the *miso* paste, soy sauce, sugar and wine, and stir well. Set aside.

● Boil plenty of water in a pan and add the *udon*. Cook for 4–5 minutes for fresh or 8–15 minutes for dried *udon*, or according to the instructions on the packet. Rinse with cold water. Drain and divide into four bowls.

● Place the aubergine mixture on the *udon* and pour the stock over the top. Serve immediately.

Chilled Soba with Shredded White Radish

SERVES 4

Japanese **daikon** *is the ideal ingredient for this dish. The white radish, known as* **mooli,** *makes an acceptable stand-in or, failing that, try ordinary radishes.*

400 g/14 oz dried *soba*

350 g/12 oz white radish, peeled and shredded

handful alfalfa sprouts

1 sheet *nori* seaweed, shredded

750 ml/1¼ pt dipping stock

FOR THE GARNISH

2 spring onions, chopped

2.5 cm/1 in fresh ginger, grated

2 *myoga* (optional), shredded

● Bring plenty of water to the boil in a large saucepan. Add the *soba* and cook for 5–6 minutes. Rinse and cool in cold water. Drain.

● Mix the *soba, daikon* and sprouts well in a bowl. Divide into individual serving bowls and sprinkle with the *nori.*

● Serve with the chilled dipping stock and garnishes on a separate small dish.

Chilled Soba with Nameko Mushrooms

SERVES 4

A light, refreshing lunch or part of a dinner that is quickly prepared and easily digested.

400 g/14 oz dried *soba*

approx 400 g/14 oz canned *nameko* mushrooms

350 g/12 oz white radish, peeled and grated

½ sheet *nori* seaweed, shredded

500 ml/18 fl oz dipping stock, chilled

● Boil plenty of water in a large pan and add the *soba*. Cook for 5–6 minutes, or according to the instructions on the packet. Rinse with plenty of cold water and drain well. Divide the *soba* into four bowls.

● Mix the mushrooms and white radish together in a bowl. Pile them onto the *soba* and sprinkle with the *nori*. Gently pour the chilled dipping stock over the top just before serving.

Chilled Soba with Soured Plum Sauce

SERVES 4

The bite of the soured plums in the dipping stock gives an extra zest to this cold noodle dish.

4 spring onions, sliced

3 boneless chicken breasts

12 okra

salt

400 g/14 oz dried *soba*

FOR THE SOUR PLUM SAUCE

4 large soured plums, seeded and chopped finely

500 ml/18 fl oz dipping stock

● Soak the sliced spring onions in cold water until ready for use. Cook the chicken in boiling water for about 15 minutes, or until cooked. When cooled, pull the meat into small strips with your fingers.

● Sprinkle the okra with salt, then roll each on a chopping board to remove the fine hairs. Cook for around 1 minute in boiling water, then cut into 1-cm/½-in slices.

● Put the soured plums into a mortar. Add a little stock and grind roughly into a thin paste. Return the mixture to the dipping stock, then chill in the refrigerator until needed.

● Bring plenty of water to the boil in a large saucepan. Add the *soba* and cook for 5–6 minutes. Drain and rinse well under cold running water. Drain again. Mix the *soba* with the spring onions in a bowl, then divide into four portions.

● Add the chicken and okra. Pour the soured plum dipping stock over the top, and serve at once.

Chilled Soba
with Nameko Mushrooms

Chilled Egg Noodles with Chicken and Peanut Sauce

SERVES 4

A well-loved Chinese noodle dish. It can be prepared with any type of peanut butter, depending on your preference for smooth or crunchy.

450 g/1 lb boneless chicken breasts

450 g/1 lb fresh thin egg noodles

2 tsp sesame oil

2.5-cm/1-in piece cucumber, thinly sliced diagonally, then cut into long matchsticks

FOR THE PEANUT SAUCE

8 tbsp peanut butter

6 tbsp sugar

4 tbsp vinegar

5 tbsp chicken stock

3 tbsp light soy sauce

1 tbsp dark soy sauce

4 tsp sesame oil

3—4 tsp chilli oil

- Put the chicken in a large pan of water. Bring to the boil and simmer for 20 minutes, skimming off the scum from time to time. The poaching water can be put toward making stock. When the chicken is cooled, shred with your fingers or with a knife.

- Mix the peanut butter, sugar, vinegar, chicken stock, soy sauce, sesame oil and chilli oil together in a bowl.

- Bring a large pan of water to the boil and add the noodles. Cook for 3 minutes, rinse and drain. Toss the noodles in the sesame oil, then arrange them on four individual plates.

- Place a quarter of the shredded chicken and cucumber onto each serving of noodles. Pour the sesame sauce over the top of the shredded chicken, then serve immediately.

Chilled Egg Noodles with Chicken and Pepper Salami

SERVES 4

Pepper salami is not an authentic topping, but it really goes well with chilled noodles.

450 g/1 lb fresh or 350 g/ 12 oz dried thin egg noodles

1 tbsp sesame oil

FOR THE SAUCE

generous 250 ml/8 fl oz chicken stock

120 ml/4 fl oz light soy sauce

4 tbsp sugar

120 ml/4 fl oz vinegar

4 tsp sesame oil

2 tbsp squeezed ginger juice

FOR THE TOPPING

2 boneless chicken breasts

2 eggs, beaten

2 tsp sugar

1 tbsp vegetable oil

13 cm/5 in piece cucumber, thinly sliced diagonally and cut into long matchsticks

8 slices pepper salami, cut into long matchsticks

4 tsp red pickled ginger (optional)

4 tsp toasted sesame seeds

- Boil plenty of water in a pan and add the noodles. Cook for 3 minutes, then rinse with cold water. Drain, then toss the noodles in 1 tablespoon sesame oil. Arrange on four shallow dishes.

- To prepare the sauce, heat the stock, soy sauce and sugar in a pan, and simmer for 3 minutes. Turn off the heat and add the vinegar, 4 teaspoons sesame oil and the ginger juice. Mix well before refrigerating.

- Boil the chicken in a pan for about 15–20 minutes. Let it cool, then pull into shreds with your fingers or a knife. Set aside. Keep the water in the pan as stock for another use.

- Mix the beaten egg and sugar together in a bowl. Heat 1 teaspoon of oil in an omelette pan and pour a third of the egg mixture into it. When the egg is half set, turn it over. Repeat this to make two more thin omelettes, using fresh oil each time. When the omelettes are cooled, cut them in half and shred.

- Arrange the chicken, egg, cucumber and pepper salami on the noodles. Put the red pickled ginger (if using) on top, and sprinkle with the sesame seeds. Pour the chilled sauce over prior to eating.

Chilled Somen with Pork

SERVES 4

An invigorating combination of chilled noodles with pork and broccoli stir-fried in a hot sauce.

400 g/14 oz *somen*

500 ml/18 fl oz dipping stock

FOR THE TOPPING

1½ tbsp vegetable oil

4 cloves garlic, sliced

350 g/12 oz lean pork, sliced on a slant into bite-sized pieces

1 tbsp *mirin*

2½ tbsp soy sauce

2 tsp chilli bean sauce

8 small broccoli florets

pinch of salt

● Heat the oil in a pan, then add the garlic and fry for about 1 minute. Add the meat and fry for a further 2–3 minutes. Then add the *mirin*, soy sauce and chilli bean sauce, and stir-fry for 2 minutes.

● Bring plenty of water to the boil in a large saucepan. Add the *somen* and cook for 1–2 minutes. Drain and rinse well under cold running water. Drain again, then divide into four portions.

● Meanwhile, bring a pan of water to the boil, add a pinch of salt and boil the broccoli for 1–2 minutes. Drain and rinse.

● Place the meat and broccoli in the four bowls. Serve immediately after pouring in the dipping stock.

Chilled Somen with Sesame Dipping Stock

SERVES 4

Fried vegetables make the chilled **somen** *more nutritious and filling, while the combinaton of the sesame sauce and dipping stock imparts a rich and delicate flavour. It is a good idea to make the dipping stock in advance; it will keep in the refrigerator for a few days.*

400 g/14 oz *somen*

FOR THE SESAME DIPPING STOCK

500 ml/18 fl oz dipping stock

1 cm/½ in fresh ginger, peeled and squeezed for the juice

5 tbsp sesame sauce

2 spring onions, finely chopped

FOR THE TOPPING

sunflower oil for frying

350 g/12 oz aubergine, thinly sliced and soaked in salted water

4 large shiitake mushrooms

1 small green pepper

4 *myoga* (optional), finely chopped

● Heat the dipping stock, and add the ginger juice and sesame sauce. When it comes to the boil, add the spring onions and turn off the heat. Refrigerate.

● Bring plenty of water to the boil in a pan and add the *somen*. When the water returns to the boil, add 120 ml/4 fl oz cold water. The second time the water comes back to the boil, the *somen* will be ready. Rinse with the cold water and drain. Put the *somen* onto four plates.

● Heat 2 tablespoons of oil in a wok or frying pan. Fry the aubergine slices first, then the mushrooms and pepper. If you need more oil, add another 2 tablespoons.

● Place the aubergine, mushrooms and pepper beside the *somen*, and, if using, put the sliced *myoga* on top. Serve immediately with small bowls of the sesame dipping stock.

Chilled Somen with Pork

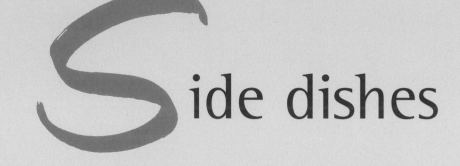

Side dishes

Use these recipes to create a wide range of side dishes. Allow the
flavour of fresh ingredients to dominate the dish by combining one
or two vegetables with herbs or seasoning, but taking care not to let
the flavour become too overpowering. The dishes include satisfying
rice, grain and bean ensembles, as well as light vegetable mixtures.
The secret to successful Asian dishes is that the ingredients should
be perfectly fresh and only lightly cooked, and all the recipes
include tips on cooking times and presentation.

Five-spice Bean Curd

SERVES 4

4 cakes bean curd

3 tbsp light soy sauce

2 tbsp dark soy sauce

1 tsp salt

1 tbsp white or brown sugar

3 tbsp rice wine or dry sherry

2–3 spring onions

2–3 slices fresh ginger

2 tsp five-spice powder

● Place the bean curd in a saucepan and cover with cold water. Bring to the boil, cover and cook over a high heat for 10 minutes. By then the bean curd will resemble a beehive in texture.

● Reduce the heat and add the soy sauces, salt, sugar, wine, spring onions, ginger, and five-spice powder. Bring to the boil gently under a cover and simmer for 30 minutes. Turn off the heat and leave to cool.

● Remove the bean curd and cut it into small slices or strips. Serve them either on their own or as part of a mixed hors d'oeuvre.

Szechwan Bean Curd

SERVES 4

10 g/¼ oz dried wood ears or
  dried Chinese mushrooms

3 cakes bean curd

1–2 leeks or 2–3 spring onions

3 tbsp oil

1 tsp salted black beans

1 tbsp chilli bean paste

2 tbsp rice wine or dry sherry

1 tbsp light soy sauce

1 tsp cornflour mixed with
  1 tbsp cold water

Szechwan pepper, freshly
  ground to garnish

● Soak the wood ears in water for 20–25 minutes, rinse them clean, discard any hard roots and then drain. If you use dried mushrooms, they should be soaked in hot or warm water for at least 30–35 minutes. Squeeze them dry, throw out the hard stalks and cut into small pieces, retaining the water for later.

● Cut the bean curd into 1 cm/½ in square cubes. Blanch them in a pan of boiling water for 2–3 minutes, remove and drain.

● Cut the leeks or spring onions into short lengths.

● Heat the oil in a hot wok until it smokes and stir-fry the leeks or spring onions and the wood ears or mushrooms for about 1 minute. Add the salted black beans, crush them with the scooper or spatula and blend well. Now add the bean curd, the chilli bean paste, rice wine or sherry and soy sauce and continue stirring to blend. Add a little water and cook for 3–4 minutes more.

● Finally add the cornflour and water mixture to thicken the gravy. Serve hot with freshly ground Szechwan pepper as garnish.

Fu-yung Bean Curd

SERVES 4

In most Chinese restaurants, fu yung means 'omelette', but strictly speaking, it should mean scrambled egg whites with a creamy texture.

1 cake bean curd

4 egg whites

1 cos lettuce heart

50 g/2 oz green peas

1 spring onion, finely chopped

½ tsp fresh ginger, finely chopped

1 tsp salt

1 tbsp cornflour mixed with 2 tbsp water

4 tbsp milk

oil for deep-frying

1 tsp sesame seed oil

● Cut the bean curd into long, thin strips and blanch in a pan of salted boiling water to harden. Remove and drain.

● Lightly beat the egg whites. Add the cornflour mixture and milk.

● Wash and separate the lettuce heart. If you use frozen peas, make sure they are thoroughly thawed.

● Wait for the bean curd to cook and then coat with the egg whites, cornflour and milk mixture.

● Heat the oil in a wok or deep-fryer until it is very hot. Turn off the heat and let the oil cool a little before

adding the bean curd coated with the egg whites and cornflour mixture. Cook for about 1–1½ minutes and then scoop out with a slotted spoon and drain.

● Pour off the excess oil leaving about one tablespoon in the wok. Increase the heat and stir-fry the lettuce heart with a pinch of salt. Remove and set aside on a serving dish.

● Heat another tablespoon of oil in the wok and add the finely chopped spring onion, and ginger followed by the peas, salt and a little water. When the mixture starts to boil, add the bean curd strips. Blend well, add the sesame seed oil and serve on the bed of lettuce.

Green Peppers and Deep-fried Bean Curd

SERVES 4

1 tbsp groundnut or corn oil

2 thin slices fresh ginger, peeled

4 large leaves Chinese cabbage, cut into 2.5 cm/1 in lengths

1 large green pepper, seeded and sliced

salt

oil for deep-frying

4 x 2.5 cm/1 in square cakes bean curd, drained and cut into rectangles, 3 per cake (use kitchen paper to drain)

FOR THE SAUCE

1 tsp potato flour

5 tbsp mushroom water

2 tbsp oyster sauce

2 tsp thick soy sauce

2 tbsp vegetable oil

1 clove garlic, finely chopped

2 spring onions, cut into 2.5 cm/1 in sections, white and green parts separated

4 large dried Chinese mushrooms, soaked, squeezed and cut into thin strips (water to be reserved)

● Prepare the sauce by mixing together the potato flour, mushroom water, oyster saucer and soy sauce. Heat a wok and add 2 tablespoons oil and swirl around. Add the garlic, letting it sizzle and then add the white spring onion and then the Chinese mushrooms. Stir for about 30 seconds and pour in the potato flour mixture. Lower the heat and continue to stir until the sauce thickens. Remove from heat.

● Heat 1 tablespoon oil in a wok over a high heat until it starts to smoke. Add the ginger and when it starts to sizzle, add the cabbage and green pepper. Toss for about 30 seconds. Season with a little salt, lower the heat and continue to cook, covered for a further 2 minutes. Remove and put into an earthenware pot or saucepan.

● Now half fill the wok with oil, heat to 200°F and lower the bean curd into the oil, one piece at a time, and deep-fry for 4 minutes or until golden brown, turning over from time to time. Remove with a large strainer and drain on absorbent kitchen paper.

● Lay the bean curd on the cabbage in the pot and add the green spring onion. Heat the sauce and pour this over the bean curd. Heat the pot for 2 minutes and serve.

Japanese-style Omelette

SERVES 2

Often served for breakfast in Japan, this dish requires a little more skill and patience than a Western omelette, but the delicious result is well worth the extra effort. It is essential to use a nonstick frying pan.

2 eggs	½ tbsp *dashi*
½ tbsp caster sugar	pinch of salt
½ tbsp soy sauce	vegetable oil, for frying

● Break the eggs into a bowl, add the sugar, soy sauce, *dashi* stock and salt and mix well. Heat the oil in a nonstick frying pan over a low heat. Pour one-quarter of the egg mixture into the frying pan.

● Just before the surface of the egg starts to get firm, carefully flip over the edge and roll up. Store on one side of the pan.

● Holding up the rolled omelette with a fish slice or chopstick, add a second quarter of the egg mixture, making sure that it spreads beneath the already cooked roll.

● Again, just before the egg begins to firm, roll around the completed roll and keep on the other side of the pan. Repeat this process with the two remaining quarters of egg mixture. Cool before cutting into 2.5 cm/1 in lengths. When serve as a side dish, sprinkle with soy sauce.

Stuffed Omelette

SERVES 4

This is a rapidly made lunchtime dish, more easily available in markets than in restaurants.

4 tbsp peanut or corn oil

100 g/4 oz minced pork

3 tbsp tomatoes, finely diced

3 tbsp peas

2 tbsp finely diced green pepper

2 tbsp finely diced onion

½ tbsp sugar

1 tsp fish sauce

¼ tsp ground white pepper

¼ tsp black soy sauce

3 eggs, beaten

FOR THE GARNISH

3 tbsp coriander leaves

finely sliced red chilli

● Heat half the oil in a frying pan or wok over high heat and fry the pork lightly for about 2 minutes. Add all the remaining ingredients, except for the eggs, and the rest of oil. Fry until fairly thick, about 5–8 minutes, then set aside.

● Heat a shallow nonstick or good omelette pan, add a drop of the remaining oil and pour in enough egg to thinly cover the base. Brown the omelette lightly on both sides, flipping over half-way through cooking. Place a spoon of pork mixture in the centre, fold two opposite sides toward the centre and then fold in the remaining two sides so that it resembles a square.

● Flip onto a serving plate and repeat until all the egg and pork mixture is used up. Garnish with coriander leaves and finely sliced red chilli. Serve accompanied by rice.

Hot and Sour Cabbage

SERVES 4

675 g/1½ lb white cabbage

10 Szechwan peppercorns

5 small dried red chillies

3 tbsp oil

2 tbsp soy sauce

1½ tbsp vinegar

1½ tbsp sugar

1½ tsp salt

1 tsp sesame seed oil

● Choose a round, pale green cabbage with a firm heart—never use loose-leafed cabbage. Wash in cold water and cut the leaves into small pieces the size of a matchbox. Cut the chillies into small pieces. Mix the soy sauce, vinegar, sugar and salt to make the sauce.

● Heat the oil in a preheated wok until it starts to smoke. Add the peppercorns and the red chillies and a few seconds later the cabbage. Stir for about 1½ minutes until it starts to go limp.

● Pour in the prepared sauce and continue stirring for a short while to allow the sauce to blend in. Add the sesame seed oil just before serving. This dish is delicious both hot and cold.

Simmered Cabbage

SERVES 2

Japanese cabbage has a soft texture. It is best to discard, or use for another recipe, the tougher, outer leaves of the cabbage and use only the inner leaves for this dish. Try not to overcook the cabbage or it will become limp. The leaves should be cooked but still have some crunch left in them.

185 g/6½ oz cabbage leaves, cut into 2.5 cm/1 in squares

2 rashers of unsmoked bacon, cut into 2.5 cm/1 in lengths

300 ml/½ pt *dashi* stock

2 tsp soy sauce

2 tsp vegetable oil

● Heat the oil in a pan and fry the bacon over a low heat until cooked.

● Add the cabbage and fry, stirring, for 2 minutes.

● Add the *dashi* stock and soy sauce. Simmer, covered for 10 minutes, or until the cabbage has softened. Stir occasionally. Serve as a side dish.

Chinese Cabbage and Mushrooms

SERVES 4

6–8 dried Chinese mushrooms

450 g/1 lb Chinese cabbage
   leaves

3 tbsp oil

1 tsp salt

1 tsp sugar

1 tbsp soy sauce

1 tsp sesame seed oil

● Soak the mushrooms in warm water for about 20 minutes. Squeeze them dry and discard the stalks. Keep the water. Cut each mushroom in half or into quarters depending on the size. Cut the cabbage leaves into pieces about the size of a large postage stamp.

● Heat the oil in a wok, add the cabbage and the mushrooms, and stir-fry until soft. Add the salt, sugar and soy sauce, and cook for a further 1½ minutes. Mix in some of the water in which the mushrooms were cooked and the sesame seed oil.

Spicy Cabbage—Szechwan Style

SERVES 4

450 g/1 lb white cabbage

2 tsp salt

3–4 dried hot chillies, soaked, and finely chopped

3 spring onions, finely chopped

2 tsp finely chopped fresh ginger

2 tbsp sesame seed oil

2 tbsp sugar

4 tbsp water

2 tbsp vinegar

● Discard the outer tough leaves of the cabbage and cut the tender heart into thin slices. Sprinkle with salt and let stand for 3–4 hours. Pour off the excess water and dry the cabbage thoroughly. Place it in a bowl or a deep dish.

● Heat the sesame seed oil in a pan until very hot. Add the finely chopped chillies, spring onions and ginger. Stir for a few seconds and then add the sugar and water. Continue stirring to dissolve the sugar. Add the vinegar and bring the mixture to the boil.

● Remove the pan from the heat and allow the sauce to cool slightly before pouring it over the cabbage. Cover the bowl or plate and leave to stand for 3–4 hours before serving.

Salted Cabbage and Cucumber

SERVES 2

This quickly prepared side dish makes a superb partner to fresh cooked white rice. A sharp knife will help you with the cucumber.

100 g/4 oz green cabbage (preferably the softer, inner leaves)

4 cm/1½ in cucumber, halved lengthways

1 tsp salt

1 small red chilli, seeded and finely chopped

● Cut the stalks out of the cabbage leaves, then slice the leaves lengthways, before cutting into 1 cm/½ in widths. Slice the two halves of the cucumber finely.

● Put the cabbage and cucumber in a bowl and sprinkle with the salt. Leave for 30 minutes, then squeeze out any excess liquid from the vegetables with your hands.

● Add the chilli and mix well. Leave for 5 minutes.

● Sprinkle with soy sauce just before serving.

Carrot Fritters

SERVES 2–4

Any of the dipping sauces in this book can be served to accompany these carrot slices.

2 carrots, thinly sliced diagonally

4 tbsp plain flour

1 large egg, beaten

vegetable oil for frying

sesame dipping sauce

● Coat the carrot slices lightly and evenly in the flour, then dip in beaten egg.

● Heat a 5-mm/¼-in layer of oil in a frying pan. Add the carrot slices and fry in a single layer until golden brown on both sides. Using a slotted spoon, transfer the carrot slices to absorbent kitchen paper to drain. Serve hot with a dipping sauce.

Salted Cabbage and Cucumber

Braised Chinese Broccoli

SERVES 4

450 g/1 lb Chinese broccoli

3 tbsp oil

1 tsp salt

1 tsp sugar

1 tbsp soy sauce

● Trim off the tough leaves of the broccoli and blanch the rest in slightly salted boiling water until soft. Remove and strain.

● Heat a wok until hot. Add the oil and wait until it starts to smoke. Stir-fry the broccoli with the salt and sugar for 1½–2 minutes.

● Remove and arrange neatly on a long serving dish. Pour on the soy sauce and serve.

Stir-fried Broccoli

SERVES 4

250 g/9 oz broccoli

3 tbsp oil

1 tsp salt

1 tsp sugar

2 tbsp water

● Cut the broccoli into small pieces and remove the rough skin from the stalks.

● Heat the oil in a wok until hot and stir-fry the broccoli for about 1–1½ minutes.

● Add the salt, sugar and water and cook for a further 2 minutes. Serve hot.

Chinese Leaves and Cockles in Mustard and Soy Sauce

SERVES 2

Cockles are not very common in Japan, and clams are usually used for this dish, but cockles go so well with the other ingredients that they make an excellent and economical substitute. You can use fresh cockles or those sold in jars or cans.

150 g/5 oz Chinese leaves	1 tsp mustard
4 spring onions	1 tsp *mirin*
½ tbsp soy sauce	90 g/3½ oz cockles, drained

● Bring a saucepan of water to the boil, add the Chinese leaves and cook for 3 minutes. Then, add the spring onions and boil for a further 2 minutes. Drain and rinse lightly with cold water, then squeeze out any excess water. Cut into 2.5 cm/1 in lengths.

● Mix the soy sauce, mustard and *mirin* in a large bowl. Add the Chinese leaves, spring onions and cockles and mix.

Stir-fried Greens

SERVES 4–6

Possibly the fastest dish to cook in Thailand, this is properly made with the water plant variously known as morning glory, swamp cabbage or water convolvulus.

3 tbsp peanut or corn oil

325 g/11 oz morning glory leaves and stalks, cut into 10 cm/4 in lengths

120 ml/4 fl oz chicken stock

2 tbsp marinated soya beans

1 tbsp chopped garlic

● Heat the oil in a wok or pan until very hot. Add all the ingredients at once (watch for splattering) and stir-fry for about 2 minutes.

● Serve accompanied by Boiled Rice Soup with Chicken (page 74) or steamed rice.

Spinach with Bonito Flakes and Soy Sauce

SERVES 2

Fresh spinach is vital to make this delicious, nutritious dish. Take care not to overcook the spinach or you will destroy its vitamins.

225 g/8 oz spinach leaves, rinsed and drained

pinch of salt

large pinch of *bonito* fish flakes

2–3 tbsp soy sauce

● Boil the spinach in salted water for about 2 minutes or until lightly cooked.

● Drain and quickly rinse with cold water. Holding the leaves in a bunch at the stalk, squeeze out any excess water.

● Cut the bunch into 2.5 cm/1 in lengths. Place in a small bowl or dish and sprinkle with the *bonito* flakes, followed by a drizzle of soy sauce.

Crispy 'Seaweed'

SERVES 4

You might be surprised to learn that the very popular 'seaweed' served in Chinese restaurants is, in fact, green cabbage! Choose fresh, young spring greens with pointed heads. Even the deep green outer leaves are quite tender. This recipe makes an ideal garnish for a number of dishes, particularly cold appetizers and buffet dishes.

675–800 g/1½–1¾ lb young cabbage

600 ml/1 pt oil for deep-frying

1 tsp salt

1 tsp sugar

● Wash and dry the cabbage leaves and shred them with a sharp knife into the thinnest possible shavings. Spread them out on absorbent kitchen paper or put in a large colander to dry thoroughly.

● Heat the oil in a wok or deep-fryer. Before the oil gets too hot, turn off the heat for 30 seconds. Add the cabbage shavings in several batches and turn the heat up to medium high. Stir with a pair of cooking chopsticks. When the shavings start to float to the surface, scoop them out gently with a slotted spoon and drain on absorbent kitchen paper to remove as much of the oil as possible. Sprinkle the salt and sugar evenly on top and mix gently. Serve cold.

Green Beans with Crushed Garlic

SERVES 4

1 tbsp vegetable oil

1 onion, finely chopped

4 cloves garlic, finely chopped

3 large green chillies, seeded and sliced thinly diagonally

1 tsp ground coriander

½ tsp ground cumin

2 ripe tomatoes, blanched, skinned, seeded and chopped roughly

450 g/1 lb green beans, washed, trimmed and halved

½ tsp sugar

pinch of salt

2 tbsp chopped fresh coriander

● Heat the oil in a wok and stir-fry the onion, garlic and green chillies, stirring constantly for 2 minutes.

● Add the coriander and cumin, stir vigorously and add the chopped tomatoes and beans. Stir and cover the wok for 5 minutes. Remove the cover, add the sugar and a little salt, and stir again for 1 minute. Add the coriander, stir for 30 seconds and transfer to a warm serving dish.

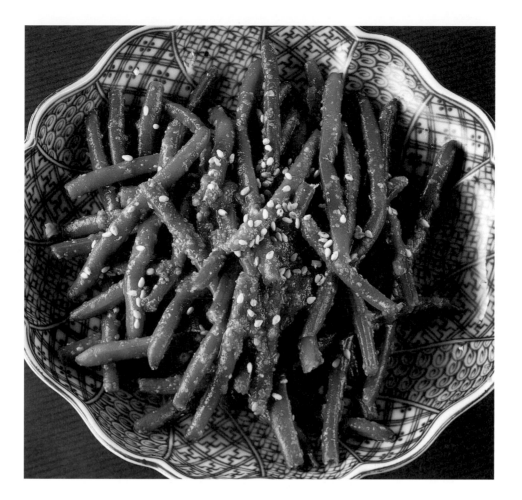

Green Beans in a Sesame Dressing

SERVES 2

Sesame enjoys a reputation for being a healthy food in Japan, and both black and white sesame are common ingredients in Japanese cuisine. To toast the seeds for this recipe, simply put them in a frying pan without oil then heat while stirring until the seeds have puffed up and you can smell the distinctive aroma of sesame.

175 g/6 oz frozen whole green
   beans

pinch of salt

FOR THE DRESSING

1 tbsp toasted sesame seeds

1 tbsp caster sugar

⅔ tbsp *dashi* stock

½ tbsp *miso* paste

1 tbsp soy sauce

● Boil the beans in a pan of boiling water for 5 minutes or until tender.

● Finely grind the sesame seeds in a pestle and mortar or in a coffee grinder. Add the sugar, *dashi, miso* paste and soy sauce and mix together well.

● Toss the green beans in the sesame dressing and serve as a side dish.

Fried Beans with Pork

SERVES 4

You can use fresh beans as a substitute for the sator beans, but really the basis for this quintessentially southern dish is the strange flavour of the latter. The recipe is included here for authenticity and just in case you are able to find the real sator beans in a Thai delicatessen or greengrocer.

3 fresh yellow or green chillies, chopped

1 tbsp chopped garlic

½ tsp shrimp paste

2 tbsp peanut or corn oil

150 g/5 oz pork loin (or chicken or prawns), cut into thin strips

250 g/12 oz fresh sator or broad beans

½ tsp fish sauce

½ tsp sugar

½ tsp lime or lemon juice

● Pound the chillies and garlic together with a pestle and mortar or in a blender to a fine paste. Mix with the shrimp paste.

● Heat the oil in a pan or wok. Add the chilli-garlic mixture, then add the pork and stir-fry for 3 minutes. Add the beans and all the remaining ingredients, plus 3 tablespoons of water if using broad beans, then fry until the beans are cooked, about 10 minutes—they should be quite firm.

● Serve accompanied by rice.

Beans with Mixed Grains

SERVES 4

The combination of red and black beans and three different grains makes this a colourful dish with many different tastes and textures.

50 g/2 oz kidney beans, soaked overnight

50 g/2 oz black kidney beans, soaked overnight

200 g/7 oz short-grain rice, washed and soaked

2 tbsp millet

2 tbsp pearl barley

● Drain the beans and add to a saucepan of boiling water. Cover and bring to the boil. Boil for 10 minutes, then simmer for 1–1½ hours until just tender; the time will depend on the beans. Drain them, reserving the water.

● Drain the rice. Put all the ingredients in a saucepan. Add 400 ml/14 fl oz of the bean cooking water and bring to the boil. Stir once, then cover and turn the heat to very low. Cook for 20–30 minutes, without removing the lid even once. Turn the heat up as high as it will go for 30 seconds, then turn it off, or remove the pan from the heat. Leave, without removing the lid at all, for 10–15 minutes before serving.

Spicy Aubergine and Tomatoes

SERVES 4

1 aubergine

2 cloves garlic, thinly sliced

2 red peppers

1 medium tomato, thinly sliced

1 tbsp fish sauce

2 tbsp rice wine

1 tbsp olive oil

● Preheat the oven to 200°C/400°F/Gas Mark 6.

● Cut slits all over the aubergine and push a slice of garlic into each slit. Place the aubergine and the whole peppers in a baking dish and bake, turning regularly to brown evenly, for 45 minutes or until all are very soft. Set aside to cool.

● Cut the stalk off the aubergine and, with your fingers or a paring knife, peel off the skin. Shred the flesh, discarding any big lumps of seeds. Place the aubergine in a bowl with the garlic slices.

● Peel the skin off the peppers and discard the stalks, cores and seeds. Cut into long, thin strips and add to the aubergine. Add the tomato, fish sauce, rice wine and olive oil, and toss to mix well.

Deep-fried Aubergines

SERVES 4

These deep-fried aubergine pieces can be served as a first course, or to eat with drinks; in which case, supply cocktail sticks for spearing the aubergine slices.

2 aubergines, thinly sliced on the diagonal

salt

plain flour for coating

Korean chilli powder, or cayenne pepper mixed with paprika

1–1½ tbsp chopped fresh coriander

1 large egg, beaten

oil for deep-frying

sesame dipping sauce to serve

● Put the aubergine slices into a colander. Toss with salt and leave for 30 minutes. Rinse the aubergine slices, drain and dry thoroughly on absorbent kitchen paper.

● Season some plain flour with salt and chilli powder, or cayenne and paprika, to taste, and add the coriander. Toss the aubergine slices in the flour to coat evenly, then dip in the beaten egg. Let the excess egg drain off.

● Heat a deep-fat fryer half-filled with oil to 180°C/350°F. Add the aubergine slices in batches so the pan is not crowded and fry until golden brown. Drain on absorbent kitchen paper. Serve hot with sesame dipping sauce.

Spicy Aubergine and Tomatoes

Aubergine with Szechwan 'Fish Sauce'

SERVES 4

Szechwan 'fish sauce' is commonly served with fish, but it does not have any fish in it.

450 g/1 lb aubergine

4–5 dried red chillies

oil for deep frying

3–4 spring onions, finely chopped

1 slice fresh ginger, peeled and finely chopped

1 clove garlic, finely chopped

1 tsp sugar

1 tbsp soy sauce

1 tbsp vinegar

1 tbsp chilli bean paste

2 tsp cornflour, mixed with 2 tbsp water

1 tsp sesame seed oil

● Soak the dried red chillies for 5–10 minutes, cut them into small pieces and discard the stalks.

● Peel the aubergine, discard the stalks and cut them into diamond-shaped chunks.

● Heat the oil in a wok and deep-fry the aubergine for 3½–4 minutes or until soft. Remove with a slotted spoon and drain.

● Pour off the oil and return the aubergine to the wok with the red chillies, spring onions, ginger and garlic. Stir a few times and add the sugar, soy sauce, vinegar and chilli bean paste. Continue stirring for 1 minute.

● Finally add the cornflour and water mixture, blend well and garnish with the sesame seed oil. Serve either hot or cold.

Fried Aubergine and Green Pepper in Sweet Miso Sauce

SERVES 2

Autumn is the season for aubergines in Japan, when greengrocers stock their shelves with the numerous varieties available. Japanese aubergines vary greatly in length, though none possess the girth of those typically produced in the United States.

2 tbsp sesame oil

1 medium onion, peeled and cut into bite-sized pieces

225 g/8 oz aubergine, cut into bite-sized pieces and soaked in water

½ green pepper, cut into bite-sized pieces

FOR THE SWEET *MISO* SAUCE

3 tbsp *miso* paste

2 tbsp caster sugar

2 tbsp water

2 tbsp *mirin*

● Heat 1 tablespoon of sesame oil in a pan and fry the onion for 3–4 minutes. Add the rest of the oil and the aubergine and continue to fry for 3–4 minutes. Add the green pepper and fry until the aubergine has softened.

● Mix together the *miso* paste, sugar, water and *mirin* in a bowl, then add to the pan, stirring for 1–2 minutes. Serve hot as a side dish.

Fried Courgette with Sesame Seeds

SERVES 4

A coating of sesame seeds gives courgette an interesting nutty flavour and a crisp texture. This picture also shows Deep-fried Aubergines (page 338), Carrot Fritters (page 326).

550 g/1¼ lb small courgettes, cut diagonally into 5 mm/ ¼ in thick slices

salt

seasoned plain flour

1 large egg, beaten

sesame seeds

vegetable oil for frying

sesame dipping sauce or vinegar dipping sauce

● Put the courgettes into a colander. Toss generously with salt and leave for 30 minutes.

● Rinse the courgettes well and dry thoroughly with absorbent kitchen paper. Toss the courgettes in seasoned plain flour to coat evenly, then dip in beaten egg. Finally, coat in sesame seeds.

● Heat a thin layer of oil in a wide frying pan. Add the courgette slices in a single layer and fry for 3–4 minutes on each side until golden on the outside.

● Using a slotted spoon, transfer to absorbent kitchen paper to drain. Serve hot with dipping sauce.

Stir-fried Courgettes

SERVES 4

450 g/1 lb courgettes

3 tbsp oil

2 tsp salt

1 tsp sugar

2 tbsp water

● Do not peel the courgettes; just trim off the ends. Split the courgettes in half lengthways and cut each length diagonally into diamond-shaped chunks.

● Heat the oil in a wok. When the oil starts to smoke, put the courgettes in and stir-fry for about 30 seconds. Add the salt and sugar and cook for a further 1–1½ minutes, adding a little water if necessary. Serve hot.

Courgettes with Beef

SERVES 2–4

This is a simple but very tasty dish that can be served in traditional Korean manner with **kimchis**, *rice, salads and vegetables, or Western-style with a green vegetable or salad.*

4 small courgettes, cut
    diagonally into 5 mm/¼ in
    thick slices

salt

225 g/8 oz lean minced beef

2 tbsp vegetable oil

2 spring onions, white and
    green parts very thinly sliced

1 tbsp sugar

1 tbsp soy sauce

½–1 tsp chilli powder

FOR THE MARINADE

1 spring onion, white and green
    part very thinly sliced

2 cloves garlic, crushed

1½ tbsp soy sauce

1 tbsp sesame oil

2.5 cm/1 in piece fresh ginger,
    finely chopped

1 tbsp toasted sesame seeds

freshly ground black pepper

FOR THE GARNISH

toasted sesame seeds

● Put the courgettes in a colander and sprinkle generously with salt. Toss together and leave for 30 minutes. Meanwhile, mix all the marinade ingredients together. Add the minced beef and leave for about 30 minutes.

● Rinse the courgettes well and dry thoroughly with absorbent kitchen paper. Heat the vegetable oil in a large frying pan over a fairly high heat. Add the beef and marinade, and fry, stirring to break up the lumps, for about 1 minute or until the beef changes colour.

● Lightly stir in the courgettes, then add the remaining ingredients. Cook for 2 minutes, stirring lightly. Lower the heat and continue to stir for another minute until the courgettes are tender but still retain some bite.

● Serve sprinkled with toasted sesame seeds.

Courgettes with Beef

Stir-fried Mange Tout and Corned Beef

SERVES 2

It has been said many times that the Japanese are a nation of innovators, and this dish illustrates the Japanese habit of absorbing a foreign influence into their culture and then enhancing it with a distinctive Japanese flavour. The mange tout should be firm, so be careful not to overcook them.

150 g/5 oz mange tout, rinsed
   and trimmed

1 tbsp vegetable oil

100 g/4 oz canned corned
   beef, chopped

1 tsp soy sauce

salt and freshly ground black
   pepper

● Boil the mange tout in salted boiling water for 3 minutes, then drain.

● Heat the oil in a frying pan. Add the corned beef and stir-fry for 5 minutes over a medium heat.

● Add the mange tout, sprinkle with salt and pepper and stir-fry for another 5 minutes. Sprinkle with the soy sauce. Serve hot as a side dish.

Stir-fried Bean Sprouts with Green Peppers

SERVES 4

450 g/1 lb fresh bean sprouts

1 small green pepper, cored and seeded

1–2 spring onions

3 tbsp oil

1 tsp salt

1 tsp sugar

● Wash and rinse the bean sprouts in cold water, discarding the husks and other bits and pieces that float to the surface.

● Cut the green pepper into thin shreds. Cut the spring onions into short lengths.

● Heat the oil in a hot wok until smoking. Add the spring onions and green pepper, stir a few times, and then add the bean sprouts. Continue stirring.

● After about 30 seconds, add salt and sugar, and stir a few times more. Do not overcook, or the sprouts will become soggy. Serve hot or cold.

Stir-fried Green Peppers, Tomatoes and Onions

SERVES 4

1 large or 2 small green peppers

1 large or 2 small firm tomatoes

1 large or 2 small onions

3 tbsp oil

1 tsp salt

1 tsp sugar

● Core and seed the green peppers and peel the onions. Cut all the vegetables into uniform slices.

● Heat the oil in a wok and wait for it to smoke. Add the onions and stir-fry for 30 seconds. Add the green peppers and continue cooking for 1 minute. Add the tomatoes, salt and sugar and cook for 1 minute more. Serve hot or cold.

Stir-fried Lettuce

SERVES 4

1 large Cos lettuce

3 tbsp oil

1 tsp salt

1 tsp sugar

● Discard the tough outer leaves of the lettuce. Wash the remaining leaves well and shake off the excess water. Tear the larger leaves into two or three pieces.

● Heat the oil in a wok or large saucepan. Add the salt followed by the lettuce leaves and stir vigorously as though tossing a salad. Add the sugar and continue stirring. As soon as the leaves become slightly limp, transfer them to a serving dish and serve.

Shredded Cabbage with Red and Green Peppers

SERVES 4

450 g/1 lb white cabbage

1 green pepper

1 red pepper

3 tbsp oil

1 tsp salt

1 tsp sesame seed oil

● Thinly shred the cabbage. Core and seed the green and red peppers and thinly shred them.

● Heat the oil in a wok until hot. Add the cabbage and the peppers and stir-fry for 1–1½ minutes. Add the salt and stir a few more times. Add the sesame seed oil to garnish and serve either hot or cold.

Stir-fried Green and Red Peppers

SERVES 4

1 large or 2 small green
    peppers, cored and seeded

1 large or 2 small red peppers,
    cored and seeded

3 tbsp oil

1 tsp salt

1 tsp sugar

● Cut the peppers into small, diamond-shaped pieces; if you use one or two orange peppers, the dish will be even more colourful.

● Heat the oil in a hot wok or frying pan until it smokes. Spread the oil with a spatula so that the cooking surface is well greased. Add the peppers and stir-fry until each piece is coated with oil. Add the salt and sugar.

● Continue stirring for about 1 minute and serve if you like your vegetables crunchy and crisp. If not, you can cook them for another minute or so until the skin of the peppers becomes slightly wrinkled. Add a little water if necessary during the last stage of cooking.

Stuffed Chillies

SERVES 4

Touching chillies can make your hands, particularly any cuts or bruises, sting, so it is a good idea to wear fine rubber gloves when preparing this dish.

450 g/1 lb lean minced pork

1 clove garlic, finely chopped

1 cm/½ in piece fresh ginger, finely chopped

4 spring onions, finely chopped

2 tsp crushed toasted sesame seeds

2–3 tsp soy sauce

16–20 large fresh red chillies

seasoned plain flour for coating

1 large egg, beaten

vegetable oil for frying

vinegar dipping sauce to serve

● Mix the pork, garlic, ginger, spring onions, sesame seeds and soy sauce together very well.

● Cut the chillies in half lengthways and remove the seeds. Break off small pieces of the meat mixture to fill the chillies. Form into torpedo shapes and use to stuff the chillies, packing the meat stuffing in firmly.

● Roll the stuffed chillies in seasoned flour to give an even coating, then dip in beaten egg.

● Heat 4 cm/1½ in layer of oil in a frying pan. Add the chillies in batches and fry for 4–5 minutes on each side until golden brown and cooked through. Remove from the oil with a slotted spoon and drain on absorbent kitchen paper. Serve hot with vinegar dipping sauce.

Spiced Sweet Potato Slices

SERVES 4

Traditionally, these potato slices are served with a dipping sauce but they can also be served as a vegetable accompaniment.

2 sweet potatoes, cut diagonally into 5 mm/¼ in thick slices

salt

plain flour for coating

chilli powder

1 large egg, beaten

vegetable oil for frying

vinegar dipping sauce to serve

● Add the sweet potato slices to a saucepan of boiling salted water and cook for about 5 minutes. Drain well and dry on absorbent kitchen paper.

● Season the flour with chilli powder, then coat the sweet potato slices evenly in the seasoned flour. Dip in beaten egg.

● Heat a thin layer of vegetable oil in a wide frying pan. Add a layer of sweet potato slices and fry for about 4 minutes on each side.

● Transfer to absorbent kitchen paper to drain. Serve hot with vinegar dipping sauce.

Stuffed Chillies

Braised Bamboo Shoots

SERVES 4

If possible, use the 'Evergreen' brand slender bamboo shoots, a speciality from Kiangsi province in southeast China; they need only be drained and they are ready to cook. The next best are 'maling' bamboo shoots from Shanghai. If you can get winter bamboo shoots, so much the better.

450 g/1 lb slender bamboo shoots

3 tbsp oil

2 tbsp rice wine or dry sherry

1 tbsp sugar

2 tbsp light soy sauce

1 tbsp dark soy sauce

2 tsp sesame seed oil

● Drain the water from the bamboo shoots and slice each shoot lengthways into thin strips.

● Heat the oil in a hot wok or frying pan, add the bamboo shoots and stir-fry until well covered with oil. Add the wine, sugar and both soy sauces and stir.

● Braise for about 3–4 minutes or until almost all the liquid has evaporated. Add the sesame seed oil and serve either hot or cold.

Stir-fried 'Four Treasures'

SERVES 4

Like stir-fried mixed vegetables, the ingredients are especially selected to achieve a harmonious balance of colours, textures and flavours.

3–4 tbsp wood ears, dried	3–4 tbsp oil
225 g/8 oz broccoli	1½ tsp salt
175 g/6 oz bamboo shoots	1 tsp sugar
100 g/4 oz oyster mushrooms	1 tsp sesame seed oil

● Soak the wood ears in water for 15–20 minutes. Rinse until clean. Discard the hard roots if any and cut the extra large ones into smaller pieces.

● Wash the broccoli and cut into whole florets. Do not discard the stalks; peel off the tough outer skin and cut them into small pieces.

● Cut the bamboo shoots into slices, or, if using winter bamboo shoots, cut them into roughly the same size pieces as the broccoli stalks.

● Wash and trim the mushrooms. Do not peel if using fresh ones. Canned oyster mushrooms are ready to cook; just drain off the water.

● Heat a wok or large frying pan over high heat until really hot. Add the oil and wait for it to smoke. Then stir the oil with a spatula so that most of the surface of the wok is well greased.

● Add the broccoli first and stir until well coated with oil. Then add the bamboo shoots and mushrooms and continue stirring for about 1 minute. Add the wood ears, salt and sugar and stir for another minute or so. The vegetables should produce enough natural juices to form a thick gravy. If the contents in the wok are too dry, add a little water and bring to the boil before serving. The sesame seed oil should not be added until the very last minute.

Stir-fried Leeks with Wood Ears

SERVES 4

The mild, subtle flavour of the wood ears is a great accompaniment to leek. Do not overcook the leeks—they should stay crunchy.

3–4 tbsp wood ears

450 g/1 lb leeks

3 tbsp oil

1 tsp salt

1 tsp sugar

1 tsp sesame seed oil

● Soak the wood ears in water for 20–25 minutes, rinse well and discard the hard roots if any. Drain.

● Wash the leeks and cut them diagonally into 5-cm/2-in chunks.

● Heat the oil in a hot wok or frying pan. Use your spatula to spread the oil so that most of the surface is well greased. When the oil starts to smoke, add the leeks and wood ears, and stir-fry for about 1 minute. Add the salt and sugar and continue stirring. Wet with a little water if necessary. Add the sesame seed oil to garnish and serve hot.

Mushrooms with Chicken and Vegetables

SERVES 3–4

Mushrooms of many different types are very popular in Korea. The most widely available of these in the West are both fresh and dried shiitake (when dried they are more commonly known as dried Chinese black mushrooms), dried wood ear, which have little flavour but a pleasing texture and attractive appearance, and stone mushrooms.

175 g/6 oz chicken breast, cut into strips

3 cloves garlic, crushed

4 tbsp soy sauce

2 tsp sesame oil

freshly ground black pepper

vegetable oil for frying

450 g/1 lb shiitake or oyster mushrooms, thinly sliced

1 red pepper, cut into thin strips

1 courgette, thinly sliced diagonally

4 spring onions, white and some green parts thinly sliced diagonally

FOR THE GARNISH

fresh coriander leaves

● Mix the chicken with the garlic, soy sauce, sesame oil and plenty of black pepper. Leave for 30 minutes.

● Heat a little vegetable oil in a large frying pan. Lift the chicken from the marinade (reserve the marinade) and stir-fry for 2 minutes or so.

● Stir in all the vegetables and cook, stirring, for about 5 minutes until the vegetables are tender but still crisp. Stir in the reserved marinade about 1 minute before the end of cooking. Serve garnished with coriander leaves.

Stir-fried Leeks with Wood Ears

'Buddha's Delight'

SERVES 4–6

The original recipe calls for 18 different ingredients to represent the 18 Buddhas. Later, this was reduced to eight ingredients, usually consisting half of dried and half of fresh vegetables.

15 g/½ oz dried bean curd skin sticks

15 g/½ oz dried tiger lily buds

3–4 tbsp dried tree ears

10 g/¼ oz dried black moss

50 g/2 oz bamboo shoots

50 g/2 oz lotus root

50 g/2 oz straw mushrooms

50 g/2 oz white nuts

4 tbsp oil

1½ tsp salt

1 tsp sugar

1 tbsp light soy sauce

1 tsp cornflour mixed with 1 tbsp cold water

2 tsp sesame seed oil

● Soak the dried vegetables separately in cold water overnight or in warm water for at least 1 hour. Cut the bean curd sticks into short lengths.

● Cut the bamboo shoots and lotus root into small slices. The straw mushrooms and white nuts can be left whole.

● Heat a wok or large frying pan. When it is hot, put in about half of the oil and wait until it smokes. Stir-fry all the dried vegetables together with a little salt for about 1 minute. Remove and set aside.

● Add and heat the remaining oil and stir-fry the rest of the vegetables and the salt for about 1 minute. Add the partly cooked dried vegetables, the sugar and soy sauce, stirring constantly. If the contents start to dry out, pour in a little water. When the vegetables are cooked, add the cornflour and water mixture to thicken the gravy. Garnish with the sesame seed oil just before serving. This dish can be served either hot or cold.

Stir-fried Celery with Mushrooms

SERVES 4

1 small bunch of celery	1½ tsp salt
100 g/4 oz white mushrooms	1 tsp sugar
3 tbsp oil	

● Wash the celery and thinly slice the stalks diagonally.

● Wash the mushrooms and cut them into thin slices. Do not peel.

● Heat the oil in a hot wok or frying pan until it smokes, swirling it so that it covers most of the surface.

● Add the celery and mushrooms and stir-fry for about 1 minute or until each piece is coated with oil. Add the salt and sugar and continue stirring. Add a little water if the contents get too dry. Do not overcook because the celery will lose its crunchy texture. This dish can be served either hot or cold.

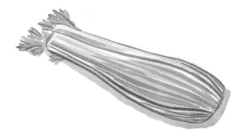

The 'Two Winters'

SERVES 2–4

The 'Two Winters' are winter bamboo shoots and winter mushrooms.

25 g/1 oz dried Chinese mushrooms

225 g/8 oz winter bamboo shoots

2 tbsp oil sauce

3 tbsp soy

1 tsp sugar

4 tbsp mushroom stock

1 tsp cornflour mixed with 2 tsp water

1 tsp sesame seed oil

● Select mushrooms of a uniform, small size. Soak them in warm water for about half an hour, squeeze dry and keep the water as mushroom stock.

● Cut the bamboo shoots into thin slices not much bigger than the mushrooms.

● Heat the oil until it smokes. Stir-fry the mushrooms and bamboo shoots for about 1 minute. Add the soy sauce and sugar and stir a few more times. Add the mushroom stock, bring to the boil and cook for about 2 minutes. Add the cornflour and water mixture and blend well. Add the sesame oil and serve.

Mushrooms Baked in Foil

SERVES 2–4

Cooking mushrooms in foil so that the aroma, flavour and juices are trapped inside is a speciality of many of Korea's older, traditional restaurants. The unseasoned mushrooms are either eaten plain, with a dipping sauce, or as a contrast to hot and garlicky dishes.

175 g/6 oz large white mushrooms, caps and stalks cut into 5 mm/¼ in slices

vinegar dipping sauce (optional)

● Cut a large piece of foil—about 50 x 30 cm/ 20 x 12 in. Put the mushrooms in the centre of the foil. Fold over the long sides of the foil, then the short sides to make a neat, secure package.

● Preheat a grill. Cook the mushroom packages about 10 cm/4 in from the heat for 5–7 minutes.

● Serve the mushrooms straightaway, accompanied by a dipping sauce if liked.

Bean Curd with Mushrooms

SERVES 4

4 cakes bean curd

3–4 medium-sized dried
  Chinese mushrooms

1 tbsp sherry

4 tbsp oil

½ tsp salt

½ tsp sugar

1 tsp cornflour

1 tbsp soy sauce

1 tsp sesame seed oil

● Soak the dried mushrooms in warm water for about 30 minutes. Squeeze them dry and discard the stalks. Keep the water for use as stock.

● Slice each square of bean curd into 5 mm/¼ in thick slices and then cut each slice into eight pieces.

● Heat the oil in a wok and stir-fry the mushrooms for a short time. Add about 120 ml/4 fl oz of the water in which the mushrooms have been soaking. Bring to the boil and add the bean curd with the salt and sugar. Let it bubble for a while and then add the sherry and the sesame seed oil.

● Mix the cornflour with the soy sauce and a little water in a bowl and pour it over the bean curd in the wok so that it forms a clear, light glaze.

Soy-glazed Pumpkin

SERVES 4

The mixture of pumpkin with ginger and soy sauce gives an attractive colour, taste and texture.

225 g/8 oz pumpkin, cut into 2.5 cm/1 in cubes

100 g/4 oz sugar

5 cm/2 in piece fresh ginger, grated

6 tbsp soy sauce

freshly ground black pepper

FOR THE GARNISH

toasted sesame seeds

garlic chives

● Cook the pumpkin in boiling water for 2 minutes. Drain well, then put into a frying pan. Add 6 tablespoons of water, the sugar, ginger, soy sauce and pepper. Heat slowly, stirring, until the sugar dissolves.

● Partially cover and simmer slowly for about 15 minutes, stirring occasionally, until the pumpkin is tender and glazed with soy syrup.

● Garnish with sesame seeds and garlic chives.

Braised Sweet Potatoes

SERVES 2

A traditional favourite, sweet potatoes are eaten throughout the year in Japan.

350 g/12 oz sweet potatoes, cut into 1 cm/½ in pieces

250 ml/8 fl oz water

pinch of salt

1 tbsp caster sugar

1 tsp soy sauce

● With a knife, bevel off the edges of the sweet potato. This will help prevent them breaking up while they are cooking.

● Put the potatoes, water, salt, sugar and soy sauce into a large pan, making sure that the pieces of potato are laid flat on the bottom. Bring to the boil, then simmer, covered, for 10–15 minutes, until the potatoes have softened, removing the lid for the last 5 minutes.

Soy-glazed Pumpkin

Salted Turnip with Lemon

SERVES 2

This dish is one of many Japanese **tsukemono** *or pickles. The freshness of the turnip is essential for the success of this dish.*

100 g/4 oz turnips peeled, halved and thinly sliced

1 tsp salt

3 lemon slices, cut into quarters

1 tsp soy sauce

● Place the sliced turnip in a bowl, sprinkle with the salt and leave for 20–30 minutes.

● Rub the turnip until it is soft, then squeeze out any excess liquid.

● Add the lemon quarters, then drizzle with soy sauce. Serve as a side dish.

Simmered Mixed Vegetables

SERVES 2

The potato is not a staple part of the Japanese diet, but it is nevertheless much used in Japanese cookery. It is usually diced and cooked with other vegetables as in this dish.

250 ml/8 fl oz *dashi* stock

100 g/4 oz carrots, peeled and chopped at random into bite-sized pieces

225 g/8 oz potatoes, peeled and cut into bite-sized pieces

1 medium onion, sliced

2 tsp caster sugar

½ tbsp *mirin*

pinch of salt

1 tbsp soy sauce

50 g/2 oz frozen, whole green beans, halved

● Put the *dashi*, carrots and potatoes in a pan. Bring to the boil and simmer, covered, for 5 minutes.

● Add the onion, sugar, *mirin*, salt and soy sauce and continue to simmer, covered, for a further 5 minutes.

● Finally, add the beans and simmer as before for 4 minutes. Serve hot as a side dish.

Fried 'Pocketed Eggs'

SERVES 4

Eggs are frequently cooked this way in China. The only preparation you will need to do is to chop the spring onion very finely. Taking a bite of the egg and finding the yolk inside the white is rather like finding something in a pocket—hence the name of this dish.

● Heat the oil in a hot wok or frying pan and fry the eggs on both sides. Add the soy sauce and a little water and braise for 1–2 minutes. Garnish with spring onion and serve hot.

4 eggs

2–3 tbsp oil

1 tbsp light soy sauce

1 spring onion, finely chopped

Eggs with Tomatoes

SERVES 4

Other vegetables such as cucumber, green peppers or green peas can be substituted for the tomatoes.

250 g/9 oz firm tomatoes

5 eggs

1½ tsp salt

2 spring onions, finely chopped

4 tbsp oil

1 tsp finely chopped fresh ginger (optional)

● Scald the tomatoes in a bowl of boiling water and peel off the skins. Cut each tomato in half lengthways and then crosscut each half into wedges.

● Beat the eggs with a pinch of salt and about one-third of the finely chopped spring onions.

● Heat about half the oil in a hot wok or frying pan and lightly scramble the eggs over a moderate heat until set. Remove the eggs from the wok.

● Heat the wok again over high heat and add the remaining oil. When the oil is hot, add the rest of the finely chopped spring onions, the ginger (if used) and the tomatoes. Stir a few times and then add the scrambled eggs with the remaining salt. Continue stirring for about 1 minute and serve hot.

Braised Soya Beans

SERVES 2

The humble soya bean is the most widely used ingredient in Japanese cuisine, forming the basis for soy sauce, bean curd and **miso.** *Soya beans are rich in nutrients and fibre and are regarded in Japan as 'meat from the earth'.*

3 dried shiitake mushrooms	50 g/2 oz carrots, peeled and diced
7.5 cm/3 in dried kelp, wiped with a damp cloth	2 tbsp caster sugar
425 g/15 oz canned soya beans, drained	1½ tbsp soy sauce

● Soak the shiitake mushrooms and kelp in a cup of water for 30 minutes. Reserve the water. Dice the shiitake mushrooms and kelp into small pieces.

● Put the kelp, mushrooms and reserved water into a pan. Add the soya beans, carrot, an extra 120 ml/ 4 fl oz fresh water and the sugar. Bring to the boil and cook, uncovered, for 15 minutes.

● Add the soy sauce and simmer for a further 10 minutes. Serve as a side dish. Any leftovers can be stored in a refrigerator for up to a week.

Sesame-grilled Seaweed

SERVES ABOUT 4

Crisp, smoky, nutty-tasting, paper-thin sheets of grilled **kim** *or laver are an extremely moreish 'nibble' to serve with drinks.*

8–10 sheets *kim*	salt
sesame oil for brushing	toasted sesame seeds to serve

● Brush both sides of each sheet of *kim* with sesame oil and sprinkle with salt.

● Hold each sheet in turn in tongs and pass backward and forward over a fairly low gas flame until crisp.

● Sprinkle the *kim* sheets with toasted sesame seeds. Let people break off pieces as they like, or cut the sheets into strips or squares.

Cucumber and Wakame

SERVES 2

Although this is a cold dish, it is not regarded as a salad in Japan. If you cannot get hold of rice vinegar, ordinary malt vinegar will do as a substitute.

200 g/7 oz cucumber, cut in
   half lengthways and then
   very thinly sliced

1 tsp salt

½ tbsp dried *wakame*, soaked
   in hot water for a few
   minutes until swollen

**FOR THE SWEET AND
SOUR DRESSING**

5 tsp rice vinegar

½ tbsp caster sugar

½ tsp soy sauce

● Put the cucumber in a bowl, sprinkle with the salt and leave for 15 minutes.

● Taking the cucumber in your hands, squeeze out as much liquid as you can. Do the same with the soaked *wakame*.

● Mix together the sugar, vinegar and soy sauce in a small bowl.

● Just before eating, mix the dressing together with the cucumber and *wakame*. Serve as a side dish.

Stir-fried Mixed Vegetables in a Fish Sauce

SERVES 4

2 carrots, finely sliced

100 g/4 oz bamboo shoots, thinly sliced

1 Chinese leaves, stalks only, diced

100 g/4 oz green beans, halved

25 g/1 oz wood ear, soaked in warm water for 15 minutes and roughly chopped

½ tsp vegetable oil

2 cloves garlic, crushed

3 slices fresh ginger, peeled and finely sliced

100 g/4 oz bean sprouts

salt

freshly ground black pepper

½ tbsp cornflour

1 tbsp fish sauce or 1 tbsp light soy sauce

● In a large saucepan half full of water boil the carrots for 10 minutes. Add the bamboo shoots, Chinese leaves, green beans and wood ear and cook for a further 5 minutes. Drain and reserve.

● Heat the oil in a wok and stir-fry the garlic and ginger for 2 minutes. Add the bean sprouts and stir-fry for 30 seconds. Stir in all the reserved vegetables and season with salt and black pepper. Stir-fry for a further 2 minutes.

● Mix the cornflour and fish sauce with a little water and fold into the vegetables to bind them.

Hot and Sour Cucumber—Szechwan Style

SERVES 4

1 cucumber

1 tsp salt

2 tbsp sugar

2 tbsp vinegar

1 tbsp chilli oil

● Split the cucumber in two lengthways and then cut each piece into strips, rather like French fries. Sprinkle with the salt and leave for about 10 minutes to extract the bitter juices.

● Remove each cucumber strip. Place it on a firm surface and soften it by gently tapping it with the blade of a cleaver or knife.

● Place the cucumber strips on a plate. Sprinkle the sugar evenly over them and then add the vinegar and chilli oil just before serving.

Stir-fried Mixed Vegetables in a
Fish Sauce

Simmered Hijiki Seaweed

SERVES 2

Hijiki *is one of the many types of seaweed used in Japanese cookery.* **Hijiki** *is a source of several minerals, including calcium and iodine.*

10 g/¼ oz dried *hijiki*

½ sheet *abura-age*

50 g/2 oz carrots, peeled, and cut into short matchsticks

2 tsp vegetable oil

250 ml/8 fl oz *dashi* stock

1½ tbsp caster sugar

1½ tbsp soy sauce

1 tbsp *mirin*

● Rinse the *hijiki* then soak in a bowlful of water for 20–30 minutes. Rinse then drain again. The *hijiki* should swell to six or seven times its original size.

● Rinse the *abura-age* with hot water, then cut into small slices, about the same size as the carrot.

● Heat the oil in a saucepan and fry the *hijiki, abura-age* and carrots for 1 minute.

● Add the *dashi* stock, sugar, soy sauce and *mirin*, then simmer, uncovered for about 25 minutes or until the liquid has almost evaporated. Serve as a side dish. Any leftovers can be kept refrigerated for 3–4 days.

Vegetarian Chop Suey

SERVES 4

Many of us know that chop suey is a creation of the West, but the Chinese have a dish called tsa-sui, which literally means 'miscellaneous fragments' or 'mixed bits and pieces'. The genuine article should have all the ingredients specially selected in order to achieve the desired harmonious balance of colours, textures and flavours. It should never be the soggy mess one often finds in a cheap take-away.

2 cakes of bean curd	1½ tsp salt
10 g/¼ oz wood ears, dried	1 tsp sugar
175 g/6 oz broccoli or mange tout	1–2 spring onions, finely chopped
175 g/6 oz bamboo shoots	1 tbsp light soy sauce
100 g/4 oz mushrooms	2 tbsp rice wine or dry sherry
4–5 tbsp oil	1 tsp cornflour mixed with 1 tbsp cold water

● Cut the bean curd into about 24 small pieces. Soak the wood ears in water for about 20–25 minutes, rinse them clean and discard any hard roots.

● Cut the broccoli or mange tout, bamboo shoots and mushrooms into uniformly small pieces.

● Heat a wok over a high heat, add about half of the oil and wait for it to smoke. Swirl the pan so that its surface is well greased. Add the bean curd pieces and shallow-fry them on both sides until golden, then scoop them out with a slotted spoon and set them aside until needed.

● Heat the remaining oil and add the broccoli or mange tout. Stir for about 30 seconds and then add the wood ears, bamboo shoots, mushrooms and the partly cooked bean curd. Continue stirring for 1 minute and then add the salt, sugar, spring onions, soy sauce and wine. Blend well and when the gravy starts to boil, thicken it with the cornflour and water mixture. Serve hot.

Salads

Salads, which are as often made with lightly steamed or fried vegetables as raw ingredients, are served simply and lightly dressed with fragrant, mouthwatering sauces. In the East, dishes such as those in this section are traditionally served as accompaniments to main dishes, but Western cooks will find here suggestions for salads and cold dishes that will win a regular place in their culinary repertoire.

Chinese Vegetable and Omelette Salad

SERVES 4

Resembling a raw stir-fry, this colourful salad makes use of Chinese vegetables. Top with shredded omelette for a special finishing touch.

450 g/1 lb young cabbage

oil for deep frying

1 tsp salt

½ tsp ground cinnamon

100 g/4 oz bean sprouts

4 spring onions, halved lengthways

50 g/2 oz canned water chestnuts, chopped

1 red pepper, sliced

1 yellow pepper, sliced

50 g/2 oz salted cashew nuts

FOR THE OMELETTE

2 eggs

½ tsp Chinese five-spice powder

FOR THE DRESSING

2 tbsp light soy sauce

1 tbsp lime juice

1 tbsp sesame oil

½ tsp ground ginger

● Shred the young cabbage. Heat the oil in a wok and deep-fry the greens for 4–5 minutes. Drain well on absorbent kitchen paper and sprinkle with salt and cinnamon. Place in a large serving bowl. Top with the bean sprouts, spring onions, water chestnuts, peppers and cashew nuts.

● Beat the eggs for the omelette with the Chinese five-spice powder. Heat a 15 cm/6 in omelette frying pan and pour in the eggs, tilting the pan to coat the base with egg. Cook for 2 minutes until the top is set. Flip over and cook for 2 minutes. Remove and cut into strips. Sprinkle over the vegetables. Mix the dressing, pour on, and serve.

Hot Egg and Shredded Vegetable Salad

SERVES 4

50 g/2 oz bean thread vermicelli

4 dried Chinese mushrooms

1 tbsp sesame seeds

2 cloves garlic, crushed

salt

2 tbsp rice vinegar

1½ tsp sugar

2 tbsp soy sauce

2 tbsp sesame oil

100 g/4 oz mange tout, thinly sliced

50 g/2 oz bamboo shoots, thinly sliced

1 small carrot, peeled and thinly sliced

1 small white radish, peeled and thinly sliced

1 small cucumber, peeled, seeded and sliced thinly

1 small green pepper, thinly sliced

1 small red pepper, thinly sliced

2 celery sticks, thinly sliced

1 small red onion, thinly sliced

salt

1 tbsp roasted peanuts, ground

fresh ground black pepper

sprigs of coriander

FOR THE EGG PANCAKES

2 eggs

¼ tsp fish sauce or light soy sauce

freshly ground black pepper

½ tsp water

1 tbsp vegetable oil

● Soak the vermicelli in warm water for 30 minutes, drain and cut into 5 cm/2 in lengths. Soak the dried Chinese mushrooms in warm water for 30 minutes, squeeze, discard the stalks, and slice thinly.

● Make the egg pancakes by beating together the eggs, fish sauce, black pepper and about ½ teaspoon water in a bowl. Heat the oil in a wok over a moderate heat. Pour in half of the egg mixture and immediately tilt the wok to spread the egg evenly over the bottom. The egg pancake should be crêpe-thin. Cook for about 30 seconds. Turn and cook on the other side for 15 seconds. Repeat with the rest of the mixture. Cool and cut into thin strips.

● Toss the sesame seeds in a dry wok over a moderate heat. Stir constantly until golden brown. This should take about 3 minutes. Set aside.

● Combine the garlic, salt, vinegar, sugar, soy sauce and sesame oil in a small bowl by stirring. Set this sauce aside.

● Bring a saucepan of salted water to the boil and put in the noodles, mange tout, bamboo shoots and mushrooms and cook for 30 seconds. Drain into a colander immediately and run under cold water for a few seconds. Dry with absorbent kitchen paper and set aside.

● Mix the carrot, white radish, cucumber, peppers, celery and red onion in a bowl and sprinkle on some salt. Toss well and let stand for 30 minutes. Rinse the salt off and squeeze the vegetables dry by hand to remove all excess liquid, and dry with absorbent kitchen paper to ensure the vegetables remain firm.

● Combine all the shredded vegetables with the blanched vegetables in a large salad bowl. Sprinkle the sauce over the mixture. Toss well. Transfer the salad to a serving platter. Sprinkle the ground nuts and black pepper over the top and garnish with the egg pancake strips and coriander sprigs.

Simple Salad

SERVES 4

1 lettuce, finely shredded

1 cucumber, peeled and cut lengthways into thin strips

2 carrots, peeled and cut lengthways into thin strips

1 large handful of bean sprouts, washed and drained thoroughly

3 tbsp chopped fresh coriander

3 tbsp chopped fresh mint

FOR THE GARNISH

2 hard-boiled eggs, quartered

FOR THE SALAD DRESSING

4 tbsp fish sauce

4 tbsp lemon juice

1 tbsp wine vinegar

3 cloves garlic, finely chopped

1 tsp sugar

1 red chilli, finely chopped

3 tbsp roasted peanuts, crushed

● Combine the lettuce, cucumber, carrots and bean sprouts. Mix lightly.

● Mix the fish sauce, lemon juice and vinegar. Add the garlic and sugar and stir thoroughly, then add the chilli and peanuts, and stir again.

● Toss the dressing into the salad and scatter the coriander and mint over the top. Garnish with the egg quarters before serving.

Cucumber Salad

SERVES 2–4

Mixing the cucumber with salt and leaving it for 1 hour draws out moisture, so preventing the sauce from being too watery.

1 long cucumber, very thinly sliced

salt

pinch of Korean chilli powder, or cayenne pepper mixed with paprika

1 tbsp sugar

2 tbsp rice vinegar

sesame oil for sprinkling

● Put the cucumber slices in a bowl. Toss with salt, then add cold water to cover. Leave for 1 hour. Drain the cucumber. If the cucumber tastes very salty, rinse it under running cold water and dry thoroughly on absorbent kitchen paper. Put the cucumber into a bowl.

● Mix the Korean chilli powder, or cayenne pepper and paprika, with the sugar and vinegar, and pour over the cucumber. Sprinkle with sesame oil and toss to mix. Cover and chill. Toss again before serving.

Simple Salad

Vietnamese Salad

SERVES 6

Most meals in Vietnam are accompanied by a salad or salad ingredients. Salads are also eaten as first courses or a side dish. A Vietnamese salad is never plain— Vietnamese are adventurous in their mixing of textures and tastes.

2 stalks fresh lemon grass (discard outer leaves), thinly sliced

50 g/2 oz each leftover roast beef, pork, lamb or chicken, finely shredded

1 bunch spring onions, washed and finely chopped

2 carrots, finely grated

1 red chilli, finely sliced

2 cloves garlic, finely sliced

3 tbsp fish sauce

9 tbsp lime or lemon juice

2 tbsp chopped fresh basil

2 tbsp finely chopped coriander

● Lightly hit the sliced lemon grass with the back of a cleaver or heavy knife to release the flavour and smell. Mix the lemon grass with the leftover meat, then add the spring onions and toss well. Mix in the carrot.

● Mix together the chilli, garlic, fish sauce and lime juice, and stir well. Add to the salad and toss well. Throw in the basil and coriander, and toss again. If you think you need more salad dressing, add equal parts of fish sauce and lime juice.

Chinese Coriander Salad

SERVES 4

This is a variation on a classic salad, made extra special by the cheese dressing, which is poured over the salad ingredients.

225 g/8 oz head Chinese leaves

1 ripe avocado, seeded

1 yellow pepper, diced

½ bunch coriander (about 15 g/½ oz), chopped

2 tomatoes, seeded and diced

4 bacon rashers, grilled and chopped

1 tsp sesame seeds

FOR THE DRESSING

25 g/1 oz grated Parmesan cheese

1 tbsp sesame oil

4 tbsp salad oil

1 clove garlic, finely chopped

1 tbsp honey

2 tbsp garlic wine vinegar

¼ tsp Chinese five-spice powder

2 tsp light soy sauce

● Wash the Chinese leaves well and cut into bite-size pieces. Chop the avocado and add to the leaves with the pepper, coriander, spring onions, tomatoes, bacon and sesame seeds.

● Mix together the dressing ingredients and pour over the salad. Toss and serve.

Shan Lee Salad

SERVES 4

3 tbsp sesame seed oil

3 tbsp orange juice, freshly squeezed

1 round lettuce, the leaves washed and separated

4 tbsp bamboo shoots

● Mix the sesame oil and orange juice together, and toss into the salad leaves and bamboo shoots.

● Serve as a simple accompaniment to a satay dish or Stuffed Chicken Wings (page 130).

Spinach Noodle Salad

SERVES 4

Young spinach leaves should be used for this recipe. The small leaves taste and look terrific with the spicy sauce and noodles.

225 g/8 oz flat rice noodles

2 tbsp groundnut oil

8 spring onions, sliced

2 cloves garlic, finely chopped

½ tsp star anise, ground

2 tsp chopped fresh ginger

2 tbsp dark soy sauce

75 g/3 oz young spinach
    leaves, washed

1 tbsp sesame oil

FOR THE GARNISH

2 tbsp chopped fresh coriander

● Cook the noodles in boiling water for 4–5 minutes. Drain and cool in cold water.

● Heat the groundnut oil in a wok and cook half of the spring onions, the garlic, star anise, ginger and soy sauce for 2 minutes. Cool completely.

● Arrange the spinach in a serving bowl. Drain the noodles and toss into the vegetables. Sprinkle over the sesame oil and place on top of the spinach. Sprinkle with remaining spring onions and serve garnished with fresh coriander.

Lotus Root Salad

SERVES 2–4

Lotus roots have a firm, crunchy texture, a taste similar to artichoke hearts, and the slices display an attractive flower-like pattern.

100 g/4 oz young lotus roots, thinly sliced

2 tbsp soy sauce

1 tbsp rice vinegar

2 tsp sesame oil

2 tsp toasted sesame seeds

1 tsp sugar

● Arrange the lotus roots in a steaming basket. Cover and put over a saucepan of boiling water. Steam for about 1 hour—the time will depend on the age and therefore toughness of the roots.

● Transfer the lotus roots to a bowl. Add the remaining ingredients and stir together. Serve warm or chilled.

Spinach Salad

SERVES 4

This salad can be served with almost any other dish and is equally good served warm or chilled.

450 g/1 lb young fresh spinach leaves

2 cloves garlic, crushed

1 tbsp sesame oil

2 tbsp soy sauce

2 tsp sesame seeds

freshly ground black pepper

● Add the spinach to a large saucepan of boiling water. Cover and quickly return to the boil. Boil for 1 minute, then tip the spinach into a colander and refresh under running cold water. Drain, then dry on absorbent kitchen paper.

● Coarsely shred the spinach, then toss with the remaining ingredients. Serve warm, or leave until cold, then cover and chill. Toss again before serving.

Bean Sprout Salad

SERVES 4–6

This is a much loved, crunchy, nutritious salad or side dish. In restaurants it may be served with your pre-dinner drinks, so you have something to nibble while you are waiting for your meal to arrive.

675 g/1½ lb soya bean sprouts or mung bean sprouts

2 cloves garlic, very finely chopped

5 spring onions, white and green parts thinly sliced into rings

1 fresh hot red chilli, seeded and thinly sliced into rings

1 tbsp crushed toasted sesame seeds

salt

● Remove the roots from the bean sprouts. Add the bean sprouts to a pan of boiling water. Return to the boil, then tip into a colander and rinse under running cold water. Squeeze as much water as possible from the bean sprouts.

● Toss the bean sprouts with the remaining ingredients. Serve either at room temperature or slightly chilled.

Spinach Salad
and Bean Sprout Salad

Carrot and White Radish Salad

SERVES 4

Both the colours and flavours of white radish and carrot complement each other in this attractive salad.

1 carrot, thinly sliced on the diagonal

225 g/8 oz white radish, cut into fine strips

salt

1 tbsp sesame oil

1 tsp soy sauce

1 tsp sugar

very small pinch of Korean chilli powder, or cayenne pepper mixed with paprika

● Cut the carrot slices into very fine strips and put into a bowl with the white radish strips. Sprinkle lightly with salt and toss together well; then leave for 1 hour. Drain, then rinse and drain thoroughly, pressing out as much liquid as possible. Dry on absorbent kitchen paper.

● Mix the vegetables with the remaining ingredients and serve.

White Radish Salad

SERVES 3–4

*In Korea, they use long, pointed white radishes, which are known in the West by the Japanese name of **daikon** or the Indian name of **mooli**. They are available in some markets as well as ethnic food shops.*

1 white radish, coarsely grated or cut lengthways into fine strips

salt

½–1 tsp Korean chilli powder, or cayenne pepper mixed with paprika

2 tsp sugar

1 tbsp sesame oil

4 tbsp rice vinegar

1 cm/½ in fresh ginger, finely chopped

FOR THE GARNISH

sesame seeds

● Put the white radish into a colander. Mix with salt and leave for 10–15 minutes.

● Rinse the radish well, then drain and dry thoroughly on absorbent kitchen paper.

● Toss the radish with the remaining ingredients, except the sesame seeds. Cover and chill. Garnish with sesame seeds to serve.

Spiced White Radish Salad

SERVES 4

White radishes have a milder flavour than Western red radishes, so respond well to being mixed with typical Korean flavourings.

1 large white radish, sliced

salt

1 tbsp soy sauce

2 tsp rice vinegar

1 cm/½ in fresh ginger, finely chopped

1 tsp sugar

2 tsp crushed toasted sesame seeds

1½ tsp chilli bean paste

1 clove garlic, finely chopped

1 spring onion, white and green part thinly sliced diagonally

● Put the white radish into a colander, mix with salt and leave for 10–15 minutes.

● Rinse the radish well, then drain and dry thoroughly on absorbent kitchen paper.

● Mix together the remaining ingredients, except the spring onions, and toss with the white radish. Scatter over the spring onions, cover and chill. Toss the salad lightly before serving.

Roasted Aubergine Salad

SERVES 6

3 long green aubergines,
combined weight approx
325 g/11 oz

25 g/1 oz minced pork

3 tbsp peanut or corn oil

50 g/2 oz dried shrimps, rinsed
in hot water and drained

50 g/2 oz shallots, sliced

5 fresh small green chillies,
chopped roughly

2 tbsp lime juice

1 tsp fish sauce

¼ tsp sugar

● Dry-roast the aubergines in a 180°C/350°F/Gas Mark 4 oven for about 15–20 minutes until soft, then cool, remove the skin and slice into 2.5 cm/1 in pieces.

● Sauté the pork in a frying pan or wok in a little oil over high heat until done, about 10 minutes. Mix the aubergine, pork, shrimps and all the remaining ingredients together well in a bowl. Serve accompanied by rice.

Aubergine Salad with Sesame Seeds

SERVES 4–6

This dish doubles as a salad and as a first course; it is usually served at the beginning of a meal, then left on the table until the end.

550 g/1¼ lb oriental aubergines, or small, slim aubergines

1 spring onion, white and green part sliced into rings

1 tbsp sugar

1 tbsp sesame oil

3 tbsp Japanese soy sauce

2 cloves garlic, finely chopped

2 tbsp rice vinegar

2 tbsp crushed toasted sesame seeds

salt

● If you are using oriental aubergines, cut them lengthways into quarters, then slice across the middle of each piece. If using ordinary aubergines, cut them into long pieces about 2.5 cm/1 in thick and 2.5 cm/1 in wide.

● Steam the pieces of aubergine in a covered container until tender and soft. Mix together the remaining ingredients.

● Leave the aubergines until cool enough to handle, then tear into long, thin strips. Put into a bowl. Pour over the dressing mixture and stir together. Serve at room temperature, or chill before serving.

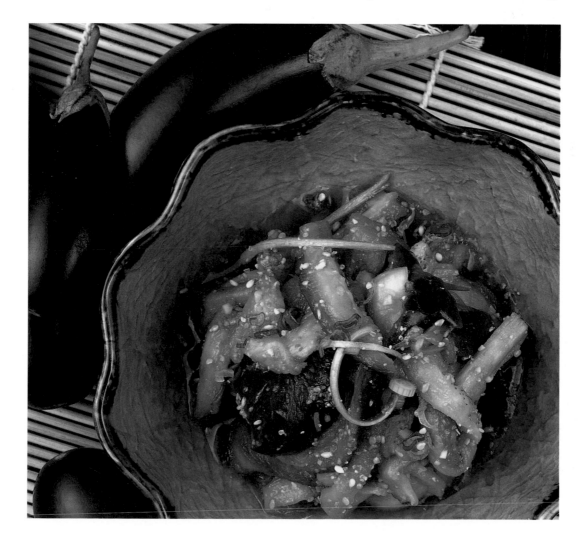

Green Bean and Red Pepper Salad

SERVES 4

225 g/8 oz green beans

1 medium or 2 small red peppers, cored and seeded

2 slices fresh ginger, thinly shredded

1½ tsp salt

1 tsp sugar

1 tbsp sesame seed oil

● Wash the beans, snip off the ends and cut into 5 cm/2 in lengths. Cut the red peppers into thin shreds. Blanch them both in boiling water and drain.

● Put the beans, peppers and ginger into a bowl. Add the salt, sugar and sesame seed oil. Toss well to coat the vegetables, and serve.

Cooked Watercress Salad

SERVES 4

Steaming the watercress rather than boiling it keeps it drier and saves having to drain it.

2 large bunches watercress

3 tbsp soy sauce

1 tbsp sesame oil

2 tsp toasted sesame seeds

salt and freshly ground black pepper

● Cut off and discard the coarse parts of the watercress stalks, then spread it out in a shallow layer in a steaming basket; you may have to cook the watercress in two batches if the steaming basket is not very large. Cover the basket and put over a saucepan of boiling water. Steam for 1–2 minutes. Remove the watercress from the steaming basket and coarsely chop it.

● Toss the watercress with the soy sauce, sesame oil and seeds, salt and pepper. Leave until cold, then cover and chill. Toss again before serving.

Tomato Salad with Spring Onion and Oil Dressing

SERVES 4

Other vegetables such as cucumber, celery and green peppers can be served in the same way.

300 g/10 oz firm tomatoes

1 tsp salt

1 tsp sugar

3–4 spring onions, finely chopped

3 tbsp salad oil

● Wash and dry the tomatoes. Cut them into thick slices. Sprinkle with salt and sugar. Leave to marinate for 10–15 minutes.

● Place the finely chopped spring onions in a heat-resistant bowl. In a pan, heat the oil until quite hot and pour over the spring onions. Add the tomatoes, toss well, and serve.

Green Mango Salad

SERVES 4

If this is too sour for some people, you can add more sugar if you like.

350 g/12 oz green unripe mango flesh, cut into long matchsticks

25 g/1 oz desiccated or grated coconut, dry-fried until light brown

25 g/1 oz dried shrimps

3 tbsp sliced shallots

5 fresh small green chillies, chopped

1 tbsp palm sugar, or to taste

fish sauce, to taste (optional)

lime juice, to taste (optional)

● Mix all of the ingredients together. If not salty enough add a little of the fish sauce; if not sour enough, add the lime juice.

Green Papaya Salad

SERVES 4

Although unripe papaya is not easy to buy in the West, this famous northeastern Thai dish is well worth the trouble. Much of the popularity of this dish, traditionally eaten with sticky rice, is its combination of sweet and sour flavours.

325 g/11 oz green papaya, peeled and cut into long matchsticks

7 fresh small whole green chillies

6 cloves garlic, chopped roughly

50 g/2 oz green beans, cut into 2.5 cm/1 in pieces

25 g/1 oz unsalted roasted peanuts

25 g/1 oz dried shrimps

6 cherry tomatoes, quartered

4 tbsp lime or lemon juice

1 tbsp palm sugar

1 tbsp fish sauce

● Take a little of the papaya, the chilli and garlic, and pound together lightly with a mortar and pestle or in a blender. Put in a bowl and stir in the beans, peanuts, shrimps, tomato and the rest of the papaya. Mix well, then stir in the lemon juice, sugar and fish sauce.

● Serve accompanied by raw vegetables chopped into bite-sized pieces—perhaps morning glory and green beans—sticky rice and roasted chicken.

Rice Salad

SERVES 4–6

This is another 'leftover' dish made with rice from a previous occasion.

350 g/12 oz cooked rice

225 g/8 oz grated coconut, browned in a 180°C/350°F/ Gas Mark 4 oven for 5–8 minutes

1 small grapefruit, shredded

50 g/2 oz dried shrimps, chopped

25 g/1 oz bean sprouts

75 g/3 oz lemon grass, finely sliced

25 g/1 oz green beans, sliced

2 dried red chillies, pounded

1 tbsp kaffir lime leaf, finely shredded

FOR THE SAUCE

250 ml/8 fl oz water

2 tbsp chopped anchovies

1 tbsp palm sugar

2 kaffir lime leaves, torn into small pieces

¼ tsp lemon grass, sliced

● Put all the sauce ingredients in a pan, boil for 5 minutes, remove from the heat, and strain.

● Place the rice in 120 ml/4 fl oz moulds or large ramekins, press and invert onto a large serving platter. Arrange the rest of the raw ingredients around the edge of the rice in separate piles. To eat, spoon some rice onto individual plates and take a little of each ingredient to mix with the rice according to taste. Spoon the sauce over the top.

Sweet and Sour Cucumber Salad

SERVES 4

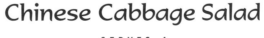

1 cucumber

2 tsp finely chopped fresh ginger

1 tsp sesame seed oil

2 tbsp sugar

2 tbsp rice vinegar

● Select a dark green and slender cucumber; the fat pale green ones contain too much water and have far less flavour. Cut it in half lengthways, then cut each piece into slices. Marinate with the ginger and sesame seed oil for about 10–15 minutes.

● Make the dressing with the sugar and vinegar in a bowl, stirring well to dissolve the sugar.

● Place the cucumber slices on a plate. Just before serving, pour the sugar and vinegar dressing evenly over them and toss well.

Chinese Cabbage Salad

SERVES 4

Green or red peppers can be added to the cabbage.

1 small Chinese cabbage

2 tbsp light soy sauce

1 tsp salt

1 tsp sugar

1 tbsp sesame seed oil

● Wash the cabbage thoroughly, cut into thick slices and place in a bowl.

● Add the soy sauce, salt, sugar and sesame seed oil to the cabbage. Toss well and serve.

Celery Salad

SERVES 4

1 bunch celery

1 tsp salt

1.7 litres/3 pt water

2 tbsp light soy sauce

1 tbsp vinegar

1 tbsp sesame seed oil

2 slices fresh ginger, finely shredded

● Remove the leaves and outer tough stalks of the celery. Thinly slice the tender parts diagonally. Blanch them in a pan of boiling, salted water. Then pour them into a colander and rinse in cold water until cool. Drain.

● Mix together the soy sauce, vinegar and sesame seed oil. Add to the celery and toss well.

● Garnish the salad with finely shredded ginger and serve.

Seafood Salad with Ponzu Dressing

SERVES 2

Ponzu *can be used as a dip sauce or as a tangy, non-oily salad dressing. It is equally good used in both ways.*

2 celery sticks

7.5 cm/3 in piece cucumber

90 g/3½ oz carrot, peeled

50 g/2 oz frozen green beans

5 seafood sticks

pinch of salt

1 quantity of *ponzu* dressing (see page 206)

● Slice the celery, cucumber and carrot on a slant then cut into matchsticks.

● Cook the beans in salted boiling water for 4–5 minutes, then rinse with cold water and cut in half.

● Mix the vegetables together on a plate or in a bowl. Then pull the seafood sticks into strands with your fingers and use to garnish the top of the salad. Drizzle with the *ponzu* dressing on serving.

Spicy Seafood Salad

The Thai versions of salad, of which this is one, are flavourful assemblies of different ingredients quite unlike those we are accustomed to in the West. Most are extremely spicy. This dish combines three of the basic five flavours: spicy, sour and salty.

150 g/5 oz sea bass or perch, cleaned, gutted and sliced thinly into strips

150 g/5 oz large prawns, shelled

150 g/5 oz squid, body and tentacles, cleaned, gutted, and sliced into 2 cm/¾ in strips

7 fresh small green chillies

5 cloves garlic

2 coriander roots

2 tbsp fish sauce

½ tsp sugar

2 tbsp lime or lemon juice

4 spring onions, sliced into 5 mm/¼ in pieces

100 g/4 oz onions, sliced thinly

50 g/2 oz celery leaves and sticks, sliced

● Cook the fish, prawns, and squid separately in salted water until cooked, about 2–3 minutes each, and drain.

● Pound the chillies, garlic, coriander root, fish sauce and sugar together with a pestle and mortar or in a blender until fine.

● Place in a bowl and mix in the lemon juice, spring onion, onion and celery. Stir in the fish and seafood and mix well. Serve immediately.

Spicy Mussel Salad

425 g/15 oz cooked mussel meat (steam approx 1.5 kg/3½ lb mussels in their shells and remove meat)

10 fresh small green chillies, finely chopped

10 g/¼ oz mint leaves

3 tbsp lime or lemon juice, or to taste

2½ tbsp fish sauce, or to taste

2 tbsp sliced shallots

2 tbsp fresh ginger, cut into matchsticks

2 tbsp finely sliced lemon grass

½ tbsp kaffir lime leaf, shredded

1 small Chinese cabbage, cut into wedges

½ small green cabbage, cut into wedges

● Mix together all the ingredients, except the cabbage, in a bowl. Taste for seasoning, adding extra lime juice or fish sauce if you like. Serve on a platter, with the cabbage leaves around the edge to be eaten with the salad.

Jellyfish, Chicken and Cucumber Salad

SERVES 4

100 g/4 oz dried jellyfish

2 cooked chicken breasts, cut into strips

½ cucumber, cut into thin strips

1 tbsp chopped fresh mint

1 tbsp chopped fresh coriander

FOR THE NUOC CHAM SAUCE

2 dried hot red chillies, cut into pieces

1 clove garlic, chopped

2 tsp sugar

½ fresh lime

2 tbsp fish sauce or 2 tbsp light soy sauce and 1 tsp anchovy essence

3 tbsp water

FOR THE GARNISH

roasted peanuts, crushed

● Make the *nuoc cham* sauce by mixing the chillies, garlic and sugar, and pounding. Squeeze the lime over the mixture. Add the fish sauce and water and stir thoroughly. Set aside.

● Soak the jellyfish in hot water for about 30 minutes. Remove and soak in cold water for 2 hours, squeezing constantly to remove the salt.

● Mix together the jellyfish, chicken and cucumber. Add the mint and coriander. Add the dressing and toss. Sprinkle with the crushed peanuts.

Minced Meat, Crab and Grapefruit Salad

SERVES 4

175 g/6 oz minced pork or beef

3 tbsp water

2 tbsp lime or lemon juice

2 tbsp fish sauce

1 green chilli, finely sliced

1 small Spanish onion, finely diced

1 cm/½ in fresh ginger, finely chopped

1 tbsp finely chopped fresh coriander

1 small can crabmeat, thoroughly drained

1 pink grapefruit, segmented then halved

FOR THE GARNISH

lettuce leaves

grated carrot

● Place the minced meat in the water and slowly cook over a medium heat until the meat turns colour and is just cooked but still tender. Remove from the heat and leave to cool slightly.

● Add the lime juice, fish sauce and chilli to the meat. When thoroughly cooled, add the onion, ginger, coriander and crabmeat and stir thoroughly. Toss the grapefruit into the salad.

● Place the lettuce leaves on a flat dish. Arrange the grated carrot on the lettuce to form a ring. Spoon the salad into the centre of the carrot.

Fresh Chicken Salad with Grapefruit, Mint and Lemon Grass

SERVES 6

vegetable oil for deep frying

about 40 prawn chips

1 tbsp unsalted peanuts

1 tbsp sesame seeds

25 g/1 oz dried shrimps, soaked in hot water for 30 minutes

50 g/2 oz belly of pork

50 g/2 oz uncooked prawns in the shell

salt

1 medium cucumber, unpeeled, halved lengthways, seeded and sliced thinly

1 large carrot, shredded

50 g/2 oz fresh bean sprouts

25 g/1 oz cooked chicken meat, cut into thin strips

1 tbsp chopped fresh mint

½ tbsp chopped lemon grass

salt

1 large grapefruit, peeled, sectioned and cut crossways into 2.5 cm/1 in pieces

FOR THE EGG PANCAKES

2 eggs

¼ tsp fish sauce

freshly ground black pepper

vegetable oil

FOR THE DRESSING

1 clove garlic, finely chopped

1 fresh red chilli, seeded and minced

½ tbsp sugar

½ tbsp fresh lime juice

½ tbsp rice vinegar

1½ tbsp fish sauce

FOR THE GARNISH

sprigs of coriander

● Heat about 5 cm/2 in oil to 180°C/350°F in a wok. Add the chips 2–3 at a time and keep them immersed in the oil with a pair of chopsticks or perforated spoon until puffy. This should take about 10 seconds. Turn and cook for the same length of time. Set aside.

● Rub down the wok, return it to a moderate heat and cook the peanuts. Stir constantly until the peanuts are golden brown—about 5 minutes. Mince with a mincer or put between a couple of sheets of clean strong paper and grind with a rolling pin or milk bottle. Toast the sesame seeds in the same way for only 3 minutes. Grind lightly to a grainy texture.

● To make the pancakes, beat the eggs, fish sauce and pepper together with ½ teaspoon water in a bowl. Brush the bottom of a nonstick omelette pan with some oil and place over moderate heat until hot. Pour in half of the egg mixture and tilt the pan immediately to spread the mixture evenly over the bottom—the pancake should be paper-thin. Cook until the egg is set—this should not take more than 30 seconds. Turn and cook on the other side for about 15 seconds. Set aside. Repeat, using up the rest of the mixture.

● Combine the garlic, chilli, sugar, lime juice, vinegar and fish sauce in a bowl. Stir to blend thoroughly.

● Drain the dried shrimps and pound or blend in a blender or processor until very fine. Set aside.

● Cover the pork with water and bring to the boil over a high heat. Lower and boil for about 30 minutes. Run cold water over the pork and set aside.

● Cook the raw prawns in boiling water until just pink—about 2 minutes. Run cold water over them, drain, peel, devein and cut lengthways in halves. Shred the prawns and set aside.

● Sprinkle salt over the cucumber and carrot, and leave to stand for 15 minutes. Run cold water over them and squeeze dry with your hands. It is imperative that the vegetables are bone dry to ensure their crunchiness.

● Dip the bean sprouts in salted boiling water for 30 seconds. Run cold water over them and drain.

● Cut the egg pancakes into strips. Combine the egg pancake strips, dried shrimps, shredded prawns, chicken, cucumber, carrot, bean sprouts, mint, lemon grass, grapefruit and sesame seeds. Mix well with your hands and pour over the dressing mixture.

● Transfer to a serving dish or serve separately, and sprinkle the ground peanuts over it. Garnish with coriander. Serve with prawn chips on which guests place bite-sized portions of the salad.

Fresh Chicken Salad with Grapefruit,
Mint and Lemon Grass

Minced Pork, Prawn and Pineapple Salad with a Fish Sauce Dressing

SERVES 2

450 g/1 lb fresh lean pork, minced or, preferably, finely chopped

2 tbsp water

225 g/8 oz cooked prawns

2 tbsp lemon juice

2 tbsp fish sauce

½ tsp dried powdered chilli

1 tsp fresh red chilli, finely sliced

2 tbsp finely sliced onion

2 tbsp spring onions, cut into 1 cm/½ in sections

2 tbsp roasted peanuts

2 slices pineapple, roughly chopped

2 tbsp fresh ginger, finely sliced

1 tbsp chopped fresh mint leaves

2 tbsp chopped fresh coriander leaves and stalks

6 large lettuce leaves

FOR THE GARNISH

roasted peanuts

1 tbsp finely sliced fresh ginger

pinch of dried powdered chilli

fresh red chilli, sliced

sprigs of mint

sprigs of coriander

spring onion curls

chilli flowers

● Cook the pork in a wok over medium heat with the water until the pork is cooked thoroughly but still tender and juicy. Remove from the heat.

● Add the prawns, lemon juice, fish sauce and dried and fresh chilli and stir. Add the onion, spring onion, peanuts, pineapple, ginger, mint and coriander leaves. Toss lightly.

● Serve on a bed of lettuce leaves. Garnish with peanuts, ginger, chilli, sprigs of mint and coriander, spring onion curls and chilli flowers.

Bean-thread Noodle Salad with Barbecued Pork

SERVES 4

The secret of success with this dish is to have good quality pork well marinated in **cha siu** *sauce, and then roast it long enough to be edible, but not so long as to overcook the centre of the meat.*

225 g/8 oz bean-thread noodles

4–5 small carrots, cut into matchsticks

225 g/8 oz cucumber, cut into matchsticks

225 g/8 oz Chinese barbecued pork, shredded

2 dried wood ear, soaked and shredded, or 2–3 shiitake mushrooms (optional)

4 tsp toasted sesame seeds

FOR THE DRESSING

4 tbsp light soy sauce

2½ tbsp dark soy sauce

2½ tbsp sugar

5 tbsp vinegar

4 tbsp sesame oil

● Soak the bean-thread noodles in warm water for 5 minutes, or according to the instructions on the packet. Rinse under water, and drain.

● Mix the soy sauce, sugar, vinegar and sesame oil together in a bowl. Add the carrots, cucumber, *cha siu* pork, wood ear or mushrooms, if using, and noodles, and mix well.

● Serve the noodles either on a large dish or in four individual dishes, and sprinkle with toasted sesame seeds before eating.

Cold Crispy Roast Lamb, Bean Sprout and Bean Salad

SERVES 4

100 g/4 oz crispy roast leg of lamb, thinly sliced and cut into 1 x 2.5 cm/½ x 1 in strips

100 g/4 oz bean sprouts, washed and dried

100 g/4 oz green beans, tossed in boiling water for 5 minutes

100 g/4 oz broccoli florets, blanched

6 lettuce leaves, preferably Chinese

3 large tomatoes, cut into wedges

1 large cucumber, peeled and sliced

½ medium pepper, cut in strips

2 medium-sized onions, finely sliced into rings

6 spring onion curls

3 hard-boiled eggs, halved

FOR THE DRESSING

50 g/2 oz unsalted roasted peanuts

120 ml/4 fl oz lemon juice

3 tbsp vinegar

4 cloves garlic

3 tbsp chopped fresh coriander

3 tbsp sugar

1 tbsp fish sauce

FOR THE GARNISH

1 hard-boiled egg, sliced

fresh coriander, chopped

chilli flowers

● Blend all the dressing ingredients in a blender using a little water to give you the consistency you want. Adjust by increasing vinegar, sugar or fish sauce.

● Arrange the salad ingredients on a large dish. Start off with a bed of lettuce and from there, you are on your own.

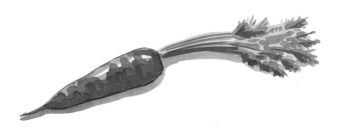

Bean-thread Noodle Salad with Prawns

SERVES 4

This is a hot Thai salad. The fish sauce, an essential ingredient in Thai cuisine, enhances the flavour of the dish. It is a good idea to prepare this salad at least 30 minutes before you serve it to allow the full sweet, hot flavour to mature.

225 g/8 oz bean-thread noodles

16 large prawns, peeled and deveined

1 tsp fish sauce

2 tsp freshly squeezed lemon juice

1 tsp palm or brown sugar

1 tbsp sunflower oil

1 small red pepper, finely chopped

2 celery sticks, thinly sliced

4–5 small carrots, cut into matchsticks

2 spring onions, chopped

4–5 lettuce leaves

coriander leaves to garnish

FOR THE DRESSING

2 shallots, finely chopped

1 dry red chilli, crushed

3 small green chilli, chopped

4 tbsp fish sauce

120 ml/4 fl oz freshly squeezed lemon juice (about 2 lemons)

4½ tbsp palm or brown sugar

1 tbsp sunflower oil

● Soak the bean-thread noodles in warm water for 5 minutes, or according to the instructions on the packet. Rinse under cold running water, and drain.

● Marinate the prawns in a mixture of 1 teaspoon fish sauce, 2 teaspoons of lemon juice and 1 teaspoon sugar for 15 minutes.

● Meanwhile, mix together the dressing ingredients.

● Heat 1 tablespoon oil in a frying pan and stir-fry the prawns thoroughly.

● Put the red pepper, celery, carrot, spring onions and noodles in a bowl, and mix together. Place a lettuce leaf on each plate, and pile the noodle mixture onto it. Put the prawns on the noodles and sprinkle with the coriander leaves.

Spicy Catfish Salad

SERVES 4

325 g/11 oz whole catfish, cleaned and gutted

1 tbsp peanut or corn oil

10 g/¼ oz mint leaves, sliced

3 tbsp lime juice, or to taste

3 tbsp sliced shallots

2½ tbsp fish sauce, or to taste

1½ tbsp sticky rice, dry-fried for a few minutes and pounded finely

1 tsp chilli powder

1 tsp kaffir lime leaf, finely shredded

● Rub the catfish with the oil and roast in the oven at 180°C/350°F/Gas Mark 4 for 40 minutes until firm but tender. When cooked, remove the skin and bones and chop the fish meat finely. Place in a bowl and stir in the rest of the ingredients—mix well. Check the seasoning, and add more fish sauce or lime juice if you like.

● Serve accompanied by raw green beans, cabbage, sweet basil and spring onions.

Bean-thread Noodle Salad
with Prawns

Fried Catfish Spicy Salad

SERVES 4–6

This crispy dish is often served as a snack to accompany drinks (an important and distinct category of dish in Thailand, where drinking tends to be separated from eating main meals).

2 whole catfish (500 g/1 lb 2 oz each), cleaned and gutted

1.2 litres/2 pt peanut or corn oil for deep-frying

1 green unripe mango, cut into matchsticks

25 g/1 oz unsalted roasted peanuts

7 fresh small green chillies, chopped

3 tbsp sliced shallots

3 tbsp fish sauce

2 tbsp coriander leaves and stems, cut into 2.5 cm/1 in pieces

● Steam the catfish for 15 minutes until well cooked. Remove all the skin and bones and chop finely.

● Heat the oil in a wok or pan until hot, about 180°C/350°F, sprinkle in the chopped fish and fry until light brown and crispy, 3–5 minutes. Remove with a slotted spoon or strainer and drain well.

● Mix all the remaining ingredients except the coriander with the fish. Place the salad on plates, and garnish with coriander and serve accompanied by rice.

Raw Beef Salad

SERVES 6

This salad from the north of Thailand differs from the better known southern version chiefly in that it does not include the roasted ground rice. Northerners also have a special liking for raw meat dishes. The origin for this and our more familiar steak tartare may well be the same.

200 g/7 oz very fresh lean beef sirloin, chopped finely at the last minute

50 g/2 oz ox liver, sliced thinly

120 ml/4 fl oz very fresh beef blood

10 g/¼ oz mint leaves

3 tbsp finely sliced spring onion

3 tbsp lime or lemon juice

½ tbsp fish sauce

1½ tsp chilli powder

● Simply mix all the ingredients together well and place on serving plates.

● Serve accompanied by raw morning glory, raw cabbage wedges, fresh basil and sticky rice.

Stir-fry Pork and Vegetable Salad

SERVES 4

The vegetables can be altered according to taste or availability.

vegetable oil for frying

100 g/4 oz piece loin of pork, cut into fine strips

1 small turnip, cut into 5 cm/ 2 in long strips

1 small carrot, cut into 5 cm/ 2 in long strips

1 small onion, cut into 5 cm/ 2 in long strips

2–3 celery sticks, cut into 5 cm/2 in long strips

50 g/2 oz mushroom caps, cut into 5 cm/2 in long strips

1 small clove garlic, crushed

1 tsp grated fresh ginger

2 spring onions, white and some green parts finely chopped

3 tbsp soy sauce

1½ tsp sesame oil

1 tbsp sugar

1 tsp rice vinegar

freshly ground black pepper

sesame seeds for garnish

● Heat about 2 tablespoons of oil in a frying pan. Add the pork and stir-fry for 3–4 minutes until cooked through. Using a slotted spoon, transfer it to a bowl.

● Add the turnip and carrot strips to the pan and fry for 5–7 minutes until just beginning to soften.

● Add the onion and celery to a saucepan of boiling water and simmer for 2–3 minutes. Drain and refresh under running cold water. Add to the pork with the mushrooms, garlic, ginger and spring onions.

● Using a slotted spoon, transfer the turnips and carrots to absorbent kitchen paper to drain.

● Whisk together the soy sauce, sesame oil, sugar and rice vinegar. Add the turnips and carrots to the pork. Pour over the dressing and toss. Leave until cold. Serve sprinkled with sesame seeds.

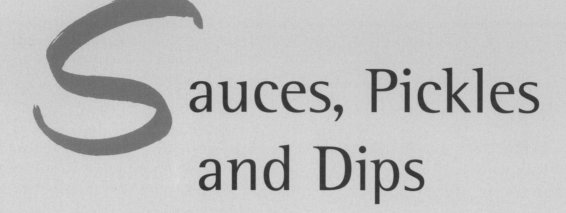

Sauces, Pickles and Dips

Many of the dishes described in earlier sections can be served with a variety of accompaniments, and some of the best known dips and sauces are included here. In addition, Asian cuisine features many preserved foodstuffs, which were developed in the days before refrigerators were available. Pickled, salted, fermented and sun-dried vegetables, meat and fish are flavoursome and economical accompaniments to plain noodles or rice.

Cabbage Pickle

FILLS ABOUT 2 2-LITRE/3½-PT JARS

*This is a standard cabbage **kimchi**. Some of the cabbage can be replaced by thinly sliced white radish, if liked.*

900 g/2 lb Chinese cabbage

salt

6 spring onions, white and green parts thinly sliced

4 cloves garlic, crushed

2 tbsp finely chopped fresh ginger

1 tbsp Korean chilli powder, or cayenne pepper mixed with paprika

1 tsp sugar

● Quarter the Chinese cabbage lengthways, then cut each quarter widthways into 5 cm/2 in pieces.

● Pour 1.5 litres/2½ pt water into a large bowl and stir in 3 tablespoons salt until dissolved. Add the cabbage and weight down with a plate.

● Cover and leave for 12 hours, stirring the cabbage occasionally. Using a slotted spoon, remove the cabbage from the bowl and reserve the salted water.

● Mix the cabbage with the remaining ingredients and 1 teaspoon salt. Pack into clean, dry jars. Pour in enough of the reserved salted water to cover the cabbage; leave a space of 2.5 cm/1 in at the top of the jar.

● Cover the jar loosely with a non-metallic lid and leave for 3–6 days until the pickle has become sour enough for your taste. Cover tightly and keep in a cold, dark place. It will keep in these conditions for up to 1 year.

Stuffed Cucumber Pickle

FILLS ABOUT 3 50-ML/¾-PT JARS

Use a potato peeler or the slicing disk of a food processor to slice the white radish. To serve, slice through the cucumbers completely and arrange on a plate.

675 g/1½ lb pickling cucumbers

350 g/12 oz white radish

2.5 cm/1 in fresh ginger

2 tbsp very finely chopped garlic

6 spring onions, white and some green parts very thinly sliced

2½ tsp Korean chilli powder, or cayenne pepper mixed with paprika

1½ tsp sugar

2 tsp salt

● Cut the cucumbers crossways, slightly diagonally, at 1 cm/½ in intervals but not going quite all the way—the slices should remain attached at the bottom.

● Pour generous 1 litre/1¾ pt water into a bowl and stir in 4 tablespoons of salt until dissolved. Add the cucumbers and weight down with a plate to keep them submerged. Leave for 3–4 hours.

● Just before the cucumbers are ready, cut the ginger into very fine strips. Cut the white radish into very fine strips. Mix with the remaining ingredients.

● Lift the cucumbers from the liquid; reserve the liquid. Dry the cucumbers with absorbent kitchen paper. Fill the gaps between the cucumber slices with as much of the white radish stuffing as they will hold easily. Put into a bowl. Add the white radish liquid. Cover and leave for 8 hours.

● Carefully pack the cucumbers fairly tightly into clean, dry 450-ml/¾-pt jars. Push any loose stuffing between the cucumbers and pour in all the juices from the bowl. Push the cucumbers down; if the liquid does not cover them by 1 cm/ ½ in, add some of the reserved cucumber soaking water.

● Cover loosely and leave for 3–6 days until the pickle has soured to your taste. Seal tightly and keep until required. It will keep for up to a year.

Spiced Turnip Pickle

FILLS A 350-ML/12-FL OZ JAR

Turnip is a very popular root vegetable in Korea, used in many everyday recipes as well as in pickles.

2 turnips, each weighing about 150 g/5 oz, peeled, halved lengthways and thinly sliced

1½ tsp salt

3 cloves garlic, finely chopped

1 spring onion, white and green part finely chopped

1 dried red chilli, seeded and coarsely crushed

● Rub 1 teaspoon of the salt into the turnip slices, then put into a bowl. Leave for 3 hours, stirring the slices every 30 minutes.

● Drain the turnips and rinse under running cold water, then mix with the remaining ingredients.

● Pack into a clean, dry jar, then cover with cold water. Put a saucer on the jar and leave for 6–8 days until the pickle turns sour.

● Cover the jar with a vinegar-proof lid and store in a cool, dry place for up to a year.

Instant Cucumber Pickle

SERVES 6–8

This is a very convenient version of **kimchi** *as it can be eaten as soon as it has been chilled (see page 413).*

450 g/1 lb cucumbers

2¼ tsp salt

1 clove garlic, crushed

9 cm/3½ in piece of white radish, cut into fine strips

2 spring onions, white and green parts thinly sliced

2.5 cm/1 in piece of fresh ginger, crushed to a pulp

1½ tsp Korean chilli powder, or cayenne pepper mixed with paprika

2 tsp crushed toasted sesame seeds

1 tbsp sesame oil

● Cut the cucumber into 5 cm/2 in lengths, then cut each piece lengthways in half. Place each half skin-side up and slice across. Put the slices in a colander and toss with 2 teaspoons of the salt. Leave for at least 3 hours.

● Drain the cucumber gently, squeezing out as much water as possible.

● Mix the cucumber with the remaining salt, garlic, white radish, spring onions, ginger and chilli powder, or cayenne and paprika. Cover and chill. Drain off the liquid from the vegetables, then toss them with the sesame seeds and sesame oil. This will keep for a day or two in the refrigerator.

Pickled Garlic

FILLS A 250-ML/8-FL OZ JAR

Green garlic is used in Korea for this recipe, but it works very well with ordinary garlic if the heads are made up of large, plump cloves. After pickling, the cut garlic heads are cut crossways to make attractive slices.

2 heads of garlic with plump cloves

120 ml/4 fl oz rice vinegar

120 ml/4 fl oz soy sauce

2 tbsp sugar

1 tsp salt

● Put the garlic in a clean, dry 250-ml/8-fl oz jar. Bring the remaining ingredients to the boil in a small saucepan, then simmer gently until reduced by half. Pour over the garlic.

● Cover tightly and leave for 2 months. It will keep for up to a year in a cool, dry place.

Stuffed Cabbage Pickle

FILLS A 250-ML/8-FL OZ JAR

Salted fish, especially anchovies, are a popular addition to **kimchis;** *the fish dissolve during the fermentation and storage, enriching the flavour of the* **kimchi,** *not giving it a fishy taste. This recipe uses fish sauce instead of salted anchovies.*

6 tbsp salt

½ Chinese cabbage, about 225 g/8 oz

175 g/6 oz piece of white radish, halved crossways

4 spring onions, coarsely chopped

4 cloves garlic, finely chopped

2.5 cm/1 in piece of fresh ginger, finely chopped

1 tbsp Korean chilli powder, or cayenne pepper mixed with paprika

1 tsp sugar

2 tbsp fish sauce

● Pour a generous litre/1¾ pt water into a large bowl and stir in all but ¼ teaspoon of the salt until dissolved. Add the cabbage and put a plate on top to keep it submerged. Leave for 8–10 hours.

● Cut the white radish into thin strips, then mix well with the remaining ingredients, including the remaining salt. Drain the cabbage well, then squeeze hard to remove as much water as possible.

● Place the cabbage cut-side up. Beginning with the outer leaves, pack the white radish mixture between each leaf.

● Fold the cabbage leaves and pack them into a clean, dry jar. Add any remaining white radish mixture. Cover loosely with vinegar-proof lids and leave for at least 3 days until sour enough for your taste. Push the cabbage down so it remains beneath the liquid that is produced. Cover tightly and keep in a cold place. It will keep for up to a year.

Stuffed Cabbage Pickle, Pickled Garlic and Instant Cucumber Pickle

Northeastern Spicy Dip

SERVES 4–6

This dip is not very spicy, but has an interesting combination of flavours.

6 cloves garlic

1 tbsp sliced shallot

1 tsp chopped galangal

2 tbsp anchovies, finely chopped

1 tbsp lemon juice

1 dried red chilli, pounded finely

1 kaffir lime leaf, torn into small pieces

½ stalk of lemon grass, sliced finely

● Dry-fry the garlic, shallot and galangal for 3 minutes over medium heat, then chop finely. Pound with the rest of the ingredients with a mortar and pestle or in a blender.

● Serve accompanied by cabbage, green beans, fresh basil and sticky rice.

Fermented Dip for Vegetables and Rice

SERVES 6–8

Northeasterners have their own special version of fish sauce, a much more substantial affair containing fish pieces, vegetables and flavourings. Quite pungent!

600 ml/1 pt thin coconut milk

75 g/3 oz dried salted mackerel (the smellier the better) or anchovies

40 g/1½ oz galangal, sliced

40 g/1½ oz lemon grass, sliced

150 g/5 oz catfish fillets, skinned and cut into pieces

6 fresh small whole red chillies

1 tbsp kaffir lime leaves, finely sliced

40 g/1½ oz *krachai*, cut into lengthways matchsticks

100 g/4 oz green beans, cut into 2.5 cm/1 in pieces

50 g/2 oz shallots, halved

50 g/2 oz bamboo shoots, cut into 5 mm/¼ in pieces

4 baby white aubergines, the size of large grapes

fish sauce, to taste (optional)

● Heat the coconut milk in a pan, add the salted fish, boil for 1 minute, add the galangal and lemon grass, boil again, then add the catfish, chillies and lime leaf and cook for another minute.

● Add the krachai—don't stir it in—and bring back to the boil. Simmer for 3 minutes, add the rest of the ingredients and cook for another 2 minutes. Taste for saltiness and add fish sauce as necessary. Serve hot or cold—this dish can be refrigerated for 2–3 days to enhance the flavours.

● Serve accompanied by raw vegetables and rice.

Spicy Dip with Mackerel

SERVES 6

3 x 100 g/4 oz baby mackerel, cleaned and gutted, or 325 g/11 oz boneless mackerel fillets

1½ tsp salt

½ tbsp shrimp paste

2 tbsp dried shrimps, finely pounded

1 tbsp sliced garlic

2 small green aubergines, peeled

15 fresh small whole green or red chillies

6 pea-sized aubergines or fresh green peas

2 tbsp lemon juice

1 tbsp fish sauce

½ tbsp palm sugar

1 fresh large red chilli, sliced into small circles

4 tbsp peanut or corn oil

● Rub the mackerel inside and out with the salt and leave in a cool place for 1 hour.

● Dry-fry the shrimp paste in foil over high heat for 5 minutes (or roast in a 180°C/350°F/Gas Mark 4 oven for 8 minutes), then remove and unwrap.

● Pound the shrimp paste, dried shrimps, garlic and aubergine together with a pestle and mortar or in a blender. Add the small chillies, pound lightly, then thoroughly mix in the rest of the ingredients, except the red chilli slices, which are used for garnish.

● Heat the oil in a frying pan over medium heat and fry the fish for 6–8 minutes on each side—the flesh should be tender but firm and white at the centre.

● Serve accompanied by fresh vegetables, such as lightly boiled cabbage and green beans.

Pickled Radishes

SERVES 4

24 radishes   1 tsp salt

2 tsp sugar

● Choose fairly large radishes that are roughly equal in size, if possible, and cut off and discard the stalks and tails. Wash the radishes in cold water and dry them thoroughly. Using a sharp knife, make several cuts from the top about two-thirds of the way down the sides of each radish.

● Put the radishes in a large jar. Add the sugar and salt. Cover the jar and shake well so that each radish is coated with the sugar and salt mixture. Leave to marinate for several hours or overnight.

● Just before serving, pour off the liquid and spread out each radish like a fan. Serve them on a plate on their own or as a garnish with other cold dishes.

White Radish Pickle

FILLS 1 JAR

Some people find that chillies and chilli powder irritate their skin; if this happens to you, wear fine rubber gloves when rubbing the chilli powder into the radish.

2 tbsp Korean chilli powder or cayenne pepper mixed with paprika

800 g/1¾ lb white radish, cut into 2.5 cm/1 in cubes

4 spring onions, white and green parts thinly sliced

2.5 cm/1 in piece fresh ginger, finely chopped

1 small clove garlic, finely chopped

2 tsp sugar

4 tsp salt

● Rub the chilli powder or cayenne and paprika into the white radish. Put in a bowl and leave for at least 30 minutes.

● Mix the remaining ingredients with the white radish and cover with cling film. Put a plate that just fits inside the bowl, on top of the cling film, and put a heavy weight on top. Leave for about 48 hours until the liquid rises above the white radish.

● Remove the weight and leave the pickle for a further 3–7 days, depending on the temperature, until it turns sour.

● Transfer the pickle to a dry, clean jar. Cover with a vinegar-proof lid and keep in a cold, dark place. It will keep for up to a year in these conditions.

Pickled Vegetables

SERVES 4

Use 4–6 of the following vegetables or more: cucumber, carrot, radish or turnip, cauliflower, broccoli, green cabbage, white cabbage, celery, onion, fresh ginger, leek, spring onion, red pepper, green pepper, green beans and garlic

4.75 litres/8½ pt cold boiled water

175 g/6 oz salt

50 g/2 oz chillies

3 tsp Szechwan peppercorns

4 tbsp Chinese distilled spirit (or white rum, gin or vodka)

100 g/4 oz fresh ginger

100 g/4 oz brown sugar

● Put the cold boiled water into a large, clean earthenware or glass jar. Add the salt, chillies, peppercorns, spirit, ginger and sugar.

● Wash and trim the vegetables, peel if necessary and drain well. Put them into the jar and seal it making sure it is airtight. Place the jar in a cool place and leave the vegetables to pickle for at least five days before serving.

● Use a pair of clean chopsticks or tongs to pick the vegetables out of the jar. Do not allow any grease to enter the jar. You can replenish the vegetables, adding a little salt each time. If any white scum appears on the surface of the brine, add a little sugar and spirit. The longer the pickling lasts, the better.

Fried Egg Strip Garnish

SERVES 1

A common garnish for Korean savoury dishes. Lightly beaten eggs are fried one at a time to keep the mixture thin. Sometimes, the eggs are separated and the yolks and whites cooked separately.

1 egg, lightly beaten

vegetable oil for frying

● Heat a very thin film of vegetable oil in a large nonstick frying pan. Pour in the egg, and tilt and swirl the pan to spread the egg out in a thin even layer.

● Fry for 1–2 minutes until set underneath, then turn the 'omelette' over and fry until set. Transfer the 'omelette' to a wooden board, or a work surface, and roll it up. Cut into 5 mm/¼ in strips.

Southern Vegetable Dip

SERVES 4

75 g/3 oz raw large prawns, shelled and cut into 3 pieces

2 tbsp fish sauce

2 tbsp lemon or lime juice

1 tbsp fresh small green chilli, chopped

1 tbsp sliced shallot

1½ tsp shrimp paste

● Boil the prawns in a small amount of water for 2 minutes and drain. Place in a bowl and mix well with the rest of the ingredients except the shrimp paste.

● Wrap the shrimp paste in foil and roast in a 180°C/350°F/Gas Mark 4 oven for 5 minutes, or dry-fry in a hot wok for 3 minutes. Remove and stir into the prawn mixture.

● Serve accompanied by green beans, broad beans, raw cabbage and rice.

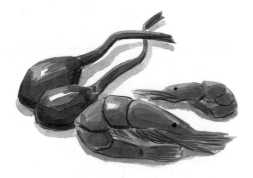

Green Chilli Dip

SERVES 6

This is high on the scale of chilli 'heat', but green and fresh-tasting. It is intended to be eaten with sticky rice and assorted raw vegetables, and as part of a larger meal. Traditionally, everyone eats from one bowl.

1 tbsp dried salted mackerel or anchovy, chopped

4 tbsp peanut or corn oil

10 fresh 5 cm/2 in green chillies, chopped roughly

10 cloves garlic, chopped roughly

6 shallots, chopped roughly

3 cherry tomatoes

2 tbsp hot water

1 tbsp chopped spring onion

1 tbsp chopped coriander leaves

fish sauce, to taste (optional)

● Fry the dried fish in the oil over medium heat for about 7–10 minutes and drain. Dry-fry the chillies, garlic, shallots and tomatoes until fragrant, about 8–10 minutes. Place in a bowl.

● Pound them lightly with the dry fish. Add the water, spring onion and coriander, and mix well. Taste to check—it should be of a saucy consistency and a touch salty; if not, add more water or fish sauce.

● Serve accompanied by a selection of raw cabbage wedges, sliced cucumbers, raw green beans and/or fried or roasted fish.

Spicy Meat and Tomato Dip

SERVES 4–6

This is a relatively mild dip, and in northern Thai fashion, guests eat from the bowl in which it is served, scooping with the pork rind, vegetables or sticky rice.

6 dried red chillies, chopped

3 tbsp chopped shallots

1 tbsp sliced lemon grass

1 tbsp chopped garlic

2 tsp shrimp paste

2 tsp salt

2 tbsp peanut or corn oil

100 g/4 oz minced pork

8 cherry tomatoes, diced

120 ml/4 fl oz water

lemon juice, to taste

fish sauce, to taste

sugar, to taste

25 g/1 oz coriander leaves

● Pound the chillies, onion, lemon grass, garlic, shrimp paste and salt together with a pestle and mortar or in a blender until fine.

● Heat the oil in a wok or pan and add the chilli mixture and the pork, and tomatoes. Cook until thick, about 15 minutes, then add the water and cook again for 10 minutes until thick.

● Adjust the seasoning to taste with lemon juice, fish sauce, and/or sugar. Garnish with the coriander leaves.

● Serve accompanied by raw or slightly cooked vegetables, sticky rice and, if you can buy it, crispy pork rind.

Crushed Toasted Sesame Seeds

MAKES ABOUT 1/3 CUP

Prepare the quantity of these that is appropriate to the amount of Korean cooking you are going to do (it is easy to increase or halve the recipe), and store them in a screw-top jar in a cool, dark place.

50 g/2 oz sesame seeds

2 tsp salt

● Heat a small, heavy frying pan over a medium-low heat. Add the sesame seeds and stir until they darken a shade and give off a toasted, nutty aroma.

● Crush the seeds with the salt in a pestle and mortar. Keep in a screw-top jar.

Vinegar Dipping Sauce

MAKES 10 TABLESPOONS

This can serve as a basic Korean dipping sauce.

7 tbsp soy sauce

2 tbsp rice vinegar

1 cm/½ in fresh ginger, grated

2 tsp crushed toasted sesame
   seeds

about ½ tsp Korean chilli
   powder

pinch of sugar

● Combine the soy sauce and vinegar in a small bowl, and add remaining ingredients. If you do not have the chilli powder, use cayenne pepper mixed with paprika.

Ginger Dipping Sauce

MAKES ABOUT 10 TABLESPOONS

There are no chillies in this sauce but ginger provides some 'hotness'. Also the predominance of soy sauce and rice vinegar are reversed.

6 tbsp rice vinegar

2.5 cm/1 in piece fresh ginger, grated

2 spring onions, white part only, finely chopped

2 tbsp dark soy sauce

2 tsp sugar

● Pour the vinegar into a small bowl. Add the remaining ingredients and mix together well.

Sesame Dipping Sauce

MAKES 6 TABLESPOONS

Sesame oil and toasted sesame seeds make a more richly flavoured dipping sauce.

3 tbsp soy sauce

1 tsp sesame oil

1½ tbsp rice vinegar

1 tsp toasted sesame seeds

pinch of sugar

1 small spring onion, finely chopped

● Combine the soy sauce, sesame oil and rice vinegar in a small bowl. Add the remaining ingredients and mix well.

Seasoned Dipping Sauce

MAKES 7 TABLESPOONS

4 tbsp soy sauce

2 tsp sesame oil

1 tbsp rice vinegar

about ¼–½ fresh red or green chilli

2 tsp toasted sesame seeds

pinch of sugar

½–1 small clove garlic, finely chopped

● Combine the soy sauce, sesame oil and rice vinegar in a small bowl. Deseed the chilli and chop finely. Add to the bowl with remaining ingredients and mix well.

Yakisoba Sauce

5–6 SERVINGS

5 tbsp brown sauce

4 tbsp light soy sauce

4 tsp tomato ketchup

4 tsp oyster sauce

4 tbsp sugar

● Mix all the ingredients together.

Fish Sauce with Chillies

This spicy sauce is found on all Thai tables and is used to add both spiciness and saltiness to dishes.

● Mix all the ingredients together well. This is good for accompanying almost all Thai food, especially rice. Just sprinkle a little on your food to liven it up.

4 tbsp fish sauce

10 fresh small green chillies,
   sliced into small circles

1 tsp sliced shallot

¼ tsp palm sugar

1 tbsp lime or lemon juice

Homemade Red Pepper Paste

This is an important seasoning and flavouring in Korean cuisine. It used to be made at home, from home-fermented soya beans, but even in Korea it is often bought ready-made nowadays. In the West it can only be purchased from oriental food shops or departments in supermarkets, but an approximation can be made at home quite easily using fairly readily available ingredients.

● Mix all the ingredients together in a small bowl. Keep in a screw-top jar in a cool, dark place. It will keep for up to 6 months in these conditions.

4 tbsp brown or red *miso*

1½ tbsp paprika

1 tsp cayenne pepper

1 tbsp sugar

Desserts

Asian meals do not usually conclude with a dessert, but these delicious treats are the perfect way to end a meal. Cakes and sweetmeats are popular throughout the Far East, and they are often served on special occasions such as birthdays and New Year celebrations. The section ends with a number of recipes for tea, the traditional accompaniment to many Asian meals.

Golden Balls

SERVES 6

20 egg yolks, duck if available

450 g/1 lb rice flour

1.8 litres/3¼ pt water

1.5 kg/3 lb sugar

4 egg shells

1 tsp jasmine water or vanilla essence

● Mix the egg yolks well with the flour in a bowl and put to one side until needed. Boil the water and sugar in a pan with the egg shells until reduced to about half, then strain through muslin, put back in the pan

and bring back to simmer. Add the jasmine or vanilla essence at this point.

● Take pieces of the egg mixture and form balls the size of large round grapes. Place them in the simmering sugar syrup; cook the balls until they float to the surface, then remove with a slotted spoon and drain. Strain the syrup, again through cloth, into a large bowl and set aside to cool until needed.

● Soak the cooked balls in the strained syrup for 30 minutes, then remove them with a slotted spoon and refrigerate. Serve when cool.

Gold Threads

SERVES 6

4 egg shells

1.5 kg/3 lb sugar

1.8 litres/3¼ pt water

1 tsp vanilla essence or
jasmine water

15 egg yolks, duck if available,
whisked lightly

● Punch about 25 small holes into the base of a can.
Wash well.

● Put the egg shells, sugar and water in a pan, bring
to the boil and simmer until reduced by about half.
Strain the liquid through muslin.

● Bring the strained syrup back to a simmer and add
the essence. Then, pour the whisked egg yolks
through the 'strainer' over the simmering sugar syrup.
Let cook for 1 minute and remove with a slotted
spoon or strainer. Repeat the process until all the egg
is used, packing the threads on a rack to drain.

Toffee Bananas

SERVES 4

4 bananas, peeled

1 egg

2 tbsp plain flour

oil for deep-frying

4 tbsp sugar

1 tbsp cold water

● Cut the bananas in half lengthways and then cut each half into two crossways.

● Beat the egg, add the flour and mix well to make a smooth batter.

● Heat the oil in a wok or deep-fryer. Coat each piece of banana with batter and deep-fry until golden. Remove and drain.

● Pour off the excess oil, leaving about 1 tablespoon of oil in the wok. Add the sugar and water and stir over a medium heat to dissolve the sugar. Continue stirring and when the sugar has caramelized, add the hot banana pieces. Coat well and remove. Dip the hot bananas in cold water to harden the toffee and serve immediately while still hot.

Banana and Pineapple Fritters

SERVES 4

vegetable oil for deep-frying

4 bananas, peeled and halved lengthways

4 pineapple rings, fresh or canned, dried on absorbent kitchen paper

icing sugar, sieved

FOR THE BATTER

50 g/2 oz self-raising flour

150 g/5 oz plain flour

½ tsp baking powder

2 tbsp vegetable oil

salt

1 egg white, beaten until stiff

● Make the batter first. Mix the flours, baking powder, salt and oil in a large bowl. Stir in just enough water to make a smooth paste. Fold in the egg white a little at a time.

● Heat some oil in a wok for deep-frying. Dip the fruit in the batter and cook in small batches (do not put more than can comfortably float on the oil) until puffy and golden. This should not take much longer than 2 minutes.

● Drain the cooked fritters on absorbent kitchen paper and sprinkle with the sieved icing sugar. Serve while hot.

Banana Cooked in Coconut Milk

SERVES 4

The addition of a little salt gives a refreshing and slightly unusual flavour. This dessert goes very well with ice cream.

2–3 small, slightly green bananas

scant litre/1¾ pt thin coconut milk

225 g/8 oz sugar

¼ tsp salt

● Slice the bananas lengthways, then in half. Pour the coconut milk into a pan, add the sugar and salt. Bring to the boil, add the bananas, bring back to the boil for 2 minutes and then remove from the heat.

● Serve, hot or cold, with the coconut milk.

Bananas in a Rich Coconut Sauce

SERVES 4

350 ml/12 fl oz coconut milk

1½ tbsp sugar

salt

6 large bananas, peeled and
sliced diagonally about 2 cm/
¾ in thick

ice cream or whipped cream to
serve

● Heat the coconut milk in a small saucepan and add the sugar and salt. Bring to the boil. Lower the heat and simmer for 2 minutes.

● Remove from the heat and stir in the banana slices. Bring back to the boil for a few seconds to coat the bananas. Serve with ice cream or whipped cream.

Imitation Fruits

SERVES 6–8

This refined dessert was invented for the court and originally was served only at the Thai Royal Palace. Even today it is hardly common, because of the time and skill needed to fashion these perfect miniatures of fruits and vegetables. They are spectacular to serve to guests, but only attempt them on a day when you have plenty of time to spare!

350 g/12 oz dried mung beans

475 ml/16 fl oz water

250 ml/8 fl oz thin coconut
  milk

240 g/8½ oz sugar

edible food colourings

250 ml/8 fl oz water

2 tbsp gelatine

● Place the mung beans in a container with the water and steam until soft, about 15 minutes, then pound them into a fine paste with a pestle and mortar or in a blender. Put in a pan with the coconut milk and 225 g/8 oz of the sugar, and heat slowly, stirring constantly, until very thick—about 15 minutes. Remove and allow to cool before using.

● When cool, shape the paste into small fingertip-sized fruit and vegetable shapes—oranges, bananas—it's up to your imagination. Stick them on cocktail sticks and stand them in a sheet of polystyrene or styrofoam. Using a small paint brush and food colourings in appropriate shades, paint the fruits.

● Heat the water, 1 tablespoon of the sugar and the agar agar in a pan until dissolved. Cool slightly and then dip in the painted fruits. Place them back on the foam and allow to dry for 15 minutes; then dip once more in the liquid, spinning the fruit slowly after removing them so that the syrup coats evenly. Leave to harden on the foam, then remove the cocktail sticks and decorate the fruits with any (non-poisonous) leaves of your choice, trimmed down to a small size. Serve as a special dessert.

Lychee and Ginger Ice

SERVES 4

100 g/4 oz lychees in heavy syrup

15 g/½ oz fresh ginger, peeled and grated

150 ml/¼ pt water

FOR THE GARNISH

fresh mint leaves

lychees

sponge ginger biscuits (optional)

● Put the lychees in a blender or food processor together with the ginger and water, and process to a fine purée. Pour the mixture into a 23 cm/9 in square baking tin and put into the freezer for 3 hours.

● Break the iced mixture into chunks and process again until slushy. Return to the baking tin and freeze once more until solid.

● Allow the mixture to soften slightly (about 5 minutes) and scoop into four champagne glasses or rice bowls. Garnish with mint leaves, lychees and a biscuit, if desired.

Lychee Sorbet

SERVES 4

This is a really simple and refreshing sorbet, which is quick and easy to make.

450 g/1 lb fresh lychees or 100 g/4 oz can lychees

1 egg white

● Peel the lychees and stone them. Purée the flesh, adding some sugared water if necessary. Pour into a container and freeze until nearly set.

● Whip up the egg white. Mix this into the nearly set lychee mixture. Put back into the freezer until solid.

Lychee and Ginger Ice

Lychee Slap

SERVES 4

1 medium jar Chinese stem ginger, drained

100 g/4 oz can lychees

1 tbsp ginger wine

● Insert a piece of the drained stem ginger into the centre of each lychee.

● Mix the liquid from the stem ginger and the lychee syrup, and add the ginger wine. Pour the sauce over the stuffed lychees.

Sticky Rice with Mangoes

SERVES 4–6

A simple dessert but always successful. It works because of contrasts: in flavour between the sweetness of the coconut milk and the yellow Thai mango, and in texture between the rice and the mango.

450 g/1 lb sticky rice

850 ml/1⅓ pt thin coconut milk

65 g/2½ oz sugar

½ tsp salt

½ tsp cornflour

2 ripe mangoes, peeled and sliced

● Soak the rice in water for 4 hours, rinse well three times in lukewarm water and drain very well. Line a strainer with muslin, add the rice and place over a pan of boiling water—do not let the water touch the bottom of the rice. Cover and steam for about 30 minutes until fairly soft.

● Mix 750 ml/1¼ pt of the coconut milk with the sugar and ¼ teaspoon of the salt. Stir in the rice.

● Mix the remaining coconut milk with the ¼ teaspoon salt and the cornflour together in a small pan, bring to the boil, simmer for 2 minutes and cool.

● Place the sticky rice onto serving plates, spoon the cornflour sauce over the top, and arrange the mango slices around the edges.

Mango and Banana Slices

SERVES 4

4 slices sponge cake

5 tbsp sherry

50 g/2 oz unsalted butter

1 ripe, but firm, mango peeled, pitted and sliced

75 g/3 oz redcurrant jelly

3 bananas, sliced

3 tbsp orange juice

● Divide the cake slices among four plates and sprinkle a spoonful of sherry over each portion.

● Melt half the butter and stir-fry the mango slices for 1–2 minutes, until they are hot. Add the redcurrant jelly and continue stir frying for a minute or so until the jelly melts and coats the mango. Divide the mango slices among the four plates, arranging them on top of the cake. Scrape all the juices from the pan over the mango.

● Melt the remaining butter and briskly stir fry the banana slices until hot. Sprinkle the orange juice over the banana, then stir for a few seconds to heat the juices. Spoon the bananas over the mango slices and serve at once.

Coconut Ice Cream

SERVES 4

300 ml/½ pt thick coconut milk

350 ml/12 fl oz cream

2 eggs

2 egg yolks

1 tsp vanilla essence

100 g/4 oz sugar

salt

FOR THE GARNISH

50 g/2 oz desiccated coconut, dry-fried until golden brown

sprigs of mint

● Heat the coconut milk and cream cook for 5 minutes without boiling over. Beat together the eggs, egg yolks, vanilla, sugar and salt.

● Place a deep bowl in a saucepan with boiling water up to the halfway mark of the bowl. Pour in the egg mixture and beat in the warm coconut milk mixture, a little at a time. Stir until the mixture thickens enough to coat a spoon. Remove from the heat, stirring occasionally as it cools.

● Pour into a bowl when it is cool enough to be put into the freezer. Freeze for 1 hour. Scoop out into a blender or food processor and process until smooth. Pour back into the bowl and freeze until solid.

● Serve in scoops, garnished with desiccated coconut and sprigs of mint.

Mango and Banana Slices

Mango Ice Cream

SERVES 4

4 ripe mangoes or 100 g/4 oz
  can sliced mango

225 g/8 oz sugar or 50 g/4 oz
  if using canned mango

1 tbsp lemon juice

1 tbsp gelatine, dissolved in
  3 tbsp water

350 ml/12 fl oz double cream,
  whipped until stiff

FOR THE GARNISH

extra mango slices

sprigs of fresh mint

● Peel and cut the mangoes, discarding the stones. Place in a bowl and add the sugar, lemon juice and dissolved gelatine. Mix thoroughly, making sure that the sugar is dissolved.

● Fold the whipped cream into the mango mixture. Spoon into a tray and put into the freezer until half-frozen. Put in a blender or food processor and process until smooth. Return to freezer and freeze until solid.

● Serve in scoops garnished with freshly sliced mango and sprigs of fresh mint.

Coconut Custard

SERVES 4

250 ml/8 fl oz thick coconut cream

4 eggs, beaten

100 g/4 oz sugar

● Beat the coconut cream, eggs and sugar together until the sugar dissolves and the mixture is thoroughly blended. Sieve the mixture through muslin. The result should be perfectly smooth.

● Place a serving bowl on top of a wooden trivet in a wok and test it for firmness. Pour the mixture into the serving bowl. Pour some water into the wok and bring to the boil. Place the serving bowl on the wooden trivet and allow to steam until the mixture is firm, about 10–15 minutes.

● Alternatively, pour the mixture into four individual bowls and steam in a large bamboo steamer.

Coconut Custard in Young Pumpkin

SERVES 4–6

This is a special version of one of the best known and best loved Thai desserts. Although more usually served in a coconut shell, a hollowed pumpkin not only looks more attractive, but its flesh gives a pleasing contrast to the sweet custard.

1 small pumpkin	350 g/12 oz palm sugar
9 duck or chicken eggs	475 ml/16 fl oz thin coconut milk

● Slice off and remove the top of the pumpkin carefully and clean out the seeds thoroughly.

● Whisk the eggs, sugar and coconut milk together in a bowl until frothy, and allow to stand for 10 minutes. Then, strain through muslin into the pumpkin.

● Steam for 30 minutes in a covered wok or steamer with the pumpkin lid steamed on the side: the custard is cooked when a skewer comes out clean.

● Cool overnight in the refrigerator. Replace the pumpkin lid before serving, then cut into wedges at the table.

Ginger Surprise

SERVES 4

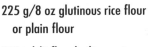

25 g/1 oz fresh ginger, crushed

225 g/8 oz sugar

350 ml/12 fl oz hot water

FOR THE FILLING

50 g/2 oz dried yellow mung
   beans, soaked in warm water
   for 30 minutes and drained

1½ tbsp sugar

4 tbsp sesame seeds

FOR THE DOUGH

225 g/8 oz glutinous rice flour
   or plain flour

250 ml/8 fl oz boiling water

● Make the ginger syrup by swirling the ginger and sugar constantly in a small saucepan over low heat, until the sugar browns. When it starts to smoke, stir in the hot water (be careful: you could give yourself a nasty burn with the spluttering) and allow to boil for about 3 minutes until the sugar is dissolved. Set aside in a cool place. Discard the ginger when cooled.

● Make the filling by steaming the mung beans over high heat for 20 minutes. Transfer to a blender or food processor, add the sugar and process to a fine paste. Put in the refrigerator for 20 minutes to firm up.

● Toast the sesame seeds by dry-frying in a wok for 2 minutes. Reserve 2 tablespoons for garnishing, put the remainder in a blender and process to a paste.

Combine with the mung bean paste and blend well. Roll 16 marble-sized balls of the mixture (1 teaspoon each). Set aside.

● Place the glutinous rice flour in a mixing bowl and quickly mix with the hot water to make a sticky dough. Cover and leave to stand for 5 minutes. Dust a work surface with flour and knead the dough for 3 minutes until soft and smooth. Divide into two equal parts. Roll each into a rope about 25 cm/10 in long and 2.5 cm/1 in in diameter. Cut each into 10 equal portions and roll each one into a ball. Cover with a damp cloth until ready to proceed.

● Flatten the dough balls, one at a time, into 6 cm/ 2½ in discs. Place a mung bean ball in the centre, gather the edges around the pinch to seal. Roll the dumplings between the palms to form perfect balls.

● Divide each of the remaining four dough balls into four, cover and set aside.

● Bring a large pot of water to the boil. Boil the filled dumplings for 2 minutes over a moderate heat. Add the smaller dumplings and cook for a further 3 minutes or until they rise to the surface. Drain.

● Reheat the ginger syrup over low heat in a large saucepan. Add the dumplings and allow to simmer for 2 minutes. Set aside to cool.

● Serve four large dumplings and four small ones to each person in individual dessert cups or rice bowls. Sprinkle with the reserved toasted sesame seeds.

Fried Bananas

SERVES 4–6

If at all possible, buy small, fragrant bananas for this (and other) banana desserts.

350 g/12 oz rice flour

250 ml/8 fl oz water

50 g/2 oz desiccated coconut

3 tbsp plain flour

3 tbsp sugar

2 tbsp sesame seeds

2 tsp baking powder

1 tsp salt

approx 1.5 litres/2½ pt peanut or corn oil for deep-frying

450 g/1 lb small, slightly green bananas, quartered

● Mix together well in a bowl all the ingredients except the oil and bananas. Heat the oil in a wok or deep pan to about 180°C/350°F.

● Dip the banana pieces into the coconut batter and then deep-fry until brown but not dark, about 3 minutes. Turn over and cook for 2 more minutes. Take out with a slotted spoon and drain on absorbent kitchen paper. Serve immediately.

Almond Junket

SERVES 4

*This junket can be made from **agar-agar**, isinglass or gelatine. When chilled and served with a variety of fresh and canned fruit, it is a most refreshing dessert.*

10 g/⅓ oz *agar-agar* or
    isinglass (or 25 g/1 oz
    gelatine powder)

4 tbsp sugar

150 ml/¼ pt evaporated milk

600 ml/1 pt water

1 tsp almond essence

1 can cherries or mixed fruit
    salad with syrup to garnish

● Dissolve the *agar-agar* or isinglass and the sugar with water in two separate pans over gentle heat. (If you are using gelatine powder, just follow the instructons on the packets.)

● Add milk and almond essence and pour the mixture into a large serving bowl. Allow to cool for at least 30 minutes and then place in the refrigerator for 2–3 hours to set.

● To serve, cut the junket into small cubes and pour the canned fruit and syrup over it.

Sweet Blackened Jelly

SERVES 6–8

This unusual dessert must be one of the few dishes anywhere in the world that makes use of the outside of a mature coconut—something that, fortunately, is usually readily available in the West.

50 g/2 oz coconut hair (hairy brown coating from outside of coconuts)

1.5 litres/2½ pt water

350 g/12 oz rice flour

½ tbsp tapioca flour

550 g/1¼ lb palm sugar

225 g/8 oz desiccated coconut

¼ tsp salt

● Take the coconut hair and roast it in a 190°C/375°F/ Gas Mark 5 oven for about 20 minutes until black, stirring occasionally, then chop well. Mix it with 250 ml/8 fl oz of the water and then strain twice through muslin.

● Put both the flours in a large bowl, mix well, then stir in the remaining water and the sugar. Stir in the 250 ml/8 fl oz black water mixture and strain again through muslin.

● Place the liquid in a stainless steel pan and slowly bring to the boil, stirring constantly, for about 20 minutes, until very thick—don't burn the bottom. When thick, pour into ungreased shallow cake tins and leave to cool for 1 hour. Refrigerate overnight.

● To remove the jelly, warm the pans by dipping them in warm water and then inverting onto a plate. Cut the jelly into bite-sized pieces. Mix the coconut with the salt and sprinkle over the top.

Jackfruit Seeds

SERVES 6-8

These are one of a range of Thai sweetmeats made with egg yolks. Kanoon, or jackfruit, is not used in the recipe—they are only called after the fruit because of the similar shape.

350 g/12 oz dried yellow mung beans	1.2 litres/2 pt water
850 g/1¾ lb sugar	10 egg yolks, duck if possible, whisked lightly
scant litre/1¾ pt thin coconut milk	

● Soak the mung beans in water for 1 hour, then drain and steam them for 20 minutes or until soft. Mash or purée in a food processor.

● Put the beans in a pan with 350 g/12 oz of the sugar and the coconut milk. Bring to the boil and then simmer, stirring, until reduced to a paste, about 15 minutes—be careful not to burn the mixture. Remove from the heat and leave to cool.

● Meanwhile, make the syrup. Boil the water with the remaining sugar until reduced by half. Remove 250 ml/8 fl oz of the syrup and put to one side. Keep the remaining syrup simmering slowly.

● Take pieces of the bean paste and shape them into small fingertip-sized ovals. Cook them in batches of eight to ten at a time. Dip first into the egg yolk and then into the pan of syrup. Wait until they float to the top, then remove with a slotted spoon and drain on absorbent kitchen paper. Place them in the reserved 250 ml/8 fl oz syrup for 30 minutes, remove, set aside and allow to dry for 5 minutes.

● Serve immediately or cover and refrigerate; serve at room temperature.

Rolled Sesame Slices

SERVES 4

These uncooked biscuits are rolled up like a Swiss roll, then cut across into slices; this is easiest to do if you use a hot sharp knife.

50 g/2 oz white sesame seeds

50 g/2 oz black sesame seeds

about 50 g/2 oz light brown sugar

8 tbsp golden syrup

● Heat the white and black sesame seeds in separate dry heavy frying pans until they just begin to pop.

● Gently heat the sugar in the golden syrup, stirring until the sugar has dissolved. Mix half with the white sesame seeds and half with the black sesame seeds.

● Spread each mixture out on a sheet of greaseproof paper. Put another sheet of greaseproof paper on each and roll out. Remove the top sheets of greaseproof paper and invert the black sesame seed mixture onto the white sesame seed mixture.

● Remove the greaseproof paper now on top. Roll up the sesame seed mixtures firmly, enclosing the black in the white and using the underneath sheet of paper to help you. Leave until cold, then cut into slices.

Biscuit Bows

SERVES 4–6

These crisp biscuits are very moreish, but if you can resist eating them all soon after they are made, they will keep in an airtight container for several days.

100 g/4 oz plain flour

1½ tbsp caster sugar

3 tbsp rice wine or dry sherry

vegetable oil for deep-frying

about 120 ml/4 fl oz clear honey

chopped pine nuts for coating

● Stir together the flour and sugar, and slowly pour in the rice wine or dry sherry to make a smooth dough; add a little water if necessary. Knead lightly on a floured surface, then roll out lightly to a thin rectangle. Cut into 5 x 2.5 cm/2 x 1 in pieces. Cut a lengthways slit about 2.5 cm/1 in long in the centre of each piece. Pull one end of each piece through the slit so the piece resembles a small bow shape.

● Heat the oil in a deep-fat fryer to 160°C/330°F. Add the bows and fry for 4–5 minutes until rich golden brown. Remove and drain briefly on a pad of absorbent kitchen paper.

● Meanwhile, slowly heat the honey (dilute with a little water if the honey is too thick). Dip the bows in the honey to coat, then sprinkle with chopped pine nuts.

Spiced Honey Cakes

SERVES 4

In Korea, there are special moulds for shaping these deep-fried cakes. To get the juice from fresh ginger, squeeze a piece of peeled fresh ginger in a taint-free garlic press.

100 g/4 oz self-raising flour

1 tsp ground cinnamon

grated rind of ½ lemon

2 tbsp rice wine or dry sherry

2 tbsp clear honey

1 tsp fresh ginger juice

2 tbsp sesame oil

vegetable oil for deep-frying

sesame seeds for coating

● Sift the flour and cinnamon into a bowl. Stir in the lemon rind, then add the rice wine or sherry, honey, ginger juice and sesame oil and enough water to make a smooth dough.

● Knead the dough, then roll out on a lightly floured surface to about 5 mm/¼ in. Using a 4 cm/1½ in biscuit cutter, cut into rounds.

● Heat the vegetable oil in a deep-fat fryer. Add the cakes in batches so they are not crowded, and fry until they rise to the surface and are light golden brown, about 3–5 minutes.

● Transfer to absorbent kitchen paper to drain. Sprinkle with sesame seeds.

Southern Flat Breads

MAKES 7–8

These are derived from Thailand's Indian connections, as the name suggests. Bread is uncharacteristic of Thai cooking, and roti are used mainly in this way, as a dessert snack.

175 g/6 oz plain flour

4 tbsp water

1 tbsp softened butter

1 egg

¼ tsp salt

250 ml/8 fl oz peanut or corn oil for frying

● Mix all the ingredients except the oil together well in a bowl; if the mixture is too wet to shape, add a little more flour. Shape the dough in bite-sized balls and flatten them into 10 cm/4 in circles by throwing them onto a lightly floured table surface—be careful to throw them quite horizontal.

● Heat enough oil to just cover the bottom of a frying pan over medium heat. Place the flattened dough balls in the pan and brown lightly, about 3–4 minutes, on each side. Drain on absorbent kitchen paper and repeat.

● Three delicious ways of serving the flat breads are: to place an egg on top of each browned roti, flipping it over to cook the egg and rolling it up to eat (perhaps with coffee); to sprinkle them with sugar and condensed milk; or to spread them with butter.

Spiced Honey Cakes

Red Bean Paste Pancakes

SERVES 4

225 g/8 oz plain flour

120 ml/4 fl oz boiling water

1 egg

3 tbsp oil

4–5 tbsp sweetened red bean paste or chestnut purée

● Sift the flour into a mixing bowl and very gently pour in the boiling water. Add about 1 teaspoon oil and the beaten egg.

● Knead the mixture into a firm dough and then divide it into two equal portions. Roll out each portion into a long 'sausage' on a lightly floured surface and cut it into four to six pieces. Using the palm of your hand, press each piece into a flat pancake.

● On a lightly floured surface, flatten each pancake into a 15 cm/6 in circle with a rolling pin and roll gently.

● Place an ungreased frying pan on a high heat. When hot, reduce the heat to low and place one pancake at a time in the pan. Turn it over when little brown spots appear on the underside. Remove and keep under a damp cloth until you have finished making the rest of the pancakes.

● Spread about 2 tablespoons red bean paste or chestnut purée over about 80 percent of the pancake surface and roll it over three or four times to form a flattened roll.

● Heat the oil in a frying pan and shallow-fry the pancakes until golden brown, turning over once.

● Cut each pancake into three or four pieces and serve hot or cold.

Barley Tea

MAKES 900 ML / 1 ½ PT

Poricha is ubiquitous throughout Korea. In winter it is served hot, in summer it is served cold, sweetened with honey or sugar. Poricha has a distinctive, smoky taste and is quite free of caffeine. Roast barley is available from Korean and Japanese food shops.

2 tbsp roast barley

900 ml/1½ pt water

● Put the roast barley and water into a saucepan and bring to the boil. Lower the heat and simmer the tea until it is as strong as you like it. Strain.

Ginseng Tea

MAKES 900 ML / 1 ½ PT

Korean ginseng is believed to be the best. In Korea (and elsewhere) ginseng is purported to cure all manner of ills, from insomnia to impotence. A favourite way of taking ginseng is in the form of a tea.

3 slices of red ginseng

1 cm/½ in piece fresh ginger, sliced

3 jujubes (Chinese dates), cut into pieces

900 ml/1½ pt water

● Put all the ingredients into a saucepan. Add 900 ml/1½ pt water and bring to the boil. Lower the heat, cover and simmer for 1 hour.

● Strain into cups. Add pieces of jujube, ginseng and ginger to each cup if liked.

Rice Tea

MAKES 900 ML / 1 ½ PT

When rice is cooked in the traditional way in large pans (although now electric rice cookers are often used) some grain invariably sticks to the bottom of the pan and burns. After all the non-burned rice is served, hot water is poured into the pot and boiled. This is then served as a digestive rice tea at the end of the meal. There are many versions of rice tea, and one can be made without first cooking and burning a pot of rice.

2 tbsp uncooked long-grain rice

900 ml/1½ pt boiling water

● Put the rice into a small heavy frying pan and cook over a medium-low heat, stirring, until the rice becomes flecked with dark patches and has a rich nutty aroma.

● Tip the rice into a saucepan and add the boiling water. Return to the boil, then simmer for 1½ minutes. Cover and remove from the heat. Leave for 5 minutes, then strain and serve the tea while still hot.

Ginger Tea

MAKES 1 LITRE/1¾ PT

In addition to being a digestive, Saenggangcha is meant to be good for coughs and colds.

3 x 2.5 cm/1 in pieces fresh ginger, coarsely chopped

strip of orange peel

4–5 tsp clear honey

ground cinnamon for sprinkling

pine nuts for decorating

● Put the ginger, orange peel and honey in a saucepan and add 1 litre/1¾ pt water. Bring to the boil, then simmer slowly for 15–20 minutes.

● Strain the tea and sprinkle a little cinnamon on top. Serve hot or cold.

Glossary of Ingredients

A clear, concise guide to the ingredients used in the recipes in this book, explaining how they are prepared and used. Many are illustrated. These ingredients can be found not only in specialist food shops and delicatessens but also in many supermarkets. Wherever appropriate, however, more easily obtainable alternatives are suggested.

Rice

RICE AND NOODLES

RICE Korean rice is a medium- to short-grain variety that becomes sticky when cooked. If you cannot find Korean rice, use Japanese rice instead.

NOODLES One of the mainstays of the Asian diet, noodles were the inspiration for spaghetti. They are used extensively throughout the area. Dried noodles should be kept in an airtight container, where they will last for several months. They are usually cooked by boiling in salted water, like pasta. _See also_ CELLOPHANE NOODLES, BUCKWHEAT NOODLES.

RICE STICK NOODLES These vary in thickness and shape. They are made from rice flour, starch and water.

BANH PHO The short, flat, white Vietnamese rice stick noodles are about 3 mm/⅛ in wide. They cook in minutes in boiling water or soup, and they should not be overdone. They are used in soup-noodle dishes, especially the Vietnamese soup known as _pho_.

BANH TRANG The Vietnamese equivalent of ravioli skins, _banh trang_ is round, semi-transparent, thin, hard and dry rice paper. It is used as the wrapping of Vietnamese spring rolls and grilled meats, with salad and herbs. It is made from a dough of finely ground rice, water and salt, with tapioca (cassava) flour as the binding agent. The dough is passed through rollers and then cut into circles 18–36 cm/7–14 in in diameter.

These are put on bamboo mats to dry in the sun. Once dry they will keep almost indefinitely. To use, they must be moistened by covering with a damp cloth until soft or by dipping quickly into warm water. To get a crisp, golden brown colour, the wrappers can be brushed lightly with a sugar water solution before frying.

RICE VERMICELLI A fine, extruded, creamy-coloured noodle, made from a dough of finely ground rice and water. It cooks almost instantly, needing only to be dipped in very hot water and drained thoroughly. Rice vermicelli can be stir-fried and served as soft noodles. It should be softened first and drained before stir-frying. To deep-fry, the dried noodles are added directly to the oil.

BEAN THREAD NOODLES or VERMICELLI _see_ CELLOPHANE NOODLES

CELLOPHANE NOODLES These noodles are also known as bean-thread noodles, glass noodles or transparent noodles. They are made from ground mung beans and are clear white, fine, dried strands that are so tough they are almost impossible to cut. They are sold in bundles and need to be soaked for 10–15 minutes before cooking. After cooking, cellophane noodles become soft, slippery and gelatinous. In Szechwan and neighbouring Tibet they are first softened in water and then stir-fried with vegetables. In Indonesia, Malaysia and Singapore, the boiled noodles are added to sweet drinks and desserts, together with palm sugar, syrup, coconut milk and diced vegetables such as yam or sweet potato or sweetcorn.

BUCKWHEAT NOODLES Known in Korea as _son myon_. These are thin dried noodles. Japanese _soba_ noodles are also made from buckwheat, but they are fatter. Japanese _somen_ noodles or Italian vermicelli or capellini are nearer in size to Korean buckwheat noodles, but they are made from wheat flour.

Cellophane Noodles

SOBA These noodles, made from buckwheat and plain flour, are very nutritious, rich in protein and lecithin. Soba is sold fresh, parboiled or dried, and it is used in hot noodle soups or as a cold dish.

SON MYON *see* BUCKWHEAT NOODLES

SOMEN Made from wheat flour and water, these noodles are sold dried. Take care when you handle them, because they are very fragile. They are often used in cold summer dishes as well as in hot noodle soups.

UDON Mainly eaten in Japan and Korea, these noodles are made from wheat flour and water. They come in various thicknesses, both round and flat, and are suitable for hot noodle soups, cold dishes and stir-fries.

EGG NOODLES Made from wheat flour, egg and water, these are eaten widely over southeast Asia in both soups and stir-fried dishes. They generally come in thin or medium thicknesses. Fresh and steamed egg noodles should be eaten within two or three days. Dried noodles can be kept almost indefinitely as an airtight container.

RAMEN Fresh egg noodles or fresh Japanese ramen noodles are best in hot noodle soups.

FRUIT AND NUTS

CANDLE NUT Round candle nuts are the fruit of the candleberry tree. They are used, crushed or ground, as thickening agents. Macadamia nuts can be used as a substitute.

WATER CHESTNUTS The water chestnut is actually a bulb, very similar in shape to the chestnut but unrelated. Water chestnuts have a crunchy texture and are used in Chinese dishes. Peeled, white water chestnuts are available in cans.

COCONUT MILK There are a number of excellent brands of canned coconut milk available, but it should be remembered that it will keep for only a few hours at room temperature or two days in a refrigerator. If there is a great deal left over, it should be frozen. Desiccated coconut can be soaked in hot water or milk, and then squeezed through muslin. The first squeeze is very rich and tends to curdle during cooking. To avoid this, continual stirring is recommended.

POMELO This large Chinese fruit resembles a grapefruit. It tapers slightly at the stalk end and has a thick, sweet, slightly rough-textured skin and a dry, semi-sweet flesh. Like many other fruits, it is sometimes eaten in southeast Asia with salt.

SOURED PLUMS (umeboshi) Green plums are salted with red shiso leaves to form a traditional Japanese preserved food. They taste quite sour, so a little goes a long way.

VEGETABLES

ABURA-AGE *see* BEAN CURD SHEET

BEAN CURD (tofu) This thick, custard-like ingredient is made from dried soya beans, soaked, puréed and boiled with water. The resulting milky liquid is strained and then mixed with a coagulant or natural solidifier, which causes it to form curds. Fresh bean curd is inexpensive and easily available. Although it is bland, it absorbs the flavours in which it is cooked. It is available in three textures—soft, medium and firm—and is best eaten on the day it is bought. It is served on its own after being sautéed, deep-fried or braised, and it is added soups, casseroles and braised dishes.

BEAN CURD SHEET Known as *abura-age* in Japan. Deep-fried thin bean curd, usually sliced and used as a garnish, or slit to make a pocket and stuffed with rice. The bean curd sheet can be frozen, but does not keep longer than 48 hours in the refrigerator. Do not confuse bean curd sheet with dried bean curd.

GOBO This is a narrow, long, edible root akin to burdock. When using fresh, scrape with a knife and soak in vinegared water to prevent discoloration. It is full of fibre and used in Japanese cooking.

KOYA DOFU Japanese freeze-dried bean curd, which will keep for up to 6 months in its dried form. To prepare for use, soak in water until the bean curd has swollen and become spongy.

BEAN SPROUTS Sprouted mung beans are eaten raw or steamed, and used in stir-fries, soups and salads.

Bean Curd (tofu)

SPRING ONIONS A much wider variety of shape and size of spring onion is available throughout the East than in the West. Use the plumpest you can find.

BAMBOO SHOOTS Sold in cans, bamboo shoots should be eaten as soon as possible after the can has been opened. They will, however, last for up to 6 days in a refrigerator if the water in which they are stored is changed every day. Cooked dried bamboo shoots, *shinachiku*, originated in China but are now frequently used as a garnish for ramen dishes in Japan.

DAIKON *see* WHITE RADISH

MOOLI *see* WHITE RADISH

WHITE RADISH Daikon is a long, white radish, which is also known as mooli in the West. It is eaten raw, grated and added to stir-fries, pickled or cooked in stews.

SPRING GREENS Spring greens are used for Chinese dishes. Spinach can be used as a substitute.

BLACK BEANS When black beans are listed in ingredients, the fermented black bean is meant—that is, the original *shih* or darkened, salted soya beans of China. Dried soya beans are cooked, salted and fermented until they become almost black and soft. They can be kept almost indefinitely in airtight jars. They should be washed and dried before use and may be cooked whole, finely chopped, or mashed.

FERMENTED SOYA BEANS (natto) The end produce of fermenting soya beans, this is a sticky substance and has a smell that many people find off-putting. It is high in fibre and protein and is used in Japanese dishes.

Chinese Mushrooms

CHINESE MUSHROOMS These are black or brown dried mushrooms. Long ago the Chinese discovered that drying mushrooms intensifies the flavour. They should be soaked in water for about 20 minutes, then squeezed to get rid of the salt. The stalks should be cut off, because they are too tough to eat.

ENOKI or ENOKITAKI MUSHROOMS These mushrooms are slender, creamy in colour, with tiny caps. They grow from a dense set of roots, which must be cut off before use. They are used in both Japanese and Chinese dishes, and have a sweet, almost fruity flavour.

NAMEKO MUSHROOMS The small mushrooms, with light brown caps, have a slippery outer coating.

SHIITAKE MUSHROOMS Dried shiitake mushrooms are widely used in Asian cookery. They have a characteristic, smoky smell. When bought dried, they should be soaked in water for at least 30 minutes before use. The water can be reserved for later use in *dashi* stock.

SHIMEJI MUSHROOMS These mushrooms grow in short stumpy clusters from a simple root. The stalks are creamy at the base, gradually becoming greyish-brown toward the cap. They have a mild, subtle flavour and are a favourite ingredient in Japanese cooking. Cut off the root before use.

STRAW MUSHROOMS The distinctly earthy taste derives from the paddy-straw on which these mushrooms are grown. They are available in cans. They are globe shaped, about the size of a quail's egg, and buff-coloured, growing grey-black as they become older. They have no stalks, but a cross-section reveals an internal stalk.

WOOD EAR Known also as black fungus, cloud ear and tree ear mushroom. This type of dried mushroom is valued for its subtle, delicate flavour, and slightly crunchy 'bite'. When soaked, tree ear expands to five times its dried size.

Wood Ear

BLACK FUNGUS *see* WOOD EAR

TREE EAR *see* WOOD EAR

HERBS AND SPICES

CHINESE STEM GINGER Probably better known as ginger preserve, this is traditionally preserved with cucumber, fruits and spices. It is used as a relish and in sweet and sour sauces.

GALANGAL (ka) A member of the ginger family and in many countries used as a substitute for ginger. It has a hot, peppery taste and is used mainly as a flavouring. In Thailand, greater galangal is ground with chillies and other herbs and spices to make a refreshing drink. Lesser galangal is eaten as vegetable, both raw and cooked. In Indonesia, lesser galangal is used as a spice. *See also* KRACHAI.

KRACHAI There is no generally accepted English word for this small, yellow-brown rhizome, which is related to ginger and galangal. It is sometimes called lesser galangal or finger root.

FRESH GINGER Ginger is a popular addition to many Asian dishes. Choose plump fresh ginger so that there is a high proportion of flesh to skin, and make sure it feels firm and has a shiny skin.

WASABI Sometimes translated as 'horseradish', wasabi is ground from the Japanese riverside plant, *Wasabia japonica*. Like mustard, wasabi can be bought ready made or in powder form, which is then mixed with a little water. Powdered wasabi is generally better than the ready-made kind, which loses its 'bite' fairly quickly.

CUMIN Although it is Mediterranean in origin, it is widely used in Asian cuisine. It is both pungent and aromatic. The seeds should be roasted in a dry pan or in a very hot oven before using, either whole or ground.

The temperature should be high enough to make them pop.

TURMERIC A native of southeast Asia, turmeric belongs to the same family as ginger and galangal. It has a bright orange-yellow flesh, with a strong, earthy smell and a slightly bitter taste. The flesh is responsible for the yellow colour associated with curry.

STAR ANISE The seedpod of one of the magnolia species, the tan-coloured, eight-pointed pods resemble stars. It has a pronounced licorice flavour, and the ground spice is one of the essential ingredients in the Chinese five-spice powder. In Vietnam it is used primarily in simmered dishes and for making stock.

GROUND CORIANDER One of the essential ingredients in curry powder, it is made from the seed spice and it is best to buy the spice whole and grind it when needed. To get the best out of coriander seeds, it is advisable to toast them first in an oven and then grind them finely.

SESAME SEEDS These seeds are widely used in Japanese, Chinese and Korean cooking. Small quantities of sesame seed are roasted in a heavy, dry pan, then lightly crushed with salt before being added to sauces, marinades, dips and salads, and to braised dishes. Black sesame seeds have a more pronounced, and slightly more bitter taste than white sesame seeds.

FIVE-SPICE POWDER This aromatic Chinese spice powder is made according to an ancient formula using three native spices—star anise, cassia bark and Szechwan peppercorns —with the seeds of wild fennel and cloves from the nearby Moluccas or Spice Islands. The five spices in their whole form can be used as an Asian bouquet garni, tied up in a small muslin bag and put into stews and the like and retrieved before serving. Five-spice powder can also be made into a dip by adding five-spice powder to heated salt.

You can make your own five-spice powder by placing 40 Szechwan peppercorns, 2 cinnamon sticks (5 cm/2 in long), 1½ teaspoons fennel seeds, 12 whole cloves and 2 whole star anise in a mortar and spice grinder and grind to a fine powder. This should produce about 25 g/ 1 oz powder. Store in a tightly closed jar.

SEVEN-FLAVOURS CHILLI POWDER (shichimi) A Japanese chilli powder, ground and blended with a mixture of red chilli pepper, black pepper, sesame seeds, poppy seeds, *nori*, hemp seeds and *sansho* pepper. It is used as a seasoning over udon or soba noodle soup and other Japanese dishes.

Sesame Seeds

PAPRIKA Also known as capsicum or peppers, paprika can be used as both a vegetable and a spice.

CHILLI There are many different varieties of chilli and each variety has its own flavour and hotness. Size is not an infallible guide to hotness, but, in general, the larger the chilli, the less intense the heat. Chopping a chilli increases the amount of 'fire' in a dish, as does including the seeds. Chillies add flavour as well as hotness, and for a milder dish, instead of reducing the number of chillies, leave the chillies whole if possible and discard the seeds. **NOTE:** Chillies should always be handled carefully because they contain a substance that can irritate the skin. If you have a cut, bruise or scratch on your hands or if your skin is sensitive, wear thin rubber gloves.

CHILLI POWDER The chilli powder from Korea is among the best in the world. It is relatively mild, a glowing carmine colour and coarsely pounded. It tastes somewhat like a cross between paprika and cayenne pepper (which can be used as a substitute if necessary). It is added to dishes in generous quantities, imparting not only flavouring and adding 'heat', but giving a characteristic vibrant colour.

GROUND CHILLIES Made from dried pods, which are also used whole, broken or desiccated, the pods are best dried by roasting in a hot oven or in a dry pan. They are then ground to a coarse powder, which can be added to ground rice. This mixture is used as a strongly flavoured thickener or coating for fried foods. It may also be sprinkled over foods as a condiment.

CORIANDER These leaves are used extensively in southeast Asian cooking, although they are hardly used in Japan. The flavour is fresh, strong and earthy.

CORIANDER ROOTS In Thai cooking, the roots are ground together with the stalks for curry pastes and sauces. The leaves are used in salads and as a garnish.

KAFFIR LIME LEAVES These leaves are widely used as a flavouring in Thai cuisine and in some Malaysian and Indonesian dishes. They are sold fresh or dried.

LEMON GRASS Also known as citronella, this herb is named for its distinctive lemon flavour. It is best used fresh, but can be kept, loosely wrapped, in the refrigerator for about 10 days. To store, the bulb end should be rinsed and dried, then finely sliced or chopped. When ready for use, it should be slit open lengthways to release the flavour.

SZECHWAN PEPPERCORNS The aromatic, small, red-brown seeds from the prickly ash tree are known as *fagara*. The whole 'peppercorns' can be kept for years without loss of flavour if they are sealed in a tightly sealed jar away from light, heat and moisture. In China, they are mixed into heated fine salt to produce pepper-salt, a fragrant, salty dip for grilled and fried foods and often used in marinades.

PALM SUGAR Made from the sap of the coconut palm, palm sugar is used throughout southeast Asia. It is light brown in colour and has got a distinguishing sweet toffee smell.

SUGAR CANE Available from some Asian market stalls, it is cultivated exclusively for its sweet sap that is made into sugar. The sugar cane bought for cooking consists of the stalk, the leaves being chopped off in the cane field. The cane should be carefully peeled with a sharp knife.

SEAFOOD

BONITO FLAKES (katuso-bushi) Bonito is a member of the tuna family. When dried and grated into flakes, it is an essential ingredient in Japanese cuisine. It is mainly used for making *dashi* stock, but is also an ingredient in other dishes and as a garnish.

DRIED JELLYFISH Although it has little taste, it is valued for its crunchy texture. It is the salted and sun-dried skin of the mantle of the jellyfish. It should be soaked in warm water for several hours and does not require cooking, which only serves to toughen it. It is usually shredded finely and marinated in vinegar to be served in a salad. Add a little sesame oil to transform it into a delicious and crunchy salad.

DRIED SHRIMPS OR PRAWNS These salty, hard, whole shrimps are used to add extra flavour. They are sometimes soaked in water before use. Dried shrimps used in Chinese and Thai recipes are very different from those sold for inclusion in Japanese cooking.

Kelp

KELP Known as *tasima* in Korea; *kombu* or *konbu* in Japan. One of the best sources of iodine, calcium and other valuable minerals, it resembles large, long leaves. It is available either folded or cut into small pieces. Care should be taken not to over-boil kelp, as it very quickly becomes bitter. To prepare for cooking, wipe the kelp with a damp cloth but do not rinse, because this will wash away many of the nutrients.

DRIED LAVER Known as *nori* in Japan; *kim* in Korea. The most widely used seaweed in Japanese cooking. It is vitamin- and mineral-packed, and there are many varieties and qualities, from dark green to purplish-black. Price is usually a good guide to quality. It is sold in paper-thin sheets. Before use, it is cooked quickly under a grill or over a gas flame until it becomes crisp. It may then be eaten as it is or crumbled over noodle or rice dishes. Some pre-cooked laver is available in the West, so check which kind you have bought before use.

KOMBU or KONBU *see* KELP

NORI *see* DRIED LAVER

WAKAME This type of dried seaweed is widely used in Japanese and Korean soups and stews, and in salads, when it is dressed with a vinegar dressing. It should never be cooked for long and can, in fact, be used after simply being dipped into boiling water. When it is bought dried, it should be soaked in cold water before being used in any recipe. It is thinner than kelp (*konbu*).

SALTFISH First imported from Newfoundland in Canada as a survival food for British colonies, saltfish somehow found its way to Vietnam, where it has become a delicacy.

Wakame

OILS/VINEGARS/PICKLES

CHILLI OIL The red-coloured oil is made from ground chillies. It is used for cooking, as a spice, and can be added to some dips.

SESAME OIL This is used as a flavouring as well as for cooking in many Asian cuisines. In Korea, the sesame oil is made from toasted sesame seeds, so has an amber colour and a nutty, sesame flavour. As it therefore provides both a distinctive flavour and colour, pale sesame oil does not result in authentic-looking and -tasting dishes. Store sesame oil in a cool, dark place.

SU *see* RICE VINEGAR

RICE WINE This is a light, slightly sweet wine used in many Asian dishes. Use dry sherry if it is not available. *See also* SAKE.

MIRIN Japanese cooking wine, a mixture of a variant of *sake* with sugar. It contains only a trace of alcohol but imparts a distinctive sweet flavour to any dish in which it is used.

SAKE Japanese rice wine, which is widely available outside Japan, is made by introducing a yeast mould to steamed rice. It is used only sparingly in Japanese cooking. If you cannot get genuine *sake*, use dry sherry instead.

RICE VINEGAR Known as *su* in Japan. Made from naturally fermented rice, clear *su* is widely available and suitable for *sushi* rice. Brown *su*, which is the unrefined basis for white *su*, can be used in any recipe when the colour of the vinegar is not important to the appearance of the finished dish. The Japanese rice vinegar is lighter and milder than Chinese versions. White wine vinegar can be used instead; alternatively, dilute three parts white distilled vinegar with one part water; if the recipe does not include sugar, add a small pinch.

Sesame Oil

Rice Vinegar

BLACK VINEGAR This dark, mild, almost sweet vinegar has only one equivalent: balsamic vinegar. It is usually made from glutionous rice or sorghum, which gives it its distinctive taste. The better varieties have a range of flavours, from smoky to wine-yeasty. In central China and parts of the north, black vinegar is used like tomato ketchup and is added to almost every dish.

KIMCHI The spicy pickle is a vital part of almost every Korean meal, including breakfast. It is also added to soups, stews, stir-fries and pancakes. Although you can make your own, bottles of ready-made *kimchi* are available. Among the more than 160 types that are produced, there are white radish, cucumber, stuffed cucumber, garlic, Chinese turnip and onion *kimchi*.

RED PICKLED GINGER (beni-shouga) Slivered ginger is pickled with a little sugar and vinegar and used as a garnish in Japanese dishes.

MYOGA This relation of the ginger plant is eaten, raw, pickled or as a garnish, in Japanese dishes.

Soya Bean Paste

PASTES/SAUCES/STOCKS

CHILLI BEAN PASTE (toban djan) This thick, dark reddish sauce, made from chilli, soya beans, and soy sauce, is used for spicing up Chinese dishes. Chilli bean sauce or paste is available from large supermarkets. *See also* KOCHUJANG.

DRIED SHRIMP PASTE (belacan) This fermented shrimp paste has a very characteristic, strong smell. Before it is used, the paste has to be fried.

SOYA BEAN PASTE Soya bean paste is made from fermented soya bean cakes, pepper and salt. The thick, brown paste has a pungent, characteristic flavour. Japanese *miso* can be used instead.

FERMENTED SOYA BEAN PASTE Known as *twoenjang* in Korea.

OYSTER SAUCE One of the most popular sauces in southeast Asia, oyster sauce is made from dried oysters. It is thick and richly flavoured. The cheaper brands tend to be more salty. The original sauce was thinner and contained fragments of dried, fermented oysters. Many people use it as a superior version of soy sauce, but Asian cooks use it as an accompaniment for stir-fried vegetables and to flavour and colour braised and stir-fried dishes.

BLACK BEAN SAUCE Black beans are salted and fermented with spices to produce the sauce. It has a strong salty taste, and is used widely in Asian cooking.

CHA SIU SAUCE This is the marinade sauce used for making Chinese barbecue pork. It is a blend of many ingredients, including Chinese five-spice powder, honey, sugar, soy sauce, rice wine and garlic.

SOY SAUCE Known as *kanjang* in Korea. This is an essential flavouring and seasoning in many Asian dishes. Light, medium and dark soy sauces are available; light versions tend to be the thinnest and most salty. The Japanese version (medium) of this combination of fermented soya beans, wheat and salt is lighter and sweeter than the Chinese equivalent. Japanese brands such as Kikkoman are now widely available in the West.

CHILLI SAUCE (sambal celek) This Indonesian chilli paste is made from crushed red chillies. It is used for cooking as well as a condiment.

YELLOW BEAN SAUCE Made according to the ancient recipe for *jiang* or pickled yellow soya beans in a salty liquid. It is normally bought in cans and jars, but if bought in a can it is best transferred to a jar in which it can be stored in a refrigerator.

YAKISOBA SAUCE A dark brown sauce, this is used in Japanese stir-fried noodle dishes. Japanese brown sauce is a good substitute, or blend your own *yakisoba* sauce.

FISH SAUCE Known as *nam plaa* in Thailand; *nuoc mam* in Vietnam. This powerfully flavoured, pungent seasoning sauce is used extensively in southeast Asia, especially Burma, Cambodia, Thailand and Vietnam. It is made by layering fish and salt into large barrels and allowing the fish to ferment for three or more months before the accumulated liquid is siphoned off, filtered and bottled. It is made into different dipping sauces by adding chillies, ground, roast peanuts, sugar and other ingredients. It is something of an acquired taste, and soy sauce can be used instead. As an alternative, use Maggi liquid seasoning.

HOISIN SAUCE This reddish-brown sauce is best used as a condiment for roast pork and poultry. It is made from fermented soya bean paste, sugar, garlic and spices (usually five-spice). Hoisin sauce should not be confused with Chinese barbecue sauce, *sha cha jiang*.

MISO A fermented, protein-rich soya bean paste used in Japanese cooking. The cooked soya beans are fermented with a type of yeast known as *koji*. *Miso* is unique for Japanese cooking, in which it is used widely both as a flavouring and as the basis for many dressings. It will keep for several months in the refrigerator. White *miso* is made from a rice-based yeast, and it is commonly used in soups; red *miso* is made from a barley yeast and is used as a general-purpose flavouring and for dishes requiring a rich flavour.

KANJANG *see* SOY SAUCE.

KOCHUJANG This is the Korean version of chilli bean paste. It is an essential seasoning and is used as a relish and as a spice. It is added to meats that are to be stir-fried, stews and dips and is served in small bowls as a sweet, spicy, hot relish. Every Korean household has a tall earthenware jar of thick, red *kochujang*—its preparation is lengthy and elaborate, using glutinous rice powder or barley mixed with malt, which is then cooked slowly to a smooth, thick paste. This is mixed with fermented chilli powder, soya bean powder and salt. If you cannot obtain Korean *kochujang*, use Chinese chilli bean paste, which is widely available in the West.

NUOC MAM *see* FISH SAUCE

NAM PLAA *see* FISH SAUCE

DASHI A stock, used in Japanese cooking, made from dried *bonito* flakes (*katsuo-bushi*) or dried kelp (*konbu*) or a mixture of the two, depending on the flavour desired. Premier *dashi* stock is used in Japanese consommé, *chawan mushi* and *miso* soup; normal *dashi* is suitable for simmered dishes and noodles or for use as a supplement to premier *dashi*. Freeze-dried *dashi* stock granules are available.

Soy Sauce

Miso

Index